T0271241

Jonas Mekas: Interviews

Conversations with Filmmakers Series
Gerald Peary, General Editor

Jonas Mekas
INTERVIEWS

Edited by Gregory R. Smulewicz-Zucker

University Press of Mississippi / Jackson

The University Press of Mississippi is the scholarly publishing agency of
the Mississippi Institutions of Higher Learning: Alcorn State University,
Delta State University, Jackson State University, Mississippi State University,
Mississippi University for Women, Mississippi Valley State University,
University of Mississippi, and University of Southern Mississippi.

www.upress.state.ms.us

The University Press of Mississippi is a member
of the Association of University Presses.

First printing 2020
∞

Library of Congress Cataloging-in-Publication Data

Names: Mekas, Jonas, 1922–2019, interviewee. | Smulewicz-Zucker, Gregory
    R., 1983– editor.
Title: Jonas Mekas : interviews / edited by Gregory R. Smulewicz-Zucker.
Other titles: Conversations with filmmakers series.
Description: Jackson : University Press of Mississippi, [2020] | Series:
    Conversations with filmmakers series | Includes index.
Identifiers: LCCN 2020017713 (print) | LCCN 2020017714 (ebook) | ISBN
    9781496829214 (hardback) | ISBN 9781496829221 (trade paperback) | ISBN
    9781496829238 (epub) | ISBN 9781496829207 (epub) | ISBN 9781496829245
    (pdf) | ISBN 9781496829252 (pdf)
Subjects: LCSH: Mekas, Jonas, 1922–2019—Interviews. | Independent
    filmmakers—United States—Interviews. | Motion picture producers and
    directors—United States—Interviews. | BISAC: PERFORMING ARTS /
    Individual Director (see also BIOGRAPHY & AUTOBIOGRAPHY / Entertainment
    & Performing Arts) | LCGFT: Interviews.
Classification: LCC PN1998.3.M44 A3 2020 (print) | LCC PN1998.3.M44
    (ebook) | DDC 791.4302/33092 [B]—dc23
LC record available at https://lccn.loc.gov/2020017713
LC ebook record available at https://lccn.loc.gov/2020017714

British Library Cataloging-in-Publication Data available

Contents

Introduction

Jonas Mekas (1922–2019) occupies a special space in the history of cinema.[1] A brilliantly innovative filmmaker best known for his diary films, Mekas was also a leading champion of independent cinema as a movement for close to seven decades. A member of the highly diverse group of filmmakers that emerged in the 1950s and early 1960s labeled the New American Cinema, Mekas was one of the movement's major theorists and an architect of its major institutions. Any discussion of Mekas's life and work necessarily entails a journey into one of the most exciting and aesthetically sophisticated artistic movements of the twentieth century. In the interviews that make up this volume, Mekas speaks of his own work as well as the movement he nurtured.

America's foremost advocate of a cinema emancipated from commercial interests and aesthetic conservatism was born in the Lithuanian farming village of Semeniškiai on December 24, 1922. Lithuania became an independent republic four years prior to Mekas's birth. Lithuania's early decades of independence were tumultuous. Throughout the 1930s, Lithuania's president, Antanas Smetona, led an authoritarian regime that repressed dissent within. At the same time, Lithuania contended with efforts by the Soviet Union and Nazi Germany to retake lands that the Russian and German empires had controlled before Lithuania's independence. With the outbreak of World War II, Lithuania was first occupied by the Soviet Union in 1940 and then invaded by Nazi Germany in 1941.

Though his early years were defined by the localized concerns of a small village of farmers, Mekas found his broader intellectual interests nourished by a theologian uncle and politically engaged older siblings. Mekas was active in resistance to both the Soviet and Nazi occupations of Lithuania. In an effort to protect Mekas and his younger brother, Adolfas (who would later direct the independent comedy *Hallelujah the Hills* and found the film department at Bard College), from reprisal for their underground activities, an uncle acquired papers to send both young men to study in Vienna. Their train was stopped in Germany, where the brothers were arrested. They spent the remainder of the war in a forced labor camp. After liberation, the brothers were assigned for four years to displaced persons camps. Both were able to briefly study at the University of Mainz.

Before his imprisonment, Mekas had begun keeping diaries and writing poetry. Following the war, during his time at a displaced persons camp in Elmshorn, Germany, Mekas composed his *Idylls of Semeniskiai*. The *Idylls* became in Mekas's homeland one of the most celebrated examples of Lithuanian poetry. Mekas's works as a diarist and poet are integrally important to the development of his style and sensibilities as a filmmaker. They explore the themes of the remembrance of homeland and the search for a new home, which also figure prominently in Mekas's diary films. While Mekas treated his experiences in intensely personal terms, they resonate with those of the many millions of refugees. He summons an old aesthetic tradition—evident in the oeuvres of Dante and Petrarch, with whom Mekas deeply identified—in which the poet's personal journey is intertwined with world-historical transformations. At the same time, Mekas's own oeuvre, ranging from his early poems and written diaries to his later films, emphasizes the aesthetic sublimity found in everyday experience. Mekas's focus on the seemingly mundane invites deeper explorations of both the joyful and painful moments that define life.

The Mekas brothers arrived in New York in late 1949. Soon thereafter, Jonas Mekas bought his first 16mm Bolex film camera and began to record life in the Lithuanian émigré community in Brooklyn. He soon began attending film screenings at the Museum of Modern of Art and the seminally important Cinema 16, founded by the film theorist Amos Vogel. Through such venues, Mekas discovered the works of avant-garde filmmakers such as Maya Deren and Kenneth Anger, who had produced important films in the 1940s, as well as emerging filmmakers like Stan Brakhage. By the early 1950s, Mekas was a member of the exciting community of artists and intellectuals who would reshape every aspect of the arts in America.

In 1955, Mekas founded *Film Culture* to answer the need for a theoretically sophisticated film journal in the United States. Three years later, Mekas began his "Movie Journal" column in the *Village Voice* to reach a more popular audience. Both *Film Culture* and Mekas's "Movie Journal" column initially gave broad coverage to mainstream as well as noncommercial film. Mekas himself, however, was becoming more excited by the advances made by the large group of independent filmmakers whom, drawing from the title of Donald M. Allen's influential 1960 anthology, *The New American Poetry*, Mekas would dub members of the New American Cinema. This included figures such as Anger, Brakhage, James Broughton, John Cassavetes, Shirley Clarke, Deren, Hollis Frampton, Jerome Hill, Ken Jacobs, George and Mike Kuchar, Gregory Markopoulos, Marie Menken, Ron Rice, Jack Smith, and Andy Warhol. In September 1960, Mekas helped found the New American Cinema Group as an organization representing the interests of these filmmakers. Two years later, Mekas managed one of the Group's main objectives, the establishment of the Film-Makers' Cooperative, a distributor for the work of noncommercial cinema.

Through his film criticism in the *Voice*, his editorship of *Film Culture*, and his work as a founding member of the New American Cinema Group, Mekas had become one of the most tireless advocates of a major artistic movement. His support of filmmakers who were daringly expanding the language of cinema beyond the confines of the narrative form made audiences aware of a real alternative to the dominance of Hollywood. Mekas would gain greater public notoriety when, in 1964, he was arrested with Ken and Flo Jacobs on obscenity charges for screening Jack Smith's *Flaming Creatures*. Smith's film was deemed pornographic for its depictions of hetero- and homoerotic sexual playfulness. Mekas did not let the matter settle, recruiting public support and reporting on the ensuing legal battle against censorship of the film in his "Movie Journal" column. He also defiantly smuggled into the United States and screened the French writer Jean Genet's homoerotic short film *Un Chant d'Amour*. Mekas's dedication to the emancipation of cinema from conservative mores made him one of the most significant anticensorship activists of the 1960s, earning him the admiration of Jean-Paul Sartre, Simone de Beauvoir, Susan Sontag, and many others.

Mekas also produced and directed his first two features, *Guns of the Trees* (1961) and *The Brig* (1964).

Guns of the Trees follows the story of two couples as they seek to comprehend the motive for their friend's suicide. The disjointedness of the film's structure communicates the moral confusion and anguish of the protagonists amidst the burgeoning social upheaval of early 1960s America.

The questioning of the rigidity of the American social order was amplified in Mekas's important second film, *The Brig*. Experimental theater pioneers Julian Beck and Judith Malina had put on a production of Kenneth Brown's play about a day in a military prison through their The Living Theatre theatrical company, but the play was shut down when Beck and Malina were charged with tax fraud. Mekas and the actors broke into the theater to film through the night a final performance. Mekas's camerawork clearly draws from the style of documentary filmmakers of the time such as the Maysles brothers and Richard Leacock. Brilliantly capturing the harsh regimentation of life in a military prison, the film was awarded the Grand Prix at the Venice Film Festival.

Though *Guns of the Trees* and *The Brig* are seminal examples of the kind of free-flowing storytelling and innovative cinematographic techniques that marked American independent cinema of the 1960s, Mekas is more closely associated in cinema history with his pioneering, influential diary films. *Walden (Diaries, Notes, and Sketches)* (1968) brings together footage that ranges in subject from mundane everyday experiences to major life events. The film is also noteworthy for appearances by Mekas's many prominent friends and collaborators. *Walden* marks the unification of Mekas's work as a poet and written diarist and as a filmmaker. The footage is complemented by Mekas's narration: experience processed and reflected upon via Mekas's sensibilities.

Because of his reputation for rebelliousness and his critique of the American military in *The Brig*, Mekas was permitted by Soviet authorities to visit Lithuania and to film in his homeland. *Reminiscences of a Journey to Lithuania* (1971) is a record of Mekas's return to his village and reunion with his family some twenty-five years after he was forced to flee. The film celebrates the refugee's return home, but also strikes a sorrowful tone as the viewer is aware of how much Mekas himself has changed as he participates in daily activities that resemble those of his youth. While the first third of the film centers on Mekas's reunion with his mother and brothers, a second, briefer portion of the film documents Jonas and Adolfas's visit to the site of the forced labor camp where they lived out the war.

Reminiscences is all the more profound as a lyrical reflection on the experience of homelessness and displacement. Far from being nationalistic in tenor, the film uses the voyage home to meditate on self-discovery as the artist finds a new home among his friends and collaborators. Mekas often declared that cinema was his country. It is through the activity of artistic production, of recording his journey, that Mekas makes a homeland for himself.

Mekas's second important film of the 1970s, *Lost Lost Lost* (1976), explores themes similar to those of *Reminiscences* from a different angle. Whereas in *Reminiscences* the viewer witnesses a kind of reconciliation with the past, in *Lost Lost Lost* Mekas most explicitly deals with the painful experience of the refugee. The film begins with Mekas's earliest footage after his arrival in New York and shows Mekas very engaged with the Lithuanian refugee community in late 1940s and early 1950s Brooklyn. He records daily life on the street, social gatherings, traditional Lithuanian customs, political meetings, and speeches by prominent exiles. Yet midway through the film, Mekas moves from Brooklyn to Manhattan, signaling his entry into the New York art scene and, thus, a kind of declaration of independence from the past.

Even as Mekas produced these major works, he maintained a busy schedule as columnist, curator, and editor of *Film Culture*. These efforts culminated in the founding in 1970 of Anthology Film Archives as a museum, library, and screening venue dedicated to the promotion of independent cinema and to the higher ideal of treating cinema as a serious, eminently important art. Along with the filmmakers Peter Kubelka, James Broughton, and Jerome Hill and the theorists Ken Kelman and P. Adams Sitney, Mekas established the Essential Cinema Repertory. The films included in the Essential Cinema list make up a canon of films exemplifying the major aesthetic contributions to cinema. The Essential Cinema program, which continues to be screened at the Anthology, remains a remarkable—and rarified—compilation of masterpieces by filmmakers like D. W. Griffith, Sergei

Eisenstein, Charles Chaplin, Fritz Lang, and F. W. Murnau alongside the major works of American independent cinema celebrated by Mekas and his compatriots.

From the mid-1970s to the 1990s, Mekas focused his energies on the Anthology Film Archives as the institution's director. His films of this period consisted primarily of portraits dedicated to his children, Oona and Sebastian, and departed friends, including Andy Warhol, George Maciunas, and John Lennon. In 2000, Mekas released the five-hour *As I Was Moving Ahead Occasionally I Saw Brief Glimpses of Beauty*. The film marked a return to the grander poetic themes of his earlier diary films. Again, Mekas celebrated the beauty found in everyday experience, this time with a special focus on his relationship with his children. At the same time, the film charts Mekas's reflections on change and its painful consequences as signaled in the end of his marriage to the artist Hollis Melton.

As I Was Moving Ahead was the last of Mekas's great diary films. Afterward, he began a new chapter in his career. Though he had flirted with video in the past, he shifted entirely to the format. His engagement with new technologies led to his *365 Day Project* in which he released one short film every day for a year on his website. The 2000s also saw an explosion of interest in Mekas and his work. Throughout his eighties and nineties, Mekas traveled the world for exhibitions and retrospectives at major museums and festivals. In 2006, *Reminiscences* was added to the Library of Congress's Film Registry. The following year, the Jonas Mekas Visual Arts Center opened in Vilnius, Lithuania. He received honors from the Austrian and French governments and was elected a member of the American Academy of Arts and Sciences as well as the Academy of Motion Picture Arts. His published diaries, *I Had Nowhere to Go*, became the basis for a film by the Scottish artist Douglas Gordon. Mekas's contributions to film criticism received renewed attention when a collection of his "Movie Journal" columns was republished. Given his consistent activity well into his nineties, Mekas became the subject of articles in the *New York Times* about how to maintain an active and meaningful life. Mekas passed away in his home in Brooklyn after a brief illness on January 23, 2019.

In conversations, Mekas seamlessly shifted between his identities as poet, filmmaker, critic, theorist, and rebel. He reveled in throwing in the occasional irreverent remark if he felt his interlocutor needed to have their deeply held assumptions questioned. At times, Mekas's tendency to seemingly adopt a view that contradicted his own earlier opinions confused and frustrated even those who knew him longest. However, this was Mekas's playful way of challenging what he saw as calcified opinions.

Mekas always welcomed interviews, whether with celebrated film scholars or students. At the same time, many longtime friends recorded interviews with Mekas. These conversations often illuminate aspects of Mekas's thought that were only evident to the people with whom he was closest, such as the architect Raimund

Abraham, filmmakers Peter Bogdanovich, Stan Brakhage, and Jim Jarmusch, curator Hans-Ulrich Obrist, and the artist and actor Benn Northover. For this book, *Jonas Mekas: Interviews*, I have also included the transcripts of conversations the filmmaker had with audience members, often university students, at screenings of his films. Any conversation with Mekas was full of fresh and spontaneous insights on a variety of subjects.

The interviews collected here capture something of the man's multiple attributes. The reader will find Mekas's insights into his own films as well as into the art of filmmaking. He/she will also gain knowledge of the New American Cinema. But, perhaps more importantly, these interviews communicate Mekas's ethos. His passion, enthusiasm, and vision for the arts as a vehicle for humanity's highest capacities speaks to all lovers of the arts. Mekas mentored and nurtured three generations of artists and intellectuals. These interviews preserve that voice so that it might speak to future generations. We need Mekas's unique blend of artistic and intellectual commitment and anarchistic joyfulness in our culture now more than ever.

Acknowledgments

After editing the second edition of his *Movie Journal: The Rise of a New American Cinema*, Jonas Mekas and I were soon brainstorming about other projects. As he prepared a collection of interviews he had conducted with filmmakers, a book of interviews with him seemed a natural complement. Jonas generously gave me access to his personal archives. I spent hours in his Brooklyn loft going through the many binders of material he had accumulated over the years. Unfortunately, Jonas did not live to see the result of our effort. Even at ninety-six, Jonas's passing seemed unexpected. He was always planning the next project. I do not think he had to see this one come to fruition. The interviews collected here were part of his history, and he was always looking forward. Nevertheless, I would have liked to see him grin as he flipped through these pages, only to toss this book aside and begin planning the next project.

Jonas's children, Oona and Sebastian, have been wonderfully supportive of this project. Sebastian read through drafts and checked facts. I look forward to our future collaborations. Two of Jonas's dearest friends, the film theorists P. Adams Sitney and Amy Taubin, graciously answered the questions that—despite twenty years of friendship—I had neglected to ask Jonas. Benn Northover, whom I met on my first day as an intern at Anthology Film Archives, was one of Jonas's closest friends and collaborators for almost two decades. He has been an indispensable supporter of this book and has shared his deep insights. Alexa Zucker performed the arduous task of copyediting the manuscript and deciphering often faded Xeroxes of old interviews. I am grateful to Timothy Scott Johnson, Michael J. Thompson, and Hedda Smulewicz for their comments. My thanks to the many interviewers included in this volume who helped record Jonas's life and achievements.

Gerald Peary made this book possible by recommending it for University Press of Mississippi's series. Craig Gill and Emily Bandy turned that possibility into a reality. They have been patient and extraordinarily helpful editors. Valerie Jones did an exceptional job copyediting the book. It has been a pleasure to work with them all.

It goes without saying that any errors contained in this book are my responsibility. I would dedicate this book to my friend were it not for the fact that I know this is merely one of many projects to come that celebrate his life and work. And so, in the spirit of Jonas's tireless work ethic, on to the next film, the next book!

GSZ

Notes

1. For more detailed assessments of Mekas's work, see my "Introduction to the Second Edition" in Jonas Mekas, *Movie Journal: The Rise of the New American Cinema, 1959–1971*, ed. Gregory Smulewicz-Zucker (New York: Columbia University Press, 2016). Also, note David James's excellent edited collection, *To Free the Cinema: Jonas Mekas and the New York Underground* (Princeton: Princeton University Press, 1992).

Chronology

documentary category at the Venice Film Festival. He is arrested on obscenity charges for screening Smith's *Flaming Creatures* and Jean Genet's *Un chant d'Amour*. Mekas serves as one of the cinematographers for Andy Warhol's *Empire*. Becomes director of the Film-Makers' Cinematheque, a predecessor of Anthology Film Archives.

1968   Begins working as film curator for the Jewish Museum in New York. Subject of *Jonas*, a short film profile by Gideon Bachmann.

1969   Releases *Walden* (*Diaries, Notes, and Sketches*).

1970   Anthology Film Archives opens at Lafayette Street location with Mekas as its director.

1971   Returns to Lithuania for the first time since 1944. Appears in John Lennon and Yoko Ono's *Up Your Legs Forever*.

1972   Releases *Reminiscences of a Journey to Lithuania*. First edition of *Movie Journal*, a collection of Mekas's columns from the *Village Voice*, is published.

1973   Mekas profiled in an article by Calvin Tomkins for the *New Yorker*.

1974   Mekas marries Hollis Melton. Daughter, Oona, is born. Anthology Film Archives moves to 80 Wooster Street location.

1975   Ends his "Move Journal" column for the *Village Voice*.

1976   Releases *Lost Lost Lost*.

1977   Receives a Guggenheim Fellowship.

1979   Anthology Film Archives purchases the Second Avenue Courthouse building.

1981   Son, Sebastian, is born.

1983   Releases his first series of stills taken from his films to help raise money for the renovation of the new building for Anthology Film Archives.

1988   Anthology Film Archives moves into the renovated location at 32 Second Avenue.

1990   Lithuania breaks from the Soviet bloc. Releases *Scenes from the Life of Andy Warhol*.

1991   Peter Sempel's film about Mekas, *Jonas in the Desert*, released. *I Had Nowhere to Go: Diaries, 1944–1954* is published.

1992   Film scholar David James edits *To Free the Cinema: Jonas Mekas and the New York Underground*, which is published by Princeton University Press. Releases *Zefiro Torna or Scenes from the Life of George Maciunas*.

1995   Receives Lithuanian National Prize.

1996   *There is No Ithaca*, a collection of Mekas's poetry translated by Vyt Bakaitis, is published.

1997   Receives Pier Paolo Pasolini Award. Releases *Scenes from Allen's Last Days on Earth as a Spirit*.

1999   Releases *This Side of Paradise*.

2000   Releases *As I Was Moving Ahead Occasionally I Saw Brief Glimpses of Beauty*. Steidl publishes *Just Like a Shadow*, a collection of stills from Mekas's films.

2004   Releases *Letter from Greenpoint*. Mekas appears in Peter Sempel's second film about Mekas, *Jonas at the Ocean*. Receives the Siegfried Kracauer Award for Film Criticism from *Logos: A Journal of Modern Society and Culture*.

2005   Mekas and Hollis Melton divorce. Mekas moves from Manhattan to Brooklyn.

2006   *Reminiscences of a Journey to Lithuania* is selected for preservation in the Library of Congress's National Film Registry.

2007   The Jonas Mekas Visual Arts Center opens in Vilnius, Lithuania. Over the course of the year, Mekas releases the *365 Day Project*. Adolfas Mekas's translation of the *Idylls of Semeniskiai* is published.

2009   *Jonas Mekas* published by Walther Konig.

2011   Brother, Adolfas, passes away. Releases *My Paris Movie*.

2012   Releases *Out-takes from the Life of a Happy Man*. Retrospective of Mekas's work at Serpentine Galleries in London.

2013   Receives Commandeur de l'Ordre des Arts et des Lettres from the French Ministry of Culture. Elected to the American Academy of Arts and Sciences. The final film in Peter Sempel's Mekas trilogy, *Jonas in the Jungle*, is released.

2015   Receives Yoko Ono Courage Award. Kino Lorber releases *Walden* and *Lost Lost Lost* on Blu-ray. Mekas is profiled in the *New York Times* "85 and Up" series.

2016   Columbia University Press publishes a second edition of *Movie Journal* with a foreword by Peter Bogdanovich. Scottish artist Douglas Gordon's documentary, *I Had Nowhere to Go*, based on Mekas' diaries is released.

2017   Elected member to the Academy of Motion Picture Arts and Sciences. Second edition of *I Had Nowhere to Go* published.

2018   Mekas is interviewed for the oral history archive of the United States Holocaust Memorial Museum.

2019   On January 23, Mekas passes away at the age of ninety-six.

Filmography

Cup/Saucer/Two Dancers/Radio (1965/1983), 23 min.

Guns of the Trees (1962), 75 min.

Film Magazine of the Arts (Summer 1963), 20 min.

The Brig (1964), 68 min.

Award Presentation to Andy Warhol (1964), 12 min.

Report from Millbrook (1965/1966), 12 min.

Walden (Diaries, Notes, and Sketches) (filmed 1964–68, edited 1968–69), 3 hrs.

Hare Krishna (1966), 4 min.

Notes on the Circus (1966), 12 min.

Cassis (1966), 4 min.

The Italian Notebook (1967), 15 min.

Time and Fortune Vietnam Newsreel (1968), 4 min.

Reminiscences of a Journey to Lithuania (1971–72), 82 min.

Lost Lost Lost (1976), 2 hrs. 58 min.

In Between: 1964–8 (1978), 52 min.

Notes for Jerome (1978), 45 min.

Paradise Not Yet Lost (a.k.a. Oona's Third Year) (1979), 96 min.

Self-Portrait (1980), 20 min., video

Street Songs (1966/1983), 10 min.

Erik Hawkins: Excerpts from "Here and Now with Watchers"/Lucia Dlugoszewski Performs (1963/1983), 6 min.

He Stands in a Desert Counting the Seconds of His Life (1969/1985), 2 hrs. 30 min.

Scenes from the Life of Andy Warhol (1990), 35 min.

A Walk (1990), 58 min., video

Mob of Angels: Baptism (1990), 61 min., video

Mob of Angels at St. Ann (1991), 60 min, video

Dr. Carl G. Jung or Lapis Philosophorum (1991), 29 min.

Quartet Number One (1991), 8 min.

Zefiro Torna or Scenes from the Life of George Maciunas (1992), 34 min.

The Education of Sebastian or Egypt Regained (1992), 6 hrs., video

Imperfect 3-Image films (1995), 6 min.

On My Way to Fujiyama (1995), 25 min.

Happy Birthday to John (1996), 24 min.

Cinema is Not 100 Years Old (1996), 4 min., video

Memories of Frankenstein (1996), 95 min.

Letters to Friends (1997), 1 hr. 28 min., video

Birth of a Nation (1997), 85 min.

Symphony of Joy (1997), 75 min.

Scenes from Allen's Last Three Days on Earth as a Spirit (April 1997), 67 min., video

Letter from Nowhere—Laiškai iš niekur N.1 (1997), 75 min., video [in Lithuanian]

Song of Avignon (1998), 5 min.

Laboratorium Anthology (1999), 63 min., video

This Side of Paradise (1999), 35 min., 16mm

Notes on the Factory (1999), 64 min., video

Notes on Film-Maker's Cooperative (1999), 40 min., video

Autobiography of a Man Who Carried his Memory in his Eyes (2000), 53 min., video

As I Was Moving Ahead Occasionally I Saw Brief Glimpses of Beauty (2000), 4 hrs. 48 min.

Mozart & Wien and Elvis (2000), 3 min.

Silence, Please (2000), 6 min., video

Requiem for a Manual Typewriter (2000), 19 min., video

Remedy for Melancholy (2000), 20 min., video

Letter to Penny Arcade (2001), 14 min. 33 sec., video

Ein Märchen (2001), 6 min., video

Ar Buvo Karas? (2002), 2 hrs. 28 min.

Mysteries (1966/2002), 34 min.

Williamsburg, Brooklyn (1949/2002), 15 min.

Travel Songs 1967–1981 (2003), 28 min.

Letter from Greenpoint (2004), 80 min., video

Notes on Utopia (2003–5), 55 min., video

Father and Daughter (2005), 4 min. 30 sec., video

Notes on an American Film Director at Work: Martin Scorsese (2005), 1hr. 20 min.

Scenes from the Life of Hermann Nitsch (2005), 58 min., film and video

First Forty (2006). Forty short films, using materials from earlier films, re-edited specially for internet and installations.

365 Day Project (2007). 365 short films, one for each calendar day of the year 2007.

Lithuania and the Collapse of the USSR (2008), 4 hrs. 49 min., video

I Leave Chelsea Hotel (2009), 4 min.

Sleepless Nights Stories (2011), 114 min.

My Paris Movie (2011), 2 hrs. 39 min.

My Bars Bar Movie (2011), 86 min.

Correspondences: José Luis Guerin and Jonas Mekas (2011), 99 min.

Re: George Maciunas and Fluxus (2011), 87 min.

Mont Ventoux (2011), 3 min.

Happy Easter Ride (2012), 18 min.

Reminiszenzen aus Deutschland (2012), 25 min.

Out-takes from the Life of a Happy Man (2012), 68 min.

Jonas Mekas: Interviews

An Interview with Jonas Mekas

Salvatore J. Fallica / 1966

From *Sequoya Magazine,* Spring 1966. Reprinted by permission.

There are two aspects of contemporary American cinema: one which operates mainly as an industry and another which discards the "business" aspect and concerns itself with what it considers artistic aims. The former is commonly associated with Hollywood: the latter can be found virtually anywhere. This second aspect, the New American Cinema, has historic and contemporary roots in Hollywood, yet it is new, unconventional, poetic—the *avant-garde* or "underground" cinema. Mr. Jonas Mekas, the principal exponent of this New American Cinema, is the founder of the Film-Makers' Cooperative and the Cinematheque—the means the new cinema uses to convey its art. The interview was conducted at the Cinematheque, 125 W. 41st Street, by Sal Fallica.

Sal Fallica: How would you describe the American cinema?
Jonas Mekas: At least ten years ago it was possible to divide it into four categories. There were the old Hollywood masters like Hitchcock operating with budgets of about $5 million. Next came the so-called "Hollywood Independents" such as Stanley Kramer, who were working with $500,000 to $1 million a film.

The third group was working with a lower budget, somewhere around $200,000 to $300,000. This was the New York school, and included Maurice Enger, Shirley Clarke, Lionel Robeson, and others.[1] And then there was the fourth low-low-low-budget school, the experimental school. In the last few years the two middle categories have disappeared, and we now have the "Underground Empire."

SF: What exactly is the film "underground"?
JM: In 1959–60 I wrote an essay in *Film Culture*, which described a new excitement in cinema here and abroad. Someone started to describe whatever we were doing as the "New American Cinema," which was originally the title of my essay. At the same time we began having difficulties with the police because we refused

to license our films on the ground that art should not be licensed. There was more and more nudity freely shown in the films without any inhibitions and this also irritated the censors. So, we often had to hold our screenings in small places, and a number of our screenings were closed and some of us have been arrested. Then people started using the term "underground." The connection is almost like wartime France or Ukraine where there was a political underground, and in a sense we are an underground also.

SF: Do you think the term "underground" does justice to your films?
JM: The connotation to the public is usually that the films are dirty or pornographic, which is not true. We are not ashamed of the title because it keeps us outside the "official" cinema and we can create our art in peace. However, we do not want to connect ourselves with any one term because then the term goes down in history and is forgotten and so are those who are associated with it. I think our work itself is much more important than the words which are used to describe it.

SF: What is the difference between your cinema and the more conventional cinema?
JM: In every art there are two extremes. Man expresses himself through stories, characters, and impersonation. And yet man also expresses himself in more condensed forms, more subtle forms, and then we came to poetry and abstract non-objectives. We see this in music: we have opera and we have John Cage who works only in complete sound. We can see the same thing in painting and literature. In the cinema, storytelling was long considered the only legitimate cinema, which is completely wrong because this is only one-half of man and the most subtle part of man was not expressed in film. The cinema of poetic expression started really in France in the first avant-garde, then was picked up in America in 1943–44 by Curtis Harrington, John Hugo, William Moss, Marie Menkan, Gregory Markopoulos, and others.[2] Each of these waves sort of came, grew, and slowly faded out. The second avant-garde started fading out in 1952–53, followed by a period of silent searching. Approximately 1960–61 the third avant-garde started and that is where we are now. This avant-garde is exploring and expanding the vocabulary of the poetic cinema.

SF: What were the contributions of these three avant-garde movements?
JM: The first avant-garde, the French one, succeeded in bringing the dream aspect into cinema. The novelistic cinema was broken into pieces through surrealism and this dream reality. The second avant-garde, which started in the United States, gave to this dream reality a formal aesthetic and succeeded in detaching the cinema from other arts. The main function of the third avant-garde, or underground cinema, is to free cinema from all other arts and develop a fuller poetic vocabulary. By now, the filmmaker is free to express himself in a film poetry almost as free as written poetry.

SF: How have film audiences reacted to the new cinema?

JM: Audiences are still looking at films through the eyes of their childhood, through the eyes of Hollywood. Since the work of the avant-garde is falling more to the aspect of poetry, it will never really have the audience of millions.

SF: To whom is a filmmaker responsible?

JM: The major responsibility is to yourself, and in doing this you are equally responsible to others. Creative responsibility means a search into ourselves for that reality which we feel is beautiful and needs and forces itself to be expressed as perfectly as possible. Since we are not cut off from other people, this work of art does something, it speaks to others and changes them. One single brush line, like in some Zen masterpiece, can change one's life more deeply than some huge blood-running social revolution.

SF: Then social criticism is a part of the artist's responsibility?

JM: Oh, yes. Aesthetic feelings cannot be detached from social criticism because they are deeply interrelated. Some say abstract cinema is only for the eyes; we say that the eyes are not detached from our other senses, they are part of us and part of our soul. Therefore, whatever you see changes you.

SF: Are artists fulfilling their responsibilities?

JM: The best ones, the very few creative artists, are.

SF: What are your views on film censorship?

JM: All censorship, of any kind, should be abandoned. The human body is beginning to come back into painting, into art, into sculpture, and the same with the cinema. We feel that if one is telling a story, like Gregory Markopoulos's *Illiac Passion*, the story of Prometheus, the artist doesn't have to dress his characters in twentieth-century clothing. In some scenes he presents nude figures, and he does it very beautifully. And *Illiac Passion* may be the first film which will show that the cinema is mature enough to deal with the human body aesthetically as in other arts. This is where censorship comes in and this has nothing to do with pornography and those cheap exploitation movies one sees on Forty-Second Street. What we are presenting are aesthetic views of the human body.

There are some signs that film censorship is returning in New York, but the feeling is that it would be impossible to stop the liberation, the opening up, and I think that censorship will have to go.

SF: How expensive is it to make a film?

JM: One of the first misconceptions that we had to eliminate was the so-called million-dollar myth, that only Hollywood could produce films because of the expense. Today it is cheaper to make a film than to publish a book of poetry. A book of poetry—sixty-four pages, five hundred copies—will cost about four or five hundred dollars. We can make a film for twenty dollars, therefore we are more free. The flexibility of equipment made the filmmaker more free and opened up new subjects. Of course, it comes down to knowing how to use the machinery.

SF: Is the filming carefully planned or is it improvised?

JM: Some filmmakers stressed spontaneity and unplanned films only as a reaction, because everything else was overplanned and cinema became just a translation of books. So there was a reaction and we exaggerated to make a point. Now I would say that there is no set pattern. Some improvise without a script, some use a rough outline or notes, others follow a script very closely.

SF: What relation do you see between the cinema and other arts?

JM: We have roots in life, everything is related to our childhood or families and neighbors. We have the same in art: all arts are interrelated. Perhaps you go to the Museum of Modern Art and you watch moving color patterns. The line between cinema and painting and literature: the sharp lines disappear and there are no sharp lines. When cinema was young, we had an inferiority complex and wanted to be separate from other arts, but now we do not have such inhibitions and feel free to use literature if needed.

Cinema is no longer a minor art and is closely related to other arts.

SF: Will your cinema keep changing?

JM: Cinema is changing with each generation. There are always new sensibilities and change in the air, and so one has a tendency to be interested in something else. New aspects are explored, and cinema changes.

SF: Where would you like an expansion of cinema?

JM: An important area which should be pointed out is the journalistic cinema. I have sort of an idea to open a workshop for Harlem children and give them 8mm cameras and let them record their own reality and show it on a screen. This journalistic aspect is not done on television, not done in the underground, not done anywhere. Journalistic cinema has unlimited possibilities because you do not know, for instance, what is really happening in the South; we see it from a distance and not as a very clear reality. Take Los Angeles, for example. If that reality within their homes would be filmed by Negroes fourteen or fifteen years old and brought to the screen, it just would not be the same as *Nation* magazine writing that, oh yes, the revolt took place and aren't living conditions terrible?

SF: What exactly is your role in the New American Cinema?

JM: In one aspect I am a filmmaker, but this is a very small part. In another aspect I would consider myself a sort of midwife who watches what is coming and helps it to come. My eye is always directed to new forms, and I help point them out. I am a watcher, but I am not leading; that always ends in misleading. No one has a right to do this because things will come by themselves where there is a proper sensitivity and intelligence, and if you don't have this, you cannot produce art anyway. Critics often preach about where cinema should go and what it should be, but you just cannot give directions and expect everyone to follow. We say we do not know what cinema is. We could go into a number of directions; it is a completely open field and this is when creative things begin to happen.

SF: What is the function of the Film-Makers' Cooperative and the Cinematheque?

JM: About five years ago there was a new cinema emerging but nobody would distribute our films and so we created the Film-Makers' Cooperative. We had to take care of showing and introducing the films to the public and the critics, and we conducted showcases so that the filmmakers could see their work shown properly and learn from each other. Gradually the distribution grew, and it was impossible for the Cooperative to take care of both distribution and showcasing. We split these two functions, and the Cooperative now handles distribution, and the Cinematheque takes care of showing the film. Some nights are open to anybody, sort of open house, and constantly we are watching what is happening in other cities.

SF: Would you like to see more Cinematheques opening around the country?

JM: They will. They will be opening very soon in Boston and Los Angeles. They will have different names, but they will be theaters devoted only to this cinema. Matter of fact, we just created a new branch of the Cooperative which will deal only with this aspect: the distribution and enlarging.

SF: A national magazine recently divided the New American Cinema into three schools, namely, the Sensualist, the Documentalist, and the Abstractionist. What was your reaction?

JM: These are not schools, really. Each filmmaker is doing something different. Each has his own vision, each is a school in himself. There might be some who fall into categories, but you could find not three or five but many schools. There is always a tendency to reduce, to departmentalize people in art, but we are trying to open everything. We are still opening, and this is not the time to close us into groups or terms.

SF: Will the New American Cinema remain permanently separated from Hollywood?

JM: I think Hollywood in the very end must be replaced and I think it will be replaced without accepting any of Hollywood's corruptions and clichés. This is always the problem because once you go directly there, you must accept that system and that system determines the kind of work you can do. This is what happened to the French New Wave. After a deep creative and financial crisis around 1960, French directors went to Hollywood and accepted the system. French cinema today is in a crisis. It changed its face and the old craggy French cinema is now covered with Madison Avenue plastic surgery. This is the difference between the New Wave and the New American Cinema. The New Wave was the same old cinema under a different face while the underground is a free, organic outgrowth and therefore it has all the possibilities of growing. The New American Cinema grew up like an ugly child: nobody liked it, they kicked it, they hoped it would die. And this child did not compromise, did not accept the establishment; this child did not respect, and was in fact spitting on his parents. And now this child is growing and is very independent.

SF: In the final analysis, what makes a film great?

JM: It is the same thing that makes any creation a great work of art. When form, content, and style reach the most perfect expression, this is art. To create a perfect work of art one has to have accumulated and absorbed within himself a sensitivity to reality, to know what man's preoccupations are; he has to experience what man is right now and then express it in a most perfect manner. One has to be a complete master of all the techniques available to him: he does not have to know all the techniques, just those which are suitable to his art.

SF: Could you give us a final comment on the difference between the New American Cinema and the established cinema?

JM: A work of art cannot continue clichés and the same old routines. Very often I have been reproached for advocating the new. I feel that only the new is moral, because if a work is only repeating something like an old record, the growth of man is stopped because only what is new is growth. We are creating cinema. The rest is immoral, outdated, a continuation of dead matter. The only new, and therefore the only moral cinema, is the New American Cinema.

Notes

1. There are several errors in the original printed version of this article. "Maurice Enger" refers to Morris Engel. "Lionel Robeson" refers to Lionel Rogosin.

2. "John Hugo" more likely refers to Ian Hugo. "William Moss" is likely a mistaken transcription of Willard Maas. Marie Menken is misspelled as Menkan.

Jonas Mekas at Massachusetts Institute of Technology

Massachusetts Institute of Technology Q&A Session / 1971

Previously unpublished. Printed by permission of the Estate of Jonas Mekas.

Editor's Introduction: This is a transcription of a question and answer session in which Mekas participated at Massachusetts Institute of Technology, January 19, 1971. It is worth noting that the filmmakers Stan Vanderbeek and Richard Leacock also partici-pated in asking Mekas questions. Some audience questions could not be transcribed due to poor sound quality.

Question: How do you prepare your soundtracks?

Jonas Mekas: I am still working on them. The first volume of the *Diaries* that I have issued for the public is called *Diaries, Notes & Sketches*, also known as *Walden*. First draft. That is, the image will remain, more or less, as is. But the soundtrack may change. I am still searching for the proper sounds. In some cases I am using actual sounds, of the actual scenes, situations, events; in some cases I use them as they originally came, in others greatly condensed, changed. Still in other cases I am using music, blocks of sounds and music, for structural purposes, or to tie certain bits together, or to stress certain aspects. The basic background, for the first volume, is the New York street and subway noise; that's the background against which all other sounds are placed.

Question: What do you think about video?

JM: I don't know much about video. I can only speak about cassettes. I think they'll have revolutionary implications; they will revolutionize the dissemination of what we call films. And since the dissemination will be changed, automatically it will af-fect the movies themselves, that is, how they will be produced, how they'll be made, the length of the movies—a number of conventions that have been established, like, for instance, that the movie has to be two hours long, such conventions will simply disappear, they won't have any meaning any longer. There will be movies made that will run for days and days, and you'll be watching them like you read books. You don't read the entire *War and Peace* in one sitting, you read twenty pages today, twenty perhaps tomorrow, etc., and it doesn't bother you at all. Same will be with movies.

Question: Is your goal to recreate your subjective reality?

JM: It doesn't matter what goal I set for myself: whatever you do, you are the center of what you do. You cannot be objective. Whatever you do you do through yourself. When we say that we are aiming at objectivity, what it means usually is that we are aiming at certain realities which we, for sake of convention, call objective or objectivity. Still, they are chosen and presented through our own personal self, eyes. I'd almost say, the rule is, that the more subjective one is, the more objectivity one can attain. The deeper you go into yourself, the more you'll touch the others, at some point. But if you begin to want to be very objective, to want everybody to see the same, you're forced to stick to a certain defined level, and you remain on the surface, and reveal really nothing of value to others.

Question: [something about lyrical "pace" of *Diaries*]

Jonas Mekas: You see, the lyrical pace, the epic pace, these are qualities determined by the content and the form. The prose, in literature, has one kind of pacing, one kind of reality; the poetry is much more concentrated, there are many more levels of content touched there, the language is more complex also, the rhythms and pacing more complex.

Stan Vanderbeek: I am fascinated with what Jonas was saying. Because my interest now is in another level of image manipulation, of mixing them together. Jonas is more interested in the process of shooting. It may be opposite, two opposites.

JM: We say, these are the opposites, but maybe it's not. The only thing is that you, Stan, are after one kind of reality, a reality that has to do with your entire past, and I am after another kind of reality that has to do with my entire past, determined by my past.

SV: That's exactly so. That's quite fascinating that you assume that it has to do with former realities.

JM: I definitely think so. Because when we say, that really, I am shooting, and I am trying to catch the moment as is, an event as is . . . you see, I don't end up with that.

If you'd see, say, the three-hour version of my *Diaries*, you'd find that the basis is New York City, the seasons as they go by, notes, sketches of events. But these are not exactly objective sketches, pieces of reality, because I ended up with a New

York that nobody recognizes as the actual New York. It's my own dream, fantasy New York, and really even the wedding sequence that you saw (*Peter's Wedding*) is my dream, fantasy wedding, because the groom and the bride had a very different, completely different impression of the wedding. They made a tape of the wedding, during the wedding, and the tape has a completely different attitude to everything. Peter likes my wedding film, but that wasn't what he saw, not how he felt during the wedding; it's rather how he feels now, in retrospect. That's how my movie is, and that's why he likes it now. So that I ended up with my own artificial, concocted, subjective reality there, but not with an objective wedding, or an objective New York, etc. So now, you, Stan, you pick up bits from there and there and there, and you work in the editing room, and you change all the materials, and you end up with completely something else also, with a different kind of reality. It's just another concocted, fantasy reality that corresponds to whatever needs you have, and it's as personal as mine. It's neither present nor future.

SV: I think that the detail that I'm particularly interested in examining, is the cinéma-vérité type of thing, where you have to be there at the moment to make that come alive. That's the film I understand you are trying to make. And that's what I'm trying to understand, because it's very opposite from what I'm making.
JM: I could try to understand why I'm doing this and why you are doing that. The way I see it, when I try to understand why I am doing things *my way*, it goes like this: I was born, I grew up somewhere else, you see. I am very stable, I never leave a place, unless I really have to, unless somebody's pushing me, unless somebody takes me almost by force somewhere. I just sit there. I begin to grow my roots in, you know. You drop me into a desert, next day you come back, I'll have roots in . . . I was uprooted from my home, really, by force. And I couldn't go back. I grew up, until I was fifteen, I grew up, I lived in the fields, with the cows, and sheep, and trees, and nature, almost 90 percent of the time.

So then, when you cannot go back, you are constantly preoccupied with it. I say, I am very stable—but no place is really my place, that's why wherever I'm dropped, I let my roots in, I want to be with it, there, and nowhere else, because I don't belong anywhere.

I belong somewhere in my old home—of course, maybe I don't belong even there, but because I was pulled out by force of circumstances, and I couldn't go back, I keep thinking that I belong there. I would go back there, and you know, I may not belong there either. Now, you don't have that kind of problem, that specific reality, that preoccupation. I may be at a point of maybe escaping that reality too. I catch myself more and more often thinking about doing something completely artificial, working with imaginary, fantasy realities, materials, and forms. But I got stuck, for a very long time, with my childhood reality, so much that even my

New York becomes my childhood. If you see my *Diaries*, you see all those seasons, winters, snow, snow, a lot of snow. What is this, how much snow does New York really have? But my New York is full of snow. How come? Because I grew up with snow. So it's a fantasy. I am a romantic, you see, and you are . . .

SV: I understand your point. What I am prodding here, is technotronics, these machines that we use to translate these freedoms, or whatever we call them; we try to get away from the reality that . . .

JM: Maybe I am trying to keep certain fragments of reality, maybe I am more sentimental, I have these sentimental attachments. Now, you are trying, you say, to destroy all this old reality, old meanings. So you throw in five, six different images there, on that screen. So you are wiping out really, all the meanings, in your films, so that they become "meaningless" bits of visual impacts, lines, spaces: the meaning of medium itself . . .

The question of meaninglessness is not that simple. For instance, from the student films that I have seen during my stay here, those films became sort of interesting to me when the obvious meaning disappeared. There were many very literal, one-, two-, three-meaning films, certain stories, certain jokes, certain anecdotes, certain very simple documentaries, and they were very clear what they were all about. And then, one or two films, in one or two films the meanings and clarity disappeared, it was not very clear what they were all about. There were certain images, forms, but their meaning wasn't too clear. Those films became more interesting to me. Whenever the obvious, literal meanings disappear, there is a mystery of something else. Because, let's face it: we know that there is nothing, absolutely nothing without a meaning, and everything affects everything else. So that those films, those images, those paces, those rhythms of that film that seemingly has no meaning—in truth these films have their own meanings there.

They are never literal, or too literal, they are on other levels. There are meanings or impacts in them that affect us. So that there it becomes interesting. That's where Stan's work, when I am watching your work, that's where your meanings are, on that other, not literal, level. It's easy to say: oh, just images! But it's not that simple, because this film that you call a *Newsreel of Dreams*, you could find equivalents of that form, in literature, it's like a Sutra, like one of Ginsberg's *Sutras*, the *Wichita Sutra*, for instance—there are glimpses, bits of images of reality around you, like in Ginsberg's *Sutra*. The meaning of Ginsberg's *Wichita Sutra* is not in the words alone, in the sense of words or sentences alone; it's also in how it works, in the movements of those words, what it does.

So that the meanings of your sutra and Ginsberg's *Sutra*, no matter how confused both may seem to some, their meanings will become clearer and clearer as time goes. We can never escape reality. We say, oh, he's an escapist. No, you can't escape reality. You maybe are escaping some obvious realities, which we recognize as realities, the popular realities, the obvious ideas and meanings, but you cannot escape those that are already here but are not that obvious and not that clear yet, but some of us, like Stan, reflects them anyway, and those meanings are not Stan's meanings, and meanings of my movies are not exactly my meanings: because we are not an island, Stan is not an island, we are connected with everybody very deeply and no man is an island. Like all of you, like everybody. There it is: how can you escape reality?

SV: What I am doing here, you see, is reality of the machine. I am trying to deal with some kind of technological reality. This was done in a TV studio in alarmingly high speed, done in real time. We are dealing with this immensely delicate technology. . . . What I am dealing with here, in a practical sense, is an anthology of images, and I am not really interested in the literal part or in the social content. I am more in the area of the dreams, and I want to absolutely make contact with that. I want to make long films, eight hours, like *Sleep*. You come in, and I intend to put you to sleep, I want to trigger your system . . .

JM: You are talking about machines, and tools, but we never see them on the screen, same as you never see my Bolex. What we see, at the very end, is your films. So that you end up with as personal a work as I do in my own different way. Because I have watched your *Dream Newsreel* at a number of different projections, at different stages, and I see it becoming more and more personal, as you develop it, as it keeps growing—same, as my film diaries. We cannot escape our subjectivity.

[New reel]

JM: I sent the *Notes on the Circus* to Stan Brakhage, and it became his children's favorite film. Then, one day, the Ringling Brothers' Circus came to Denver, and the children heard of it, and they said, "Oh, Jonas's Circus is in town, we have to see Jonas's Circus!" So they went, and after ten minutes Stan had to take them home, they were crying: "This is not Jonas's Circus! We want to see Jonas's Circus!" Make out of this story whatever you want. But I was not interested in recording the circus. I was interested in recording certain movements, colors, certain memories of movement and color, and certain bits of realities.

Question: [something about "one feels like watching a bad dream," referring to Vanderbeek films]
JM: What's wrong with bad dreams: Why not bad dreams?

Question: [Summary: While watching Stan Vanderbeek, and Jonas's *Diaries*, she came to the conclusion that Stan's movies are more intellectual than those of Jonas's. . . . But she feels that both, Stan's and Jonas's films lacked emotions.]
SV: Sure, I am involved in this difficult problem, sure. My movie making at the moment, is setting up the technology, is structuring with technology, is taking these systems that we now have and exploring them in an entirely new context. What I am hoping for is that there is some common denominator of emotion. I am groping for it.

JM: I think your film was full of emotion. How do you put emotion on film? Either through certain images or through certain rhythms and pacing and movements. Really, should the film really cry hot tears through every frame, and spell by name every emotion, every feeling? Because the truth is that it's you who is responding and reading the images. It's there. In Stan's *Sutra* I felt all kinds of movements and emotions there, from desperation to I don't know what. One could react to it and feel it. As for myself, the *Diaries*—probably I'm too emotional in my films, and maybe that's the problem with me. Maybe the lady could explain herself better to us, why she can't feel any emotions in Stan's or my work. Our films are dripping with emotions. You see, not to feel, not to see emotion in something is not always the fault of the film or book or . . . because one cannot produce anything without having in it some emotion. So it's all up to you to which images you respond and to which you don't. It may be your own problem.

   . . . The same I'd say about those who are looking in films, Stan's or mine, for some very concrete and contemporary "social" or "timely" meanings, and they miss them. Because we are used to seeing only very obvious, literal, on-the-surface recognizable meanings, responses to reality, what's happening today around us, on a certain level.

   But when that is placed on a deeper level, then we think maybe it's not there, although we feel, if we are really open to it, that it is there. You'll feel that it's there, and maybe on a much more important, more subtle level, where it will affect you and will impart knowledge to you more subtle than if you'd say, okay, Nixon is stupid, cops are pigs, the world stinks. Stan's film may be a more political film than those which, you know, sometimes you hear, everybody says, "Oh, this is a political film." Those are not political films! Those are propaganda films on certain very obvious matters that everybody knows; they are only repeating the same and the same and there is no meaning in them and no affect.

Question: [unclear]
Richard Leacock: . . . I will work with 8mm sync sound which will give me a lot more freedom. I'd like sort of inch in the direction of Jonas, in making notes. How

one works out these things, it's no problem, I don't know. I don't know all the answers. But it seems to be in that direction. And that's what I feel is important now, which way you are heading.

Question: [something about *Circus*]

JM: I didn't start filming because I found myself at the circus. I made, I had to make special arrangements to get into the circus, to film it, and I was waiting for it for a number of years. Because I wanted to record certain movements, certain details, certain memories, certain preoccupations concerning with that subject, with that event.

Jonas Mekas at Findlay College

Findlay College Q&A Session / 1971

Previously unpublished. Printed by permission of the Estate of Jonas Mekas.

Editor's Introduction: The following is taken from a transcript of a question and answer session at Findlay College (now the University of Findlay) in Findlay, Ohio, January 21–22, 1971. Audience questions are summarized due to poor sound quality.

Jonas Mekas: Before you see the films, I wanted to say something about the subject of this session, "The Changing Language of Cinema," and about the films that you are going to see. The cinema is changing, the language of cinema is changing. When the language of cinema is changing, what kind of changes are those? It always comes down, when one begins to try to understand those changes, it always comes down to the subject matter that is changing, and the attitudes. That is, one begins to look at the subject from a new angle, and that new way of looking affects the syntax and affects the language. The content is inseparable from language, from form, the two always go together.

Here we are speaking about the changing language of cinema. When we look at a regular movie, the Hollywood movie, that is 99 percent of cinema that you usually see today, the European Art Movie and the Hollywood movie—it tells a story, these are storytelling, narrative fiction movies. The story is being told, there is a certain pace, there are all those characters there, we follow the characters, their actions. The language of fiction, of narrative film is bent towards presenting the story and the protagonists who enact the stories. There is a certain pace involved in this language, you can't rush too much, because speed is concentration and concentration runs into abstraction. You have to stay with the protagonist for a certain length of time and proceed at a certain pace. They cannot move too fast, the camera cannot move too fast, so that you are always there, with those characters, they don't disappear into abstract patterns, they are there, as "real" as possible. Because that is basically the storytelling cinema. And that's what about 99 percent of cinema was and still is today.

There is much talk about the underground filmmakers, about the underground cinema. You get all kinds of distorted impressions from the press, what's all about.

Usually, if we are going to follow the opinions of the press, what the underground film is all about, it's a movie that deals with the sensational aspects of life, most of the time, sex. Which, in reality, has nothing to do with what the underground film is really all about. What the underground filmmaker has been doing, mainly, during the last ten years, has been this: As in any other art—music, literature, painting—you have always these two extremes of expression: on one hand, you have the narrative, the reenactments of certain myths, experiences via the protagonists, and through the story; and on the other hand, we turn to the more indirect forms of expression, the symbols, and metaphors, further and further from the conventional narrative language and forms. So we have this in cinema now too, the narrative and nonnarrative cinema; we express ourselves through both of these extremes. If we would have only the narrative forms available for expression, it would mean, that one part of us, a great part, is being neglected, not expressed. But in cinema, till now, we had basically only the storytelling cinema. What the avant-garde filmmaker has done, he has developed the language, the vocabulary, the syntax, the forms, the approaches, the technology, the techniques of the nonnarrative film. So that the cinema has been brought to a certain fullness, as an art. You don't have, in cinema, to tell only the stories today. As in other arts, there are other forms available to you now in cinema. You may do a film "short story," or you may make short, one-minute "film poems," or, as you have in literature, you may choose the form of a haiku; or you may make longer film poems. You have in cinema today all these possibilities, the cinema is open to a very wide number of nonnarrative forms, more varieties of different content are being touched, dealt with, revealed, opened.

We spoke about the pace of prose, how one has to stay within certain movements, in order to follow the protagonists. As soon as we go to the forms of poetry, of nonnarrative cinema, the language immediately changes. Because we are dealing with a different content. There are compounds of meanings. There, many more things are touched, presented in the space of, say, one page. Take Ezra Pound, a page from *Cantos*, and compare it with a page from any prose book. We deal with compounded meanings here, presented only by suggestion, indirectly, through bits, fragments, through metaphors, or collage relationships—by all the means available to, say, poetry. The language changes because the form and the content changed. The rhythms, the paces of language are affected, the construction, the emphasis; the language leaves naturalism of prose to become a heightened language of poetry.

Now, besides these changes from form to form, from narrative to nonnarrative forms, there are other changes. There are changes between generations. The language, the feelings, the emotions of the generation of the sixties and seventies are not radically different, but they differ in many subtle ways, they differ in their inflections, in their subtle movements, subtle rhythms, innuendos, etc., etc., and these are caught by the artists and reflected in their art. The literature of one generation doesn't differ from that of the next one *radically*—nobody invents the dictionary from scratch—but it differs in many subtle ways, which sometimes become quite wide. We say that the last decade had made a big jump; we see much bigger, than usually, differences in the contemporary art.

Particularly in the development of the nonnarrative cinema. If there was no urgency for its coming into existence before, it means only that the content with which avant-garde film dealt with had no urgency to come into the open yet. But now it's coming out.

There is some kind of internal logic whenever the language of art changes, logic for that change. When the songs of poets change, the walls crumble—how does that old saying go?

What example could I give you that would illustrate the basic and new differences between the contemporary narrative and nonnarrative film, at least some aspects of it?

Say, you film a tree. A tree is standing there. You shoot it, say, for fifteen seconds, and you project it on the screen. It's fine, a tree is there, but there is something missing. It isn't a tree you really saw. What you saw, when you decided to film that tree, you saw it from a certain state of being. What's missing in that tree on the screen is you, what you felt when you noticed the tree, when you thought about filming it. Because there was a reason why you looked at the tree. Why did you look at that tree that moment? Some memory, some circumstance, some reason that leads far into your past, had to do with why you looked at that tree. So that the problem becomes: how to catch with the camera that tree, and yourself at the moment of looking at the tree, your state, your feeling, your thoughts.

How to achieve this? No doubt, there are several ways of doing it. Like, you could indicate it with qualities of light, or qualities of your camera movement. At least that it's how it was done till recently. But recently, another thing came in. It's as follows.

The projector throws image on the screen, twenty-four frames per second. The filmmaker came gradually to realize that these twenty-four frames per second are, practically, equivalent to twenty-four notes per second with which he can write his films. Like a composer writing down his music. So he began restructuring reality by means of these single frame notes. And this became the basis of practically all contemporary modern nonnarrative cinema. It became one of the basic principles of the film language. So that when now I film this tree that I was speaking about, now I completely restructure it. One frame, three frames, blank, one frame—each time different pacing, different movement. Into these twenty-four frames so much more rhythmical and textural and emotional (movement) information is concentrated that it begins to combine, express not only the reality that's filmed, the tree, but also that reality that is *filming* that tree: the author, his state of feeling, of being, that moment.

Both are being merged here now into one unity, the filmed representational reality, and the indirect reality of the filmer, of the filmmaker.

This kind of language, this kind of filming, however, is connected, almost automatically, with other requirements. It requires that the filmmaker be in total mastery of his tools because most of the structuring, what's known as editing (the meaning of which is now being redefined) has to be done during the moment of filming, during the moment of immediate response to the reality, to our tree. Same as in written poetry, all the structuring, all the pacing of it and etc., etc. is done during the actual writing of it.

You are structuring the painting when you are painting it. And you can't think, when you are painting, which way you should move the brush, which way should the hand move the brush, right or left, or how much pressure to exert, and exactly how long the stroke should be, and etc., etc. So the same is with the filmmaker. The camera had to become an extension of his hand, of his eye, of his mind; he uses it as the painter is using the brush, intuitively and automatically.

[end of tape]

* * * * *

Question: [about editing]

JM: The ideas about editing are changing. There are different stages in the history of editing. Where we are now, basically we have this: In the narrative film, there are at least two obvious stages of editing, or structuring—because editing is really structuring: there is editing, structuring during the shooting, on the set, movements of camera, movements of actors, movements of light, movements of voices, and etc., etc.—within the shot. Then, there is what's called post-editing: editing, structuring with parts of the shots, in the editing room. There is one style of narrative film today, which developed from the cinéma-vérité tradition, films like Mailer's films, or Morrissey's films, where practically all structuring is done during the shooting. In the editing room, it's not editing that is done, but trimming of ends, tails, selecting best takes, etc., which is not editing, really: it's assembling. Still, when we look at the procedures in writing, we find these different habits and procedures between prose and poetry writers. Say, Mailer, I read the other day somewhere, he said, every day he gets up, and between 9:00 a.m. and 1:00 p.m. he sits and writes. Every day. And that's normal, a normal, good procedure for a novelist. Now, can you imagine, have you ever heard of a poet writing poems every day from 9:00 a.m. to 1:00 p.m.? Working within such a routine? So that we have these different procedures not only between different arts but even in one single art, between two different forms of that art, between the narrative and nonnarrative forms. The procedures in most of the nonnarrative cinema, are similar to the procedures of other nonnarrative art forms: either you get it now, when you are responding to something, either you get it now, or you won't get it; certainly you won't be able to "create" it in the editing room if you didn't get it to begin with your camera. Exactly, like in painting or writing: either you wrote it or not. You can make some changes, improve it here and there, later: but, essentially, the poem or painting is already there. The camera will move, the structure will respond, will correspond to your immediate reaction to the reality that is happening right there and now.

Question: [about Joyce]

JM: For those who did not hear the question, I will sum it up: The gentleman said, that according to Joyce, he stated it somewhere, ideally the artist should strive to merge or coincide his inner illumination with that of the reader. The gentleman says, the filmmakers he has spoken to, usually refuse to comment on that aspect.

The difficulty here is that if an artist is really concentrating on what he's working on, be it a simple event or a complex set of ideas and events, he really is involved in creation and he is not very conscious of himself, he is sort of oblivious of the facts of how he is doing it. There is so much of an intuitive process involved here that he doesn't exactly know what his own state is. I guess, there are others, who have more distance from themselves during the moment of creation; maybe Joyce had that distance. But it is very difficult for him, the artist, to analyze the relationship to his work, to speak about his own illuminations and those of the reader; he doesn't know, most of the time, what and how he did it—except on a superficial level. To ask, really, the question: "How did you create it," this question—which is approximately what you are asking—is as unanswerable as the question: "What is Art?" In truth, how many things, really, are there in life about which you can say anything with a certainty, what they really are? We keep asking, what is that all about, what is art all about, what is this work all about, what is this artist all about? But these are complex processes, and they cannot be reduced to one meaning or one idea. We always want to reduce everything to one answer. But there are many answers: any formula for one answer has to include time: answers change and multiply with time, in space and time.

There are many answers, many directions, it's complex. So I don't blame the artists for not really answering your question. They could answer it, of course, they could make an attempt. They could try to look back, they could abstract it, they could trace back. That has been done. Still, then the question is whether such tracings are true or not. The artist is speaking already from another point in time:

not from the illumination of the moment of creation, but from the moment of reflection, much later, what one feels about it now, what it means to the artist now, etc. One can fantasize—which, in fact, may be more illuminating and useful than if one would be telling the "truth." You see, the processes of filmmaking, the techniques, these are very concrete: there is the camera, there is film, there are twenty-four frames, there is a wedding that is taking place and which I'm filming. . . . But beyond that point, it's no longer that clear, it becomes more complex.

Even if you'd be shooting a most simple detail, like my example of a tree standing in the park. Because, fine, you are filming it, but *why* are you filming it, why did you choose to film this tree and not the other, next to it, and *why* the tree and not something else there. The complications come in, memories and past and present determined why you chose this and not that, etc. Then you begin to film and there are so many ways of doing it. But you do it only one way. Something from inside, your entire past, directs you that you do things this and that and that way. So that you don't really film the tree: you film your memory. That tree attracted you, there was a reason, and the tree is a fantasy, no longer just an object, it's surrounded with all kinds of complications. And so you film the tree, say. But when you look on the screen, at that tree, you realize that what you see on the screen is not what you saw in that tree when you filmed it. So you have then to find a way. You have to film not only the tree, but all the memories, all the reasons that caused, that pulled you into the filming that tree. You have to combine both the reasons and reality, and you cannot intellectualize, you can record on film your reasons and yourself only by restructuring that tree that you are filming, breaking it down to individual single frames and restructuring it frame by frame. If not frame by frame, then movement by movement, etc., etc.—there are many ways of restructuring reality. You can also do it by juxtapositions, by cutting to the face of the protagonist, say, and his face may reflect the reason, etc., etc. But I do it by means of single frames, pacing, movement, light, and a number of many other means.

And you can't just sit and work out everything on paper. Either you get it while filming it, or you don't. Because that camera is an extension of your total being, like the artist's brush is the extension of his eye, of his total being. The artist cannot think about such details as: should my hand pull the brush now to the right or left or down, and how much to press, the pressure on the brush—if he'd start thinking consciously about all these secondary matters, he would just stop dead in the middle of the stroke. All this must be an automatic process. It's like walking. You make your art like you walk. Or let's say, you make your art as you walk a tightrope. . . . So that's my answer to your question. You see, I have no answers to anything, I can only ramble around the questions, round and round.

Question: [something about reality; whether artists are coming closer to reality or going away from it]

JM: The fact, what is reality, keeps shifting. The abstractions of 1910 became very real realities of 1960, our new reality. What was called abstract art, nonobjective or objective art, today we find that we can discuss it already in terms of reality. Light, for instance. They used to say: what is this, this is just light! But light is also reality, reality on a number of levels. Any energy, any color, is reality. Different shapes affect you differently, do something to other reality. Not only the table or a bowl of fruit, nature-morte, is reality: anything that has any impact, that can be perceived in any way, acts upon us: all is reality. So that to speak about trends, as you ask: are the artists coming closer to reality or away from it—a question like that has less and less meaning. Okay, so we have those who paint very naturalistic landscapes, the concept realists. Scenes, people, either from photographs or real life. Then there are those whom we call abstractionists or some other names. But they are working with different realities, as real as the other realities. As a matter of fact, to me they are greater realists, their realities are even more real than the realities of the so-called realists, because the so-called realists deal with the very surface aspects of reality. The structuralists, the minimalists, what Frampton is doing, or Snow, or Paul Sharits, they are to me the true realists of cinema.

So that we have here these two ends, or opinions on reality.

Question: [about Marie Menken's *Notebook*, a reference to the fact that to the viewer it seemed that some of the things or parts were self-conscious, like the playing with the moon bit]

JM: It is true that Menken, in a number of her films, there are parts where she is very conscious of what she's doing, and this we call self-conscious. She has said herself I think that some parts of this film were made to entertain, to keep company to a sick friend, passing time. But this self-consciousness, that note of self-consciousness can be also taken as part of a certain style, part of the content. I don't see it as taking something away from the work, but as adding to it. Also, it may look as a wrong note when you see only one work of an artist; but it becomes part of the artist's style when you see a group, a larger body of the artist's work. After all, Marie Menken is not working within a style of slick, impersonal cinema. She doesn't even look at her films as works of art, no. These are very simple, very personal home movies. That's closer to the way she sees them.

She wants to talk to you very personally, and very closely.

She is not talking to you with a voice that is clean, formal voice, but she speaks with little hesitations, mistakes, self-consciousness—these things give her films a certain warmth and truthfulness, directness.

JM: [answering a question about *Serene Velocity*] How to approach, how to analyze a film like *Serene Velocity*, or other works of the structural kind? One thing I could say, it doesn't work on the emotional and memory levels. It works on a sort of mental level. Yes, there are certain details in it of representational reality. But it all works only through its structure, rhythm, time. It works on the mental plane where it does something, provokes, acts upon, sets in motion certain rhythms or waves corresponding to what we see, a sort of meditational rhythm. There is such a thing. You know, there are institutes now which work with the alpha waves, connected to certain parts of the brain, and certain frequencies are being sent to those parts of the brain, and depending on the frequencies, natures of waves, and time we are exposed to them, we are put into certain states of feeling, into certain attitudes—depression, happiness, meditation, etc. And after certain time, after certain number of exposures to these rhythms, one can evoke them by one's own will. . . . So that's what the scientists are working on. But that sort of thing, it seems to me, deals with the same area of our experience as the structural art or the concept art: the mental area. What this is, really, is exploring a different area of experiential reality. During the centuries of our evolution we have explored the reality around us and inside us so much that it has become, this knowledge, like a weight deterring our further evolution, so that the evolutionary forces are pulling us now almost by force into different realities, opening to us different possibilities. So that these films, *Serene Velocity*, these are among the first signs and sights of the new reality, or waking up certain sectors of ourselves. These films are like electricity, art is electricity of a sort`.

In other words, we are still expanding, we are not shrinking. Don't get alarmed, humanity, the evolutionary necessities, Darwin's law will save us yet. There are some who say, "Oh cinema will replace all the other arts. We have a new art here that will replace them all!" We have a few apostles who say that cinema will replace all them, but they disregard the fact that humans are complex beings. If cinema came into existence, this doesn't mean now that all the other senses will be cut off; what it means is that there is one more aspect coming into existence, one more added extra to the ones we have already. That's why I think it's fantastic that films like *Serene Velocity* and Snow's films are being made. There are tremendous meanings in these films for us, and there are very few meanings in the so-called naturalist art.

JM: The title is *Diaries, Notes, and Sketches*. In literature, we keep a diary, we write. Say, in the evening, we look back, we sit down, we look back, and we write. It's a process of looking back upon what already has happened, remembering, reflecting. In cinema, if one wishes to do that, it means recreation, it means Hollywood. Such a diary is conceivable, in cinema. But the kind of diary that I was interested in exploring in cinema, was the diary of an immediate response, of immediate reaction, wherever I was. It's not looking back, it's not reflecting. What you'll see in my diaries, it's always an immediate reaction to the actual situation around me. I have been carrying my camera with me for the last ten years wherever I go every day, and I have been filming every day. Sometimes maybe just a few frames, other days maybe a few seconds, and still other days maybe a few minutes, a few rolls of film. I chose some of that footage to include in this version of the *Diaries*, in the same way, as a writer of a diary would do. The process in the selection was similar to the one that a writer of a diary would do: he would reread his diaries, he'd eliminate some of the less interesting or repetitive or badly written days. He may cross out a few paragraphs, here and there. Some days maybe interesting within the context of, say, ten pages, but would become too repetitive and would diminish the interestingness of other days, in the context of three hundred pages: it would throw the whole thing off balance. The same processes were involved in my case. I reduced the twenty hours or so of footage to three hours and ten minutes. . . . Some are just very brief notes, others are longer sketches, as long as ten minutes.

You'll notice that the basic film language principle used in my diaries is one where the starting basis is the single frame. One twenty-fourth of a second image note with which the modern filmmaker writes his films. Twenty-four notes per second.

I have been obsessed during this period with the actual reality, not with some unusual events that would stand out by themselves no matter how you film them; I am not interested in anything unusual. I am interested in how to catch very usual daily events, happenings, like street scenes, snow falling, tree in wind: how to put them there on that screen so that they would be of some interest to myself and one who is looking at it. That has been my main preoccupation. I already told you this afternoon, that the only way of filming that reality, I discovered, was by beginning with the smallest time component, one frame, and then restructuring the entire situation and introducing myself into it. I spoke already about that, that's the reason for my single frame filming. Not for reasons of abstraction: it's for reason of greater realism, of coming closer to the content. It's a method of language, it's a way of "writing," it's a style.

As you'll notice, I'm not criticizing reality, I'm not laughing at it: if anything, I am celebrating it. I am celebrating reality around me. And celebration is an attitude. This attitude—how can you celebrate it in film? It has to do with how you film it, it has to do with the rhythm and pacing. There are rhythms and paces of sadness, there are rhythms and paces of celebration, and these attitudes can be caught on film only by restructuring reality, by means, in my case, of single frames. There are other ways.

Question: I have a question, whether the use of editing and techniques were planned or it sort of fell where it may. There were several cases where I saw various densities etc. which seemed such a randomnesque use, almost like a purposeless, if not absolutely blatant dependence on accidents of photography.

JM: I know what you are driving at, and let me ramble for two minutes around it. Like, there was a time—this concerns the technical aspects, the abuses of, let's say, focus, lighting, movement. There was a time when film schools and film students and filmmakers and film studios and film directors and the cameramen knew very clearly that there is such a thing as proper exposure, a certain proper movement of the camera, of angle, of focus. There was such a thing as sharp, good focus, and if it was a little bit off, it was wrong. Now, during the last ten years, these things have changed. We came to the conclusion, the filmmaker came to the conclusion, that there was no such thing as normal exposure, normal focus. Like, you have two extremes: on one end you may totally overexpose: total white. Then you go through one million or three hundred gradations, and end up with total underexposure, total black. In movement: you can be totally static, or you go through all the variations of movement and end up with total frenzy.

In focus: you go from total out-of-focus, and all the focuses in between, and at the other end you have a very sharp focus. You may use all those steps, according to what you need for what you are after, what you need for the shot, for the scene, for the mood, for the feeling, for the rhythm, for the structure. How that is used and where, that can be very calculated, or it can be intuitive—all of this has become part of the vocabulary.

When one writes one doesn't calculate very consciously what each syllable or each word is—you don't think about every movement of the brush. The same here. My *Diaries* were filmed already with this new language of cinema, within the new film aesthetics. Yes, there are certain mistakes there, here and there, they happen when you work, and maybe you didn't want it exactly that way. But sometimes you see them, you incorporate the little chances and mistakes within the structure—there is an area within which they are also part of the controlled language. Like you control the structure of bars, but permit chance within the bars. Really, it's like in any other art. You control the brush stroke, but what the brush does, is all chance: no two brush strokes are ever really the same.

Question: The image of yourself, the image that you have of yourself, is that important to this film?

JM: The image of myself . . . You see, I had twenty hours of film, before I began editing this version. I reduced it to three hours and ten minutes. Now, that cutting out of say seventeen hours of film, it was a footage that was badly written, etc.—but maybe also . . . You see, one has no control over one's own image. But whatever I left, whatever is there, you can tell from this film more about me than I could.

Because, maybe what I left in tells more about me than what I took out, because I was more conscious of myself in the footage I took out than in the footage that I left. . . . It's an open book, I'm the living character of these film pages. . . . That is, if you know how to read it. Because, yes, it's New York there on the screen, but then, it's not New York "as is." Because everybody hates New York "as is," it's a very bleak, and morbid place, they say, a depressing place. But those who see my film, they say, "Oh, I'd like to live there." But it's my fantasy New York. So there is no such thing as filming reality as it is. All these seasons and snow! Who sees snow in New York? There is no snow in New York.

But there is plenty of snow where I come from, see. I am shooting my childhood, so it's a fantasy. The camera eye doesn't lie? Yes, it films your fantasies in full-color truth.

An Interview with Jonas Mekas

Babette Mangolte / 1971

Previously unpublished. Printed by permission of Babette Mangolte.

Editor's Introduction: The following is a transcript of an interview Mekas conducted with Babette Mangolte on November 27, 1971. Mangolte is best known for her collaborations with Chantal Akerman, which include serving as cinematographer for Jeanne Dielman, 23 quai du Commerce, 1080 Bruxelles *(1975). She is also the director of many experimental films and documentaries. The interview was discovered in Mekas's personal archives with only the interviewer's initials given. Fortunately, Mekas had saved his diary entries from that day.*

Jonas Mekas: Did you give some thought to what you want me to talk about?

Babette Mangolte: I think you are the right kind of person to make a manifesto, if it's not presumptuous, on the new independent film.
JM: Not a manifesto, but a brief introduction into what is being done.

BM: Yes.
JM: I will try to summarize what has been done during the last ten years, the directions.

BM: Since the creation of the Film-Makers' Cooperative?
JM: Yes. One main achievement during last ten years, of course, is the legitimizing of the nonnarrative forms of cinema as part of the totality of cinema. As it's well known, the nonnarrative film till about ten years ago, and outside of the United States even today, is relegated to the position of "short" film, or "experimental" film—it's discussed in any terms but those of filmic forms. It's looked upon as a step to "serious" cinemas, as "apprenticeship" stage, etc., etc. So at least in America, we have brought cinema into a certain maturity by creating a body of works, by working out the language, the styles, the techniques, the syntax, the technology

of the neglected nonnarrative part of cinema, so that now cinema is an art with two extremes, the narrative and the nonnarrative—like any other art. That I would consider our main achievements: bringing cinema to its fullness.

The second achievement was the liberation of the filmmaker from the Hollywood mentality, and technology and attitudes, which automatically called for new methods of film dissemination. And that's where the Film-Makers' Cooperative comes in. A new system of noncompetitive, anticapitalist, co-operative system was created which by now has been adapted by most of other countries in which there are active independent filmmaking movements. For the purposes of this interview, we'll avoid any detailed discussion of individual filmmakers, or films or styles. I'd like instead to cover these practical aspects, like the Cooperative. The Film-Makers' Cooperative was organized in 1961 as a branch of the New American Cinema Group, an organization created by filmmakers in 1960. Somehow when we are discussing this period, we usually start it with *Shadows* and *Pull My Daisy*; *Shadows* by John Cassavetes and *Pull My Daisy* by Alfred Leslie and Robert Frank, both from the year 1959. These two films, maybe more than any other film, of that period, generated new interest in low-budget independent films. There was a movement, it was called the experimental film movement in this country, which began somewhere around 1943 in San Francisco and New York, with people like Maya Deren, Frank Stauffachen, Willard Maas, Sidney Peterson, James Broughton, Francis Lee, Kenneth Anger, Gregory Markopoulos, Curtis Harrington, which went for almost a decade, and then it began slacking, going down. In 1959, after *Shadows* and *Pull My Daisy*, things started moving again.

What started as a low-budget movement filmmaking movement which was at that time known as the New York Film School, was a mixed group of filmmakers. Some were interested in commercial films, some were interested in just purely experimental films, as they were called in those days. So they created their own organization to explore the possibilities of production, distribution, and dissemination; to help each other to fight censorship, etc., etc. Out of that, in 1961, the Film-Makers' Cooperative was created as their own cooperative distribution center. Now the way that it happened was that those who were more interested in feature-length commercial narrative films, they had bigger dreams! They kept going to the big companies, writing scripts and trying to sell them, or get sponsorship to interest larger companies, United Artists for instance. As the years went by, nobody really sponsored them, they made only a few occasional films. Shirley Clarke, Rogosin, De Antonio, they eventually abandoned their attempts and they turned to new methods of sponsoring films, they adopted the Off-Broadway theater system, that is, individual investors on a limited partnership basis. But somehow they felt that the Film-Makers' Cooperative was too small for them, so the Film-Makers' Cooperative attracted only those filmmakers whose films had no commercial possibilities. Nobody wanted to distribute them, so they had no other place to go. Even some existing avant-garde distribution organizations such as Cinema 16 rejected us, because they thought that this was not cinema what we were doing, this was just fooling around.

So that's all the avant-garde, experimental, mostly nonnarrative filmmakers, gravitated to the Co-op. They established their own small brotherhood and they stuck to it; they did not run around looking for bigger companies. They stuck to this little center, and it started growing, it became a very concentrated small center, which generated a tremendous excitement. After we collected a good number of films, we realized that we had to also organize the screenings, we had to organize theaters. We opened our own showcases, we started screenings which brought our films to the attention of the press. So they started attacking us, and the more they attacked us the more news about us spread across the country and other cities got interested in our films, began renting them. At the same time filmmakers started slowly to organize themselves in San Francisco, into Canyon Cinema Group which was basically the work of Bruce Baillie, which became a cooperative in 1964 but the basis was laid in for it in 61–62.

There were many different directions, not one kind of filmmaking, there were many different personalities involved. It is not totally correct to say that our main interest and achievement in the last ten years was only in the nonnarrative cinema, because when I say that the main preoccupation and the main exploration took place in the nonnarrative cinema, I'm sort of exaggerating, I am just showing the extremes, because the main emphasis was there but not totally. When we start to speak of the narrative and nonnarrative, it's important to know that we are speaking about two extremes—and that we don't forget that there is a middle where narrative and nonnarrative merge and where new forms of narrative come into existence, and much work has been done in that middle. Some of the major work of Brakhage, Markopoulos, even Jack Smith are in that area, like *Dog Star Man* by Brakhage or Markopoulos's *Twice a Man*. Most of Gregory Markopoulos's work falls under this new form which T. S. Eliot referred to as Mythical. The only thing is that usually the narratives of Markopoulos or Brakhage are not taken as narratives. But they are. They are complex modern narrative films.

To go into more detail I don't know where to begin because basically we have to discuss the work of different directors because this cinema is defined by different personalities, different artists, and by their work. Maybe in general what might be said is that the French avant-garde of the twenties was influenced and had a very close relationship with the literary and art movements of that period and basically was an extension of the surrealism and Dadaism. We can see that the American film avant-garde is also closely connected with the main movements in other arts; we cannot dismiss the connection with the Abstract Expressionism for instance.

The only thing is that the avant-garde of the twenties and the avant-garde of the forties were always following the tail of other movements.

But beginning with *Pull My Daisy* and *Shadows*, American cinema picked up speed and pace and line and went almost parallel to what was happening in other arts and sometimes even led so that other arts had to pull up and look what was happening in cinema and very often the cinema was an influence on the other arts, like dance and painting of this period, and by watching cinema they had to pull themselves forward and catch up with new developments and new forms— though one would have to document it more precisely to prove that cinema was leading in the arts during this period in the United States, at least one could say without much mistake that it did not follow but went together with the other arts. So that the value of the achievements in the cinema of the last ten years is equal to the achievements of the other arts—in the originality and the impact, in content and form.

BM: There are no independent films in France because there are no institutions like the Film-Makers' Cooperative.

JM: Maybe I should tell you what the basic principles of the Film-Makers' Cooperative are because they are quite connected in a sense with what happened.

The basic four or five points on which the Film-Makers' Cooperative was founded were decided in the beginning and they remain so now. One, that no film is rejected (all other distribution set-ups are selective). Cooperative is completely open, no film is rejected, your film is your passport, your membership card. Now this was very disputable and some other countries rejected this (though later they adopted it).

The quality will go down, they said, and everybody will have their films there, you're encouraging bad filmmaking. But what happened, we discovered, was that Darwin's law exists in the arts also: the law of natural selection in art helps works of quality as it does in nature in general. So that those films which were really bad were sitting there and nobody was interested in them, nobody rented them; and those films which contained formal and other interest were rented and the interest in the films grew on its own. So when we look back now, we discover that that was the right thing to do because the bad films sat there and nobody knows about them and the good ones are being rented and shown.

Principle number two: no advertising of any kind is used. In other words, the Cooperative is not advertised, the films are not advertised, the catalogue is not advertised. If a commercial filmmaker has a bad film, or United Artists has a bad film, they will take a full-page ad in the *New York Times*, day after day they will push it, people will go to see it and they will establish this bad film as a public success. So their values can be easily distorted by advertising. Now, we do not advertise, we leave it totally to the film itself to grow by itself, to make it on its own. Now one more aspect of this is this: suppose the film was bad, we all thought the film was bad; nobody rented it, we did not like it. But it was in the Cooperative, the chance was given it and it was sitting there and three years later the "bad" filmmaker made three or four other films and they became more interesting to us as he went along. Then we looked back at his first film and we discovered that we missed the value of this first film completely, that it was not clear what he was about, that he was advanced more than we thought and we missed it—but the film was not killed, was not rejected, it was in the Cooperative and it survived, so that now, later, in the perspective of his other work, this first film takes also a place in his work and begins to live, or in other words, gains life again.

Number three principle is: no contracts are signed. You put the film into the Co-op of your own free will, nobody asks you; if you want to be part of it you come and leave your film there and anytime you want you can take it out, no contract is signed.

Number four: you can distribute it at the same time through as many other distribution cooperatives as you wish because you don't sign the contract, therefore, you are free to do whatever you want. No monopolistic ideas will be supported. Co-op has it (the film) and others can have it. So the filmmaker gains many other outlets. All the income goes to the filmmaker except the percentage which the directors of the Cooperative decide is needed to run the Cooperative. At the very beginning we decided that 25 percent from every film should stay with the Cooperative to cover the expenses and that still remains so, and 75 percent of every dollar that comes in goes to the filmmaker.

BM: And the prints, do they belong to the filmmaker?

JM: They are the filmmaker's property, he provides the prints and the Cooperative can only deal with the finished filmmaker's print.

The last point: the policies of the Cooperative are controlled by filmmakers elected yearly. Seven directors are elected by mail every year and come together once a month to discuss whatever problems arise, and they guide the policies of the Cooperative.

BM: They are elected by whom?

JM: By the filmmakers themselves. At this moment the New York Film-Makers' Cooperative has 460 filmmaker members. The seven directors for 1971 were Ken Jacobs, Robert Breer, Ed Emshwiller, Stan Brakhage, Michael Snow, Jud Yalkut, and myself. The seven filmmakers in the Committee are elected once a year (we are having elections right now). The actual work is done by hired people, paid with the 25 percent we take from every film. So these are basically the principles of the Cooperative.

It happened, for instance, in Italy that they started a Cooperative. They wanted to be very selective, and a year later they discovered that some of the filmmakers they thought were good and selected did not produce any more interesting work and those that they rejected came up with more interesting work—so they had to open up the Cooperative to all. Selectivity in a cooperative system does not work. This applies basically to all the advanced forms of art in the avant-garde and during periods when form and content is firmly established, like classical periods, the changes are very small so that you cannot make much mistake, you have a certain perspective. But today to pass judgment, when everything is changing, is very difficult unless one really has wide perspective to what is happening and those who practically run the cooperatives cannot have such perspectives. Cooperatives must be open to everybody, we cannot act as critics. So these are basic facts about the Cooperative. At this moment I think we have five Cooperatives in the United States, there are two in Germany, two or three in Italy, in Sweden also, in England and in Canada, in Australia and really in a good number of other countries, based on exactly the same principles.

BM: But there are none in France?

JM: I don't know of one in France—there were several attempts, but they all failed. Now I think Noel Burch with some friends are organizing one, but I don't know where that will lead.

BM: Perhaps you can tell us about the filmmakers.

JM: We have 460 filmmakers who belong to the New York Film-Makers Cooperative; there are two hundred who belong to the Canyon Film-Makers' Cooperative in San Francisco; some of them belong to both. Nobody can expect that all five hundred are good, but we can say that maybe twenty are doing really interesting work and five or six are known on a really high level. So to know what our cinema really is, one has to see all the work of those twenty or so filmmakers because really each one is exploring a different direction. Each one of these twenty have their own minor followers. The key figures are Stan Brakhage, Gregory Markopoulos, Andy Warhol, Kenneth Anger, Jordan Belson, Jack Smith, Harry Smith, Robert Breer, Ed Emshwiller, Marie Menken, Michael Snow, Ken Jacobs, Peter Kubelka, Paul Sharits, Bruce Baillie, Bruce Connor, Stan Vanderbeek, James Broughton, Robert Welson, Joseph Cornell, George Landow, Ernie Gehr, Andrew Noren, Robert Beavers, and a few others.

The key personality for a long time was Stan Brakhage who changed just by himself the whole visual vocabulary and attitude to reality. The next influence was Andy Warhol and Gregory Markopoulos, for different reasons, and now during these last two years, Michael Snow with Ken Jacobs have a great influence in the structural minimal direction.

BM: You have written in the *Village Voice* in September 1971 that the Nouvelle Vague has delayed the independent movement in France for ten years. Can you expand your ideas about this?

JM: I said in the *Voice* that the way I see it, the Nouvelle Vague has retarded the development of French cinema by one generation, by ten years (ten years is one generation by Berenson's description of one generation in art, usually it takes ten years for styles and subjects to change). What I simply meant was that the Nouvelle Vague revolted against the cinema in France of that day, but the source where they looked for their inspiration, for the revolution against the staleness of the contemporary (say, 1950–1960) French cinema, was Hollywood. And because they were young and temperamental, no matter where their sources came from, there was a certain dynamism in the Nouvelle Vague films. But the further they went, the more they settled down and the more they *became* Hollywood, some of the best of Hollywood there was. Chabrol, Truffaut, and Louis Malle became very good second-rate Hollywood masters, though with French touches. But in this country, the break was more radical. A new technology was coming in, and all kinds of changes were taking place in the world of ideas. We did not go to Hollywood for our sources and roots, we said, "Hollywood is there and let it die by itself, it is one kind of animal and we are a different kind of animal." So some of the work of that time, even in the narrative form—Ron Rice, *The Flower Thief*, made in 1960, was a total break. Even now it remains one of the really radical, advanced narrative films in its style and content, for this country at that period. It was not a gradual break from Hollywood; it was a radical break.

Now I did not mention Godard before—because I put him in different place by himself. Though he started together with others like in *Breathless*, we felt that with every film he was coming closer to what we were doing here. He was going away from Hollywood, while others were coming closer to Hollywood. As we used to say when they asked us "Do you think that Godard is part of the new cinema?" (I remember it was in 1966 at a symposium at the Museum of Modern Art). "No, but he will become part of the new cinema the day he takes the camera into his own hands and starts shooting!" Now Godard did that during the May 1968 days in Paris, and I have even a photograph of him shooting with the camera. In any case, somewhere from there on, he became an independent filmmaker and part of the new cinema. So I consider Godard an exception. I don't know what is happening in France now, but I think that if it hadn't been the Nouvelle Vague, during the last ten years maybe something else much more radical would have happened. But now it couldn't happen because any new young filmmaker there always looks at the Nouvelle Vague. Here in this country they have the precedence of the underground, the independent filmmaker as a revolt against Hollywood. In France any young filmmaker that wanted to be radical, looked at the Nouvelle Vague as a radical movement, which it was not, or which was in a very deceiving way a radical movement, and was absorbed into it and the whole generation of filmmakers who might have created real new cinema for France were absorbed and eaten up by the Nouvelle Vague, so that there is no new cinema in France.

Of course, there are certain individual artists of great personality, the classicists like Bresson, like Rivette, or Marcel Hanoun. We respect these artists greatly. No doubt we find certain contributions made by Resnais also, but basically to the commercial avant-garde, which is neither here nor there, if there is such a thing, which is neither fowl nor fish, which is commercial avant-garde.

BM: There is no new cinema in France, but do you think there are new critics?
JM: Not from what I see. I see no new line in *Positif*, and no new line in cinema, and *Cahiers du Cinéma* went down, I don't see any new line of criticism there. Maybe in some provincial papers, semi-underground—I don't know what student papers there are—maybe some new voices are there, but those I don't see. But in the official film press, definitely not. The official film magazines all over the world, it can be clearly stated (over one thousand exist) devote themselves every month, every week to the discussion of the same old conventional or classicist cinema, and they ignore and they kill immediately any signs of the new cinema. I think that the only magazine that is devoted consciously to the new cinema is *Film Culture*.

BM: Is it also a fact that *Film Culture* was important in the rise of the new American cinema?
JM: Yes, it was our meeting ground. Criticism is the worst part here also in this country. There are only a few, four or five people, who have knowledge and vision and ability to discuss the new cinema and see its values, and I have in mind—P. Adams Sitney, Ken Kelman, Annette Michelson, Fred Camper, and I guess that is about it. But one good thing that is happening is when one watches what is happening in the universities in this country, one sees that the university film departments (and there are I think about two hundred by now across the country) are becoming very advanced and new cinema is being accepted by them, that is, the new aesthetics, the nonnarrative cinema: the achievements of the last ten years are being incorporated into the general pattern of learning, so despite the lack of discussion of the new cinema in some of the press, or despite the primitiveness of some of the discussion, I think that it is gaining roots through the learning institutions, through the universities. I am quite optimistic about what is happening in this country in this respect.

Cinema is no longer discussed, as in most other countries, only as a narrative fictional commercial film, but it is discussed in its wide variety of forms. In other words, a two-minute-long film by Bruce Baillie called *All My Life* is being analyzed, presented, and discussed as seriously as any Antonioni feature or D. W. Griffith's *Intolerance*, which is three hours long. Because this little, two-minute film, *All My Life* by Bruce Baillie, is a film form equivalent to a "haiku" form in poetry—and is as great an achievement within that form as let's say—*Intolerance* or *Ugetsu* or *Rules of the Game*, which are achievements in the narrative form. So that is already being accepted in this country, but not, I think, in any other country or any cinematheque. That is really where Anthology Film Archives comes in because we don't divide films here by length or budgets or the time in the history when the film was made. Each is a film and has to be judged for what it is within its own form, within the tradition and within the achievements of that form. So that is a new development.

BM: But the most interesting part of the Anthology is that you repeat the same films every two months. You are the only cinematheque that does that. What is your reason for this?

JM: We thought we needed one place, one archive in which a very carefully selected history of cinema, that is, not history in time, but essential works representing different forms of cinema, the essential achievements of cinema could be presented in a practically accessible time period, let's say two-month periods—the whole of cinema, say, reduced to one hundred or so programs (which no doubt cannot represent all the good that has been done but can only represent the main achievements, directions, tendencies) so that the student who is interested in film could have a place and come, spend two months there and get there the basic introduction into cinema. Why only one hundred programs?

You really cannot redefine the art of cinema in any other way, because the whole of cinema is now around two hundred thousand films, so for practical reasons you can only work with certain numbers of films that you discuss, re-see, and argue about as we are doing at the Anthology, and then select the best ones and make them available to people.

So that every few months we add a few films; but it is a very slow process, and that's why we consider Anthology Film Archives not a museum, not really an archive, but as a system or a method of investigation of cinema, or redefining the art of cinema.

And since we have only a limited number of films, we can afford to rescreen them and rescreen them on a repertory basis. We reach the end of the list and we begin from the beginning again, so that there is a repertory situation, and if one is new in cinema and is studying cinema, this provides him an occasion to re-see the films again and again.

Most of the books of film history were written after one or two viewings, so I think those history books might be thrown out now, because I think most of us, around the Anthology, particularly when it comes to the films of the last ten years, have seen these films not two or three, not ten, but twenty, thirty, or forty times, so that we know them very, very well. So that whatever didn't work after three or four viewings, just falls out, and others that remain we see again and again, and they are tested by those numerous screenings, so that there is another aspect of it.

BM: Do you think this constitutes a different position on cinema and will give you the possibility of establishing a new theory on cinema?

JM: I don't know, but I think it is connected because, you see, there is another reason for Anthology. We had ten years, a whole decade of very productive work. I said, we have 460 filmmakers in the new catalogue of the Film-Makers' Cooperative. There are sixteen hundred films listed there—so that if a university, say in Texas, wants to show some of these films to the students to give an example of what is being done, then where do they begin? They have 460 names there and sixteen hundred titles! So they call usually on me, or P. Adams Sitney and ask for advice, they write letters, "could you help us." So I ended up with such big piles of those letters that I could not do anything. So then we thought—we had to solve this problem in some way. You face a selection when you have to advise, you select those films which you think are really essential. So we came to the conclusion that we had to have either one place where we could screen them or select and to prepare a certain list. Instead of each time answering the letter and advising, we could just send them our very carefully prepared list. This at the very end became the Anthology Archives selection list, so that we are in a sense advising, serving the learning institutions with a selection of essential films. Once they look at a few programs of the selected films, they can then take their chances and try something else—like in literature, after reading all the classics you go and take chances with secondary work. By now there are already a few books available for those who do the programming at universities, books which provide a basic introduction into the new cinema, so that the process is exactly like in any other art.

You don't go into the store and buy the first book that you see: you must have some background information and maybe you read some literary magazines, and the book was reviewed and you go by certain sources of information, and then you look for that book and you buy it. The same here. One cannot just blindly choose one title from sixteen hundred in this catalogue; one has to have certain information about what one is looking for. Therefore, it becomes a necessity for one to read those basic books that are on the subject and to follow the institutions like Anthology and see what is being selected. We have five filmmakers and critics on our selection committee, therefore at least five heads, five minds come together, not one. And since we are selecting, there are certain standards, certain guiding lines that are being established, a theory is being created there; our very selection, our list itself presents our theory of cinema. The next stage of course, is the theoretical writings. It will come slowly, because I think, again, that when one watches universities—five years ago, ten years ago, even three years ago—most of the students who studied cinema, studied what one would call *applied* filmmaking, that is, filmmaking which can be used later to make money, let's say to work in television, to make commercials, to make instructional films or school films, applied filmmaking. Today there is much interest, much more than before, in the history and theory of cinema. Just take Annette Michelson's film classes, or at Yale; there are students who are actually studying theory, or studying film criticism, which is a very new development, and they are beginning to write. I think there will be a new generation coming out from the universities of young scholars who will be the new theoreticians and critics and more capable, with much more serious background than most of the reviewers who are reviewing films now.

BM: I think most of the filmmakers are teachers too?
JM: Yes. Most of the twenty or so leading filmmakers that I named earlier, most of them are teaching at one or other place, maybe not permanently, but they are holding courses for a few weeks or months and they keep travelling and leaving certain influences and impact also.

BM: And in Germany and Italy, where there are film cooperatives also, are they connected with the universities as well?
JM: I think it should be like that by now in Italy. There it started around 1967 as cooperatives and gatherings of individual underground filmmakers—in Torino, in Genoa, in Rome. They have been quite active in Italy, maybe more than in any other country in Europe. Italy has produced the most interesting noncommercial cinema in the last two or three years. Then, Germany became very active during the last two years and some of the work is very advanced, and very good. England less, not that much, they are active but not much of interest is being produced from what I have seen. But Italy and Germany have come up with some very good work, and they are very active in organizing screenings in universities, in Germany particularly. As far as criticism, I think that Italy is still more advanced. There is a monthly film magazine, *Film Critica*, which during the last two years changed its contents. Before there used to be only one: Alfredo Leonardi, who is on the editorial board, who is a filmmaker and who is really the most influential there and most active, who helped to create the first cooperative, so he was the only propagandist or writer-theoretician in this field. But now I see that there are a few others in *Film Critica*. From the last few issues I see that in every issue there are two or three articles dealing with the nonnarrative film, with new developments, with new cinema, not just the commercial cinema. So Italy has already at least one

magazine, *Film Critica*, which is their voice, but I don't see anything from Germany, though Birgit Hein published a book on underground film, *Underground*, and she has been doing much propagandizing and writing there.

BM: You are a filmmaker yourself. Can you speak a little about your own filmmaking?
JM: In a sense, *Diaries, Notes, and Sketches*, I consider my first film. The others, *Guns of the Trees* and *The Brig*, that was a different stage, something else. *The Brig* has certain value, but what I want to do is more in the direction of the *Diaries, Notes, and Sketches*.

BM: It is a good example of independent filmmaking.
JM: What it is, *Diaries, Notes, and Sketches*, is an attempt to develop the diary form in cinema, a personal notebook which I kept during the last six or so years, carrying my camera with me and shooting practically every day, reacting to certain situations and certain images in the city or out of the city, indoors or outdoors, and I tried to develop a form and technique to react instantaneously and immediately. The main challenge became how to catch reality as I reacted to it that very moment, as I saw it that moment when I was reacting. Suppose I go to the park and I see a tree and I film that tree because I looked at it and I saw something in it, then it is just simply an image of a tree, if I just place the camera there and I shoot it. So I had to work out a technique which would not only record the tree but would at the same time record my own reaction to it—at that moment when I am looking at it—which led me, no doubt, to the use of single frames, because I had to destroy the realism and recreate reality from the beginning because the only way I could put myself into that tree when I'm shooting it, was by restructuring the image, restructuring that tree by use of single frames, by introducing a different pace, different rhythms, and putting myself into it by means, by way of the pacing and rhythm, by way of structure and lighting and movement, in other words, indirectly.

So that goes through the first volume of the *Diaries*, this preoccupation, working out the techniques of immediate reaction to reality, because the *Diaries* is a record of New York, my life here during the last six or seven years (the first volume takes 1965, '66, '67, '68 and part of '69)—I was filming the actual reality, be it the streets, the seasons, snow or weddings or other occasions, that is, the actual reality, there are no recreations of any kind. I was always filming the actual reality. Still the image which one gets of New York from the *Diaries* is not exactly the New York of any other New Yorker. It is my New York, so that in a sense I am filming my fantasy New York, or my private New York; I am filming myself instead of New York. In a sense, my New York *Diaries* are as unreal as anything else, but that is more or less the subject of the first volume. I'm still continuing. I am preparing another volume and much of the footage of the second volume will be from before this volume—it will go to 1950 (I kept shooting since 1950)—so I am organizing now the earlier material. But there I was not too conscious of the diary as a form. Some editing will be done there. The only way to get the footage now, the way I'm shooting now, that is, the only way to get reality and myself to merge together is by editing as I am shooting—structuring as I am shooting—that is what I am doing now. All my editing is during the shooting, but until 1963 I was not doing the editing while shooting. I was searching; I did not know where I was. I practically used up, consumed, two Bolexes, until I began to see what I wanted.

So in 1963 I bought my third Bolex and from there on I suddenly felt I knew how I can do what I want. It took me ten years to come to it. It is like practicing piano or something like that, or violin, for this type of shooting, that is. There are other ways, it depends on, I guess, the subject, on the form in which you are working, but in my case it was this, and I had to come to that type of technique and to have much mastery of my tools. Nobody else could shoot it for me. I had to do it myself. Only I know how I react to it, to what I am seeing, how I feel at that moment. And it is not a logical, not a mental kind of reasoning—say that I am now in the middle of this wedding and I think this looks like this and that is like that, but I just have to submerge myself completely in it and then it is my fingers which do the rest. In other words, my fingers react to my inner state in the same way as the hands of a painters react or the fingers of a musician who play the violin, without him thinking or reasoning rationally how he should play. One needs about ten years or so to come to that stage, and for this type of filmmaking, so that the reaction becomes very intuitive and instantaneous and my fingers control and do and make all of the decisions during the shooting. The length, the openings of the lenses or the speeds have to be that way, otherwise I couldn't move, I would stop dead immediately.

BM: Practically all the independent filmmakers here work alone.
JM: Yes, speaking of 460 of them, at least four hundred of them shoot and edit their own films; those are one-man films.

BM: Yes, and most of them edit during the shooting?
JM: Not all, but many, more and more. Most of it is done that way. Then there is a process of elimination of certain parts. Like in my case—I eliminated some parts which I felt were badly written; but whatever remained, remained exactly as came out of the camera, because to recreate that situation later in the editing room would be impossible, impossible. So that most of the filmmakers shoot the films and edit the films themselves. Only those who have gradually gone to the more conventional fiction films, they use other cameramen.

BM: Like Michael Snow?

JM: Michael Snow still does his own camerawork. Michael Snow is completely in control of his camera. I mean people like Paul Morrissey, Andy Warhol, a good number of other people, smaller people, who are working with actors, or semi-actors, and telling little stories, very often they use friends as cameramen, because it is not as important to them, to have complete control of every aspect. So we see more and more of that.

Not all 460 are nonnarrative filmmakers. Some of them are at the Co-op just because they simply want to make films and they sympathize with the principles of the Cooperative, so they begin there and they are not very clear about what they want to do, they just want to make films. As time goes, their own interests and directions become clearer to them, they discover that they want to make fictional films, commercial films, and to make such films they have to go to certain companies and the more they are connected with other companies, the more they get involved in different styles and in different distribution. But their early films usually remain in the Cooperative—like Bob Downey or Vernon Zimmerman, whose films are now distributed by large distribution set-ups, their earlier films are still distributed by the Cooperative. Anyway some of them gravitate into the other areas, as they become clearer about what they want to do and about the best possibilities for doing it; if they want to reach more people and work with a certain kind of popular film, they have to gravitate to more popular areas.

BM: Maybe now we can talk about the future, if the Berenson's decade is over?

JM: I don't know if one can talk about the future, maybe one can only talk about the present. Take the Russian movement in the twenties, Vertov, Eisenstein, something happened there, something very important; they were very excited and the excitement came from ideology, somehow, from the revolution there. Here something happened also.

There was great excitement, a very productive movement, but it did not come from ideology, the cause was the medium of cinema itself. We became interested in the medium itself, into the possibilities of our materials, our tools, and the new vision. Then in 1967 it started already slowly diminishing (the excitement), though it's continuing now in a classical, sort of very strong way. All those who started in that period are continuing their work and there are some new developments, through certain personalities, like Michael Snow. One decade, the work of one generation, in a sense, maybe its most exciting period, is over. I think that that may be so. The creation of Anthology Film Archives was already the first movement towards something else, the second stage, that is, placing the works achieved in the last ten years in a certain perspective.

When the movement is really alive, then it just goes from sheer passion, and there is no time to look back. Now because of the fact that we are beginning to sort out and look back, it looks like we have arrived somewhere at a different point and maybe the passion is fading slowly, so we are beginning to look back, to re-evaluate, to create Anthology Film Archives so that those works that have been created, and we think are very important, would not disappear, but they would be preserved and made available to the people, because the tragedy of the forties, of the experimental films of the forties, was that nobody took care, nobody helped much and they got very frustrated and disillusioned and the movement evaporated. So we don't want that to be repeated now and it won't happen again. You ask about the future and I can only speak about now, where we are now, at the beginning of another stage, of preserving and re-evaluating—and gaining a perspective, preserving and making them available to the people, what was created, the whole neglected part of cinema. It's clear to us and we see how this makes the cinema whole, and where this cinema that we have created belongs. But still it is for the next few years, for the next ten years to persuade through education and writings and showings of these films, to persuade the writers and public, to re-educate also all the critics of all the one thousand magazines across the world and all the cinematheques and all the film museums so that they would understand that these films are not just (as now they are still considered) short, low-budget films, but that they constitute a whole new part of cinema, that new forms have been added to cinema. This is not clear at all, it is clear to only a few people, that these films are as much a part of the totality of the cinema as poetry or nonfictional forms are part of the general literature, that it is not only Melville or Zola or Flaubert who are literature, but also Baudelaire and Apollinaire are literature, but that is not yet accepted in cinema, though the whole body of works testify to the fact that the nonnarrative forms of cinema have come into existence in the last two decades in a very strong way. They existed already in the twenties, there are, for example, films by Man Ray, Buñuel or Hans Richter and Duchamp, but they were occasional works and did not constitute a form, but were exceptions from the rule, from the general rule. But it is not a question of exception, not a question of low budget, not a question of not having certain equipment and not a question of length of film. It is a question of different forms of cinema. So this is the work for the next ten years and this is the emphasis where some of the work of the future will be, because that will change the general theory of cinema and through this cinema itself. As far as the actual film work—I think that you can see that the major figures of this period are continuing in a very strong way in the direction that they started, polishing their forms, techniques, be it Markopoulos or Brakhage, Snow or Anger. The basis was established, now they are continuing, and some of them may have made their most important work already, but others may still be producing their most important works in the future.

Jonas Mekas Answers Questions after the Screening of *Reminiscences of a Journey to Lithuania*

International Film Seminar, Hotchkiss School / 1972

Previously unpublished. Printed by permission of the Estate of Jonas Mekas.

Editor's Introduction: The following text comes from a question and answer session at Hotchkiss School as part of the International Film Seminar, August 26, 1972. Filmmakers Willard van Dyke, Marcel Ophuls, and Arnold Eagle as well as scholars and curators Gerald O'Grady and Elodie Osborn were present and participated. Some audience questions are not audible due to poor sound quality.

Question: One thing in this film that I felt was contradictory to the very sensitive, very personal treatment of the place and the people, was that you identified the people in Lithuania. You identified them by names, you told us how they were related. You also identified them by their jobs. And identifying people, particularly when you see their faces, to identify them by what they do seems to me pointless.
Jonas Mekas: It's their life. There is nothing wrong with having professions, jobs. And then, I dislike any kind of mystery. The more I can tell about the people in my films the happier I am. You'll find this in all my later films, I use titles to tell what you see. I like to tell you in advance what it is, what's coming, as much as I can. Of course, there is no need to tell everything, there are limits.

And then, there is this other thing. My friends have been asking me: "Okay, what are your brothers doing there? Where do you come from? How does it look there?" etc. So I put all that information right there, into the titles, so I don't need to answer. Kostas is in charge of the granary; he has been in charge of the granary for ten years and it may be his life for another ten years. The other one is an agronomist, and he has been one ever since he came out of the agronomy school. It's his life and he likes it, and there is nothing wrong in naming his profession. In any case, it's part of the document that my film is.

Q: Could you tell us how you developed the shooting style that you're using in this film?

JM: *Reminiscences* falls into the form of a notebook, or a diary, a form into which most of my later work seems to fall. I did not come to this form by calculation. I came to it from desperation. It's because of my last fifteen years' involvement with the independently made film. I got so entangled in it that I didn't have any time left for myself, for my own filmmaking—between Film-Makers' Cooperative, Film-Makers' Cinematheque, *Film Culture* magazine, and now Anthology Film Archives, I didn't have any time left. I mean, I didn't have any stretches of time You know, you prepare a script, then you take months to shoot, then you edit, etc. I had only bits of time which allowed me to shoot only bits of film. And so all my personal work became like notes. Whatever I can do today, I should do, because if I don't, I may not find any other free time for weeks, perhaps. If I can film one minute—I film one minute. If I can film ten seconds—I film ten seconds. I take what I can, from desperation. But for a long time I didn't look at the footage I was collecting that way. I thought what I was actually doing was practicing. I was preparing myself, or trying to keep in touch with my camera, so that when the day will come when I'll have time, then I'll make a "real" film. And so I was carrying my camera since 1949, since I arrived in this country.

The second week after I arrived here, I borrowed some money from some people I knew who came before me, and I bought my first Bolex. I started practicing, filming, and I thought I was learning. Only around 1961 or 1962 I looked at my footage for the first time, all the footage that I had collected during all that time. And as I was looking at that old footage, I noticed that there were various connections in it. The footage that I thought was totally disconnected, even in that unorganized shape, as I was screening it, suddenly began to look like a notebook with many uniting threads. One thing that struck me was that there were things in this footage that kept coming back again and again. I thought that each time I filmed something, I filmed completely something else. But it wasn't so. It wasn't always "something else." I kept coming back to the same subjects, the same images or image sources. Like, for example, the snow. There is no snow, practically, in New York. But all my New York notebooks are filled with snow. Or trees. How many trees do you see in the streets of New York? Things like that. And as I was studying this footage and thinking about it, I became conscious of the form of a diary film and, of course, this began to affect my way of filming, my style. And in a sense it helped me to gain some peace of mind. I said to myself: "Fine, very fine—if I don't have time to devote six or seven months to making a film, I won't break my heart about it; I'll film short notes, from day to day, every day." I began working within the form of a diary, within the form of brief notes and sketches. And that's how it all came about.

Q: Doesn't the idea of a diary imply stylization? Going back in memory? How does that affect your filming?

JM: I have thought about other forms of diary, in other arts. But practically, when it came to actual filming, it was not so much thinking as working with the actual material I had at hand, and thinking through and with it. Of course, it soon became clear that when you write a diary, for example, you sit down, in the evening, by yourself, and you reflect upon your day, you look back. It's a reflective process. But in the filming, in keeping a notebook with the camera, the main challenge became how to capture it, how to react with the camera right now, as it's happening; how to react to it in such a way that the footage would reflect what I feel that very moment. Because, if I choose to film a certain detail, as I go through my life, there must be good reasons why I choose this specific detail from thousands of other details, why I single it out. Be it in the park, or in the street, or in a gathering of friends—there are reasons why I choose to film a certain detail. I thought that I was keeping a quite objective diary of my life in New York. But my friends who saw the first edition of *Diaries, Notes & Sketches (Walden)*, they said to me: "But this is not my New York! My New York is different. In your New York I'd like to live. But my New York is bleak, depressing. . . ." It's then that I began to see that, really, I was not keeping an objective notebook. Really, when I started looking at my film diaries again, I noticed that they contained everything that New York didn't have. . . . It was the opposite from what I originally thought I was doing. . . . What I am doing, in truth, I am filming my childhood, not New York. It's a fantasy New York, fiction.

At the same time I realized something else. At first I thought that there was a basic difference between the written diary which one writes in the evening, and which is a reflective process, and the filmed diary. In my film diary I thought I was doing something different: I was capturing life, bits of it, as it happens, I was reacting to it with my camera as it happened. But I realized very soon that it wasn't that different at all. What I am doing, when I am filming, I am also reflecting. I was thinking that I was only reacting to the actual reality. In actuality, it's not so. I do not have much control over reality at all, and everything is determined by my memory, my past. So that this "direct" filming becomes also a reflection, or a mode of reflection. Same way, I came to realize, that writing a diary is not merely reflecting, looking back. Your day, as it comes back to you, during the moment of writing, is measured, sorted out, accepted, refused and re-evaluated by what and how one is at the moment when one writes it all down. It's all happening again, and what one writes down is more true to what one is when one writes than to the events and emotions of the day that are past and gone. So that I no longer see such big difference between a written diary and the filmed diary, as far as the processes go.

Q: Besides the form of a diary itself, how did this form affect the style of shooting?
JM: By the time I decided to look at my footage, ten years of my early footage, I had used up three Bolexes. That was a time when the liberation of the independent filmmaker was taking place, when the attitudes to filming were changing radically. Like many others, during that early period, during the years 1950–1960, I wanted to be a "real" filmmaker and make "real" films and be a "professional" filmmaker. I was caught very much in the existing, inherited filmmaking conventions. You know, I was always carrying a tripod. . . . But then I looked through all my footage, and I said, okay, I see the park scene, and the city scene, and the tree—it's all there, on film—but it's not what I saw the moment I was filming it! The image is there, but there is something very essential missing. I got the surface, but I missed the essence.

So it's at that time that I began to understand that what was missing from my footage was myself: my attitude, my thoughts, my feelings the moment I was looking at the reality that I was filming. Because that reality, that specific detail, in the first place, attracted my attention because of my memories, my past. I singled out that specific detail with my total being, with my total past. And so the challenge now to capture that reality, that detail, that very objective physical fragment of reality as closely as possible to how my Self is seeing it. Of course, what I faced was the old problem of all artists: to merge Reality and Self, to come up with the third thing. That became the challenge. And it's there that I had to liberate the camera from the tripod, and to embrace all the subjective filmmaking techniques and procedures that were either already available, or were just coming into existence. It was an acceptance and recognition of the achievements of the avant-garde film of the last fifty years. And it affected the exposures, and the movements, and the pacing, everything. I had to throw out the academic notions of "normal" exposure, "normal" movement, or normal and proper this and normal and proper that. I had react with my camera instantaneously, immediately, and I had to react with my total being, I had to put myself into it, to merge myself with the reality I was filming, to put myself into it indirectly, by means of pacing, lighting, exposures, movements, etc., etc.—I had to restructure reality completely.

Those of you who have seen the first edition of *Diaries, Notes & Sketches* (*Walden*), and now *Reminiscences*, of course, you will see the difference between the two. In *Walden* the basis is the single frame. There is a lot of density there. And when I was going to Lithuania, of course, I thought, I will bring back material in the same style. But, somehow, when I was already there, I just couldn't work in the style of *Walden*, there. And the longer I stayed in Lithuania the more it changed me, and it pulled me into a completely different style. I couldn't work in Lithuania in single frames. There were feelings, states, faces that I couldn't treat too abstractly. Certain realities can be presented in cinema only through certain durations of images. Each subject, each reality, each emotion affect the style in which you film, how you respond with your memory and your camera, how you do it—if you are really with it. And, of course, the style that I used in *Reminiscences* wasn't the most perfect style for it. It is a compromise style. I'll explain why. For instance, I made one bad mistake which I'll never make again. My third Bolex died just before I had to go on this trip. I had fixed it several times, but this time I just couldn't fix it any more. So I bought a new Bolex. The Lithuanian footage was the first footage that I shot with this new Bolex. But the thing is, that even if two Bolexes were totally identical, just the very fact that you never held it in your hands, affects you. You have to get used to every new camera so that during the filming it responds to you, and you know it, its weaknesses and its caprices. Because, later, when I started filming, I discovered that my new Bolex wasn't identical with the old one at all. It wasn't enough that it wasn't identical: it was, actually, defective. It never kept a constant speed. I set it on twenty-four frames, and after three, four shots, it's on thirty-two frames. Like, you have constantly watch it, work on it, look at the speed meter, because the speeds of frames per second affect the lighting, exposure. And when I finally realized that nothing will really work, that there was no way of fixing it or locking it—I decided to accept it and incorporate the defect as one of the stylistic devices, to use the changes of light as structural means.

Q: Could you explain more why it is a stylistic or formal means?
JM: Maybe the way I just said it is not exactly the way to say it. What I did, I used it. As soon as I noticed that the speeds were changing constantly, especially when I filmed in short takes, brief spurts—I knew that I wouldn't be able to control the exposures. And I don't exactly mean that I wanted to have "normal," "balanced" lighting. No, I don't believe in that. But to work within my irregularities, within my style of clashing light values, I can only do it when I have complete control, or at least "normal" control over my tools. But here that control was slipping. The only way to control it was to embrace it and use it as part of my way of filming. I knew it was there, so I embraced it. That's how I'll put it. To use the overexposures as punctuations; to use them in order to reveal reality in literally a different light; to use them in order to imbue reality with a certain distance; to compound reality.

You see, when I went to Lithuania, I was offered a team of cameramen, and cameras, and I could have used them. But I didn't use them. I knew that although the images recorded by these technicians, following my instructions, would have been "better" professionally, they would have destroyed the very subject I was going after. When you go home, for the first time in twenty-five years, you know, somehow, that the official film crews just do not belong there. Thus I chose my Bolex. My filming had to remain totally private, personal, and "unprofessional." For instance, I never checked my lens opening before taking a shot. I took my chances. I knew that the truth will have to hang on and around all those "imperfections." The truth which I caught, whatever I caught, had to hang on me and my Bolex. You see, when you shoot with a Bolex, you hold it somewhere not exactly where your brain is, a little bit lower, and not exactly where your heart is—it's slightly higher. . . . And then, the spring, you wind it up, you give it an artificial life . . . you live continuously, within the situation, in one time continuum; but you shoot only in spurts, as much as the spring allows. . . . You interrupt your filmed reality constantly. . . . You resume it again . . .

Q: [recording unclear; about the editing of the footage]
JM: I used the process of elimination, cutting out parts that didn't work, the badly "written" parts, and leaving in practically without any change to those parts that worked. Which means I was editing. I was not editing the individual sequences. I was only throwing out certain parts, and leaving others in. I left in those parts which, I felt, captured something, meant something to me, and didn't offend me technically and formally. That means, I accepted them, they didn't bother me, or at least I could tolerate them. Even if some parts caught something of essence but bothered me formally, I threw them out. So that my editing is based on the methods of elimination. I have this joke, that Rimbaud had *Illuminations*, and I have only eliminations.

So that is, more or less, my way of editing. Of course, I spend much time figuring out, trying out how this detail or that one, this note or this sketch works in the totality of the reel. It was a lesser problem in *Reminiscences*, but with *Diaries, Notes & Sketches (Walden)* I really had to work hard and long. After you sit for two hours, watching a movie, it's important what comes during the third hour. The question of repetition comes in. Sometimes I have to eliminate even parts which I like, because too much of something is too much. In this case, in case of *Reminiscences*, the editing was very fast. Hans Brecht of Norddeutscher Television helped me to pay for the film stock and Bolex. For the rights to show it on German television, he helped me to pay the basic expenses. But then I came back, and I completely forgot about Hans Brecht. And he forgot about me. But then, on Christmas day he calls me. "Is it ready? I need it on January twentieth." "January twentieth? Why didn't you tell me this earlier?" So I went to my editing table, and I stared at it. After I came back from Lithuania, I kept thinking: "How am I going to edit it?" This footage was very, very close to me. I had no perspective on it of any kind. And even now, today, I have little perspective on it. So I didn't know how I was going to edit it. I had about twice as much as you see in the film. So now I stood there and I said to myself: "Fine, very fine. I have this emergency now. This emergency will help me to make the decisions. I'll have to make my decisions fast, one two three." For two or three days I didn't touch the footage, I thought about the form, the structure of the film. Once I decided upon the structure, I just spliced it, very fast, in one day. I knew that this was the only way I could come to grips with this footage: by working with it totally mechanically. Another way would have been to work very, very long on it, and either to come up with a completely different film, or destroy the footage in the process.

Q: The scene where you go to Kostas's house—you start out with the sequence of the goose. And then, people inside the house. Do you mean, in a section like that, you didn't edit any of it?
JM: Correct. In that sequence I didn't do any post-editing.

Q: That sequences appears just the way you shot it?
JM: Yes.

Q: [not too audible; about the effects of going home after so many years]
JM: It's beginning to affect me. I say it in the film, "the time in Lithuania remained suspended for me, for twenty-five years, and now it's beginning to move again." So that when people ask me how is life there now, I am beginning to try to answer it. But till now I have been avoiding it. I usually say: "Oh, go and see my film, everything's there, I have nothing more to say, I know nothing about it." Because, the truth is, I didn't see the *real life* there. I was always looking for what was left of the memories of what *was*, what *has been* long ago. I missed the reality of *today*, or I saw it as through a veil. Because, you see, there are two kinds of travellers, people who go away from home. One category is those who leave their home, their country on their own. You decide, "Oh, I hate it all, I'll make more money somewhere else; people are better somewhere else; the grass is greener there. . . ." And you go, and you settle down somewhere. And, of course, occasionally, then, you think about your old home, your old folks; but, eventually, you grow new roots and you forget all about it. You may occasionally think that maybe it was more beautiful there, in the old country. But you don't break your heart about it.

Then, there is the other group of people who are uprooted from their homes by force—be it the force of other people or the force of circumstances. And when you are uprooted like this, then you always think, you always want to go back home, and it stays there, and it doesn't disappear. You think about your old home, you romanticize it, it swells and it swells. And you have to see it again, to actually go back there and start it all from the beginning, you have to leave your home for the second time. Then it begins to change. That's why in the *Diaries* (*Walden*) I was shooting New York, but it was always like shooting my old home. So, now, after I went back, all this, very probably, will begin to change.

But Ken Jacobs told me that *Reminiscences* interested him in the first place because it represented the experience of a displaced person, an experience which he never had but to which he is attracted, because of his own childhood in Williamsburg, Brooklyn, which practically is no longer there. So that we have, in America, a third category of the traveller: one whose home is constantly wiped out from under the feet by the modern building code.

Q: Do you think you want now to go home and stay there?
JM: It's quite complicated. Of course, I am thinking about sailing back, some day, and maybe settling down there. But I have to complete my work here. And then, there is another aspect to it. If I'd come, for example, from the city, that would make the adoption of a new home easier. After all, a city is a city. But I grew up in the country. The country is very much in me. There is much pull back, all the time. So that I know that eventually I'll end up in the country.

Q: [about the function of the squares and numbers in *Reminiscences*]
JM: I felt that to simply string the footage together would make it too heavy. I wanted to break it up. Squares and numbers act as structural devices.

Willard Van Dyke: I thought it was a device that worked absolutely well, for me. I felt the time passage, with the numbers, and I felt that without this device the film would have lost much.
JM: Ken Jacobs, he accepts the numbers, but he wishes, he told me, they were smaller. I really intended them to be smaller, but the B&O optical lab made a mistake, and made them larger than I had asked. I have also noticed that those who are bothered by them seem to be much less bothered the second time. By the way, it says: ONE HUNDRED GLIMPSES OF LITHUANIA. I don't know how many of you noticed it, but I thought, at the end of it, I'll give you a break, and I cut the numbers, so that I have, actually, I think, ninety-three or ninety-four numbers. But when one says "one hundred," one doesn't always mean exactly one hundred, one means almost one hundred. So that I think I didn't cheat.

Q: [about film and poetry]
JM: I was reading, just the other day, looking through *The Collected Works of Valéry*, and I opened the page, and there it was, a short discourse on poetry. And he says, there are two aspects to poetry. One is the poetic attitude aspects; and then there is another thing: the result, the thing produced by putting those attitudes or those feelings into a certain form. The first one, that is, the poetic attitude, you find it not only in poems, but in everything, not only in art. But in the second case, we deal with certain defined forms which we call poems, and that we find only in literature,

and it has a history, and there are different varieties of poems, etc., etc. In other words, we shouldn't confuse the poetic feeling with the poem or poetry. The poetic feeling can be found in sculpture, painting, cinema, or life itself. So that we should keep this in mind when we speak about poetry and cinema.

Gerald O'Grady: Is the footage in *Diaries* all chronological? If not, what other considerations were there?
JM: I have shifted the time sequence only on few occasions. In *Reminiscences* I kept the time sequence. In *Diaries, Notes & Sketches* (*Walden*) in a few places, when I had two long sketches side by side, I pushed one of them further in time, or back in time, for structural reasons.

Elodie Osborn: Jonas has said, this morning, that the important thing for the artist is to transform his material, so that he's making a personal statement. I think we have all learned much from what Jonas has said. He admits that a lot of people would have thrown out some of the footage he is using, as overexposed, or underexposed, or too fast. But because he has such a strong feeling about his material, he is able to dominate it and it comes through as one thing; there isn't anything you can drop out.

Arnold Eagle: . . . When I saw the film, at the beginning, at first I was taken aback, because I couldn't get into it. He was showing some beautiful things, and I wanted to dwell on them. But just about when I get involved with it, he takes me away from it. And I felt a little bit cheated at first. But then I realized, my God, what I'm seeing is the way Jonas sees things, how he has seen things. You normally don't really dwell. But most of the films that we make, the traditional films, we want to show to the people what we want them to see, and we explain that to them, and we explore that thing for them, so that they can see the best possible way, each image. But we don't really see that way. We see only the fleeting moments. We never really dwell on anything. I don't see, for example, everybody in this room. I see a face here, a face there, a shadow. But it's a total impression that we get. And I think that's what happens with Jonas's film. Unfortunately, near the end, my eyes couldn't take it, and I had to close my eyes; not long enough to miss something, but enough time to rest the eyes, to be able to follow the thing. But what I got from the film, my first impression is that it's the most personal film I've seen. Because, really, what he has seen, and I see it now the way he sees it, I would have seen it that way, maybe, if I had been there.

Q: [about how sounds and music are selected]
JM: Whatever sounds I use, I decide later, after the filming. I collect, whenever

I can, the sounds. Usually I end up with certain footage, and certain sounds surrounding the same situation. Since I look at my footage as memories and notes, the same way I look at my sounds, collected during the same period. In the case of the music for *Reminiscences*, for the Lithuania part, it's just a coincidence that I received a record that I had admired very much. It's music written around 1910 by a young Lithuanian composer-painter, Ciurlionis, who died very young, in an insane asylum. So I wanted to use that music.

But what I did, really, I recorded it over and over, some parts of it, certain passages, over and over. There may be influences of Scriabin in it, that's what some have said, but essentially it is Lithuanian music; it's the Lithuanian feeling that comes from it. There are certain notes in it that speak to me, and I used to listen to it all the time until the record was stolen from me, about ten years ago, together with the phonograph. So that this music means something to me, is very close to me, and that's why I used it. I used it like a loop, in a sense. I thought it would help me to join all the disparate pieces together, by means of this sound loop. I used Bruckner for the Kubelka sequence, for Vienna, because Bruckner happened to be one of Kubelka's favorite composers. And the madrigal I used in the Kremsmuenster library, was one of Kubelka's favorite madrigals. So it's all very personal.

Q: [about the black squares used to separate parts of the film]
JM: I found that little black square in my early footage. I was experimenting, in 1950, trying to work out divisions in a film, like chapter marks in a book, and I thought I'd use that square to indicate the different film chapters. But I never came to using it, until I discovered it again, while working on *Reminiscences*. You will notice that I use the numbers from 1 to 100 only in the Lithuanian part. Everywhere else I use the black square for chapter separations. Or maybe it's only paragraphs. I couldn't think, under the time pressure, what else I could do about it. I did not want to use black leader. So I used the squares.

Q: [inaudible]
JM: At the same time as I went to visit my mother, my brother went also, we went together. So my brother shot another film, with his Bolex. He just finished editing it, I haven't seen it yet. But Richard Roud saw it and decided to show them both, my film and my brother's film, together, on the same program, at the NY Film Festival. He says, these are two very different films based on exactly the same event, same time and same place. And then, Pola, my brother's wife, came with us too, and she had an 8mm camera with her, and she filmed her own view of the same event. There will be, eventually, three very different views of the same trip home.

Q: When you are in the film yourself, is it that you just leave your Bolex running or somebody else films it?
JM: Sometimes somebody else grabbed the camera and shot. But in *Diaries* (*Walden*) I have many shots in which I appear which I shot myself.

Q: Have you ever thought about using an automatic Super 8 camera?
JM: No. No. I don't intend to switch. I'll stick to my Bolex. I may have to switch to another camera only because they are beginning to improve Bolex. They are introducing all kinds of things that I think are only destroying the old good Bolex.

Q: [about methods of filming real-life situations]
JM: I try to combine both. I try to live, to be part of whatever is going, and film it at the same time. And so they don't find it inhibiting or intruding. Because whatever I film, whatever I see in the situation, I don't make it into "shooting," I don't behave like a "filmmaker": I am, rather, an amateur fooling around with my camera, and I am not separated from what's happening by my camera. So that I am looking (watching) and living at the same time. Which, of course, is a challenge and a very exhausting way of living and filming. But in my kind of filmmaking I have to do that.

Q: [about "catching" or "missing" reality]
JM: Before we go further, I'd like to say something about this thing of "reality." Reality . . . reality . . . Of course, New York is there, it's "real." The street is there. The snow is falling. I don't know how, but it's there. It leads its own life, or course. Same with Lithuania. Of course, the life is going there. So, now, I come into the picture. And with the camera. And now, as I walk with my camera, something falls into my eyes. When I walk through the city, I don't lead my eyes consciously, from that to that or that. It's, rather, I walk and my eyes are like open windows, and I see things, the things fall in. If I hear a sound, of course, I look towards the direction of the sound. The ear becomes active, and it directs the eye, the eye is searching for that thing that makes that noise. But most of the time, you know, things keep falling in—images, smells, sounds, and they are being sorted out in my head. Some things that fall in strike some notes, maybe with their color, with what they represent, and I begin to look at them, I begin to respond to that or that detail. Of course, the mind is not a computer. But still, it works something like a computer, and everything that falls in, is measured, corresponded to the memories, to the realities that have been registered in the brain, or wherever, and it's all very real. The tree in the street is reality. But here, I singled it out, I eliminated all the other reality surrounding it, and I picked up only that specific tree. And I filmed it. And if I now begin to look through my footage, that I have collected, I have a

collection of many such singled-out details, and in each case they fell in, I didn't seek them out. They chose me, and I reacted to them, for very personal reasons, and that's why they all tie-in together, for me, for one or other reason. They all mean something to me, even if I don't understand why. So it is reality, my film. But a reality that is sorted out through me by way of this very complex process, and, of course, to one who can "read" it, this footage tells a lot about me—actually, it tells more about me than about any other reality; it tells more about me than about the city in which I film this footage: because, you don't see the city, you see only these singled-out details. Therefore, if one knows how to "read" them, even if one doesn't see me, speaking or walking, one can tell everything about me. So that it is a reality of my own. As far as the city goes, of course, you could say something also about the city, from my *Diaries*—but only indirectly. Still, I walk through, through this actual, representational reality, and these images are all records of actual reality, even if only in fragments. No matter how I film, how I expose, fast or slow, still, the film represents a certain actual, historical period, in its images. But as a group of images, it tells more about my own subjective reality, or you can call it my objective reality, than any other reality. So that's how I look at the question of reality in cinema. Because, let's face it: reality exists actually and objectively, too, for each of us.

Marcel Ophuls: That tree is there, whether we are seeing it or not. . . .
JM: That has been doubted, as you know. . . .

Q: Besides being a personal film, a personal statement, *Reminiscences* also presents an interesting variation on the theme of the wanderer.
JM: I think, in a sense it is. I have been doing a lot of reading, lately. I picked up Goethe's Wilhelm Meister's *Wanderjahre*, his travelling years. I had read it years and years ago. But now, I started reading it, and it had a completely different meaning to me. As Wilhelm travels and meets different people, and sees different places, I started thinking about my film diaries. I began seeing interesting connections. He also visits places and meets people, goes to monasteries, like myself in Austria. But he travels by his own choice. He decided to leave his home and see the world, to meet different varieties of people, to learn. Goethe's "The Wanderer" is from a different century. My travels represent one typical wanderer of the mid-twentieth century—and you will find this traveller in every continent and every country, today: a displaced person. The displaced person, the exile, as traveller. There is such a thing, and it's not an abstract concept. A displaced person, a DP, is a reality of today. Because of the levels and complexities of the present-day civilizations, we have a displaced person. And I happened to be one. And a displaced person is not identical with Goethe's Wilhelm. A displaced person cannot choose, hasn't chosen

to leave the home. A displaced person has been thrown out into the world, into the travel, forced into it.

Q: [about sadness of *Reminiscences*]
JM: But *Reminiscences* are not dominated by sadness. There is much joy, or playfulness in the film. It's balanced, I think. What it is, really, is that in most cases, in art, sadness is eliminated as part of human experience, as if there was something wrong with it. But there is nothing wrong with sadness. It's a necessary, essential experience. Sadness is a state that is very real. We need it. And, of course, since sadness is usually censored, then, when one sees it in a film, then they think it's too sad.

Q: [inaudible]
JM: The real difference between these two travellers is only in the beginnings of their journeys. In the first case, one is consciously seeking, looking for something; in the second case, one takes what comes. People keep telling me don't you want to go there, and there, and there, and I keep telling them: "No, I don't want to go anywhere. I never wanted to travel. I am very happy where I am." "Yes," they say, "but you have been there, and there, and there." "But no, I never wanted to go to any of those countries, I was always taken there either by force or by a necessity, when there was no other choice left for me." Wilhelm goes, and searches, and looks after certain things; he wants to educate himself, to find out about the world, to see the world. But I never wanted to see the world. I was very happy right there, in the small world, and I didn't have any need or wish to go anywhere. But here I am. . . . And it's a slightly different situation from that of Wilhelm.

But, sometimes, these two fates come together. . . .

When a displaced person becomes conscious of the travel, then the two, Wilhelm Meister and the displaced person begin to come together. At least in my case this is becoming so. Wilhelm Meister and a displaced person meet in a new home, and they discover that they both have the same home: culture.

But there will be very few cases where the fates of Wilhelm Meister and that of a displaced person will meet in culture. Most of the time they'll die, the first generation of displaced persons will die with all the memories of their old homes in their eyes.

Jonas Mekas Interview

Gerald Barrett / 1973

From *Literature/Film Quarterly* 1, no. 2 (April 1973): 103–12. Reprinted by permission.

Gerald Barrett: Dwight Macdonald has called you the patron saint of the New American Cinema. What is the New American Cinema?

Jonas Mekas: The term, the New American Cinema (or NAC), was, mainly, taken from the title of an article I wrote in *Film Culture* in 1962. It was a survey of certain films made during the previous decade and in it I discussed tendencies and individual artists such as Cassavetes, Leacock, Vanderbeek, and Brakhage; indicating, stressing those directions which were new. And I thought that there was a definite break with the traditional cinema in techniques and forms, in content and feeling, and I called all of this the New American Cinema. So, when people began referring to the things I said, the filmmakers I referred to, they usually used the term, the New American Cinema. Then, later, I myself started using the term for the same purpose. You call someone "Peter" or "Stan," and you know who you are talking about. But the name the New American Cinema has also another origin. In 1960 I got together some of the independent filmmakers, those who were working in the avant-garde film (at that time, called the "experimental film") and those who were working in the low-budget, semicommercial area, and we decided to create some kind of an organization to produce films, to distribute films, to fight censorship, and to promote our films; and we called ourselves the New American Cinema Group. We wanted to avoid terms like "experimental" or "personal" or "avant-garde." We simply wanted to call our movement "new" which we thought it was.

GB: Was the group interested in creating a new feature film movement?

JM: Some of us wanted to move in that direction. Some members of the group were interested in feature narrative films in the cinéma-vérité style, and I felt, and still feel, that that was new and was a contribution to the narrative film tradition. The work of Ricky Leacock and the Maysles brothers at the beginning, and the later branches, Andy Warhol, the first two films by Norman Mailer (not

Maidstone), those films were made by men who went directly into a life situation and stuck with a protagonist, like the Maysles' *Salesman*; and in that sense those films were narrative and dramatic. Other filmmakers, like Warhol, imposed artificial situations that nonactors had to go through, and it is here that Mailer's first two films are important. Of course, Mailer is not an actor; but he has such a great ego-personality that, just as in his writing, he had to be at the center of his films. An actor would work within certain conventions to give us the idea of a cop, but when Mailer plays the cop in *Beyond the Law*, his imagination and his temperament lead him into very strange and unconventional fantasies and meditations on a cop. I can't think of a modern novel or a film in which the cop has come out as such a complex and interesting personality. Mailer actually makes us feel what it's like to be a cop.

However, all of the narrative films referred to thus far are quite conventional, even if they are part of the New American Cinema. To talk about the really new in the modern narrative film, we have to turn somewhere else. There is another kind of narrative film, much less known than all the others, a film that deals with myth, such as Brakhage's *Dog Star Man* and Markopoulos's *Twice a Man*. It's here that the real revolution took place. These films explode the conventional narrative form and bring to the narrative film an intensity and complexity not known to cinema before.

GB: But most of the contributions of the NAC are in the area of shorter, nonnarrative films?

JM: Yes, much of the achievement in the last ten years or so is in the nonnarrative form. But this is because the narrative form in the last sixty years of cinema has been developed much further than the nonnarrative forms. By 1960, the narrative film had been explored on almost every level. But the nonnarrative film was only at its beginning. That's why, although the achievements of the avant-garde narrative (or, perhaps more exactly, mythopoeic film, to borrow P. Adams Sitney's term) are very monumental, it is still correct to say that the main achievement of the sixties was the working out of the language, techniques, vocabulary, and forms of the nonnarrative film.

GB: Let's go back to Macdonald's statement for a moment. While it's clear that your work was seminal to the NAC, I have always had the feeling that he was being a bit sarcastic in calling you the "patron saint" of the movement. Macdonald has never taken the nonnarrative films of the NAC very seriously, and he has been joined by other critics such as Pauline Kael, John Simon, and Stanley Kauffmann. **JM:** Yes, and these people have seen relatively few non-narrative, avant-garde films. They refuse to see them, but they like talking about them: they're not interested in them. It's easy to be sarcastic about things you don't know. They're more interested in producing entertaining copy—Pauline Kael, John Simon, and Macdonald are always great fun to read—than in providing the correct information on things they are writing about.

GB: They refer to those films in such terms as "undisciplined," "amateurish," "confusing."

JM: They take the same kind of stance as a Stalinist social realist attacking Picasso, or the Nazis attacking the German Expressionist artists. They say things like "your camera shakes," or "you don't know what you are doing," or "you're sloppy," or "any child could do it." They're not really carrying on a serious discussion.

GB: Does your film *Reminiscences of a Journey to Lithuania*, screened the other evening at the New York Film Festival, offer us some examples of this critical problem?

JM: Let's take, for example, the exposure of my film. I did not eliminate shots on the basis of under- or over-exposure. I cut out shots because I did not like the way they looked, what they said. Because the question of under- or over-exposure is no longer that simple as it used to be in cinema's infancy. The modern film aesthetics have thrown out such conventional textbook ideas as the "normal" exposure, or "normal" focus, or "normal" this or that. Now, we say that the exposure can be from complete white to complete dark, and you choose what you need according to what you are doing—it all depends on the feeling, on the mood, on one's style, on the rhythm, etc., etc. The same with speeds: you can film from fastest to slowest. And the same is true with every cinema technique. Of course, in other arts this has been true for many decades, or many centuries. Is there a "normal" color scale in painting? Must all trees be green? A certain green? Such ideas have been thrown out.

GB: Similarly, you generally edit in the camera, don't you?

JM: I edit most of my footage in the camera. Post-editing on the table is more a matter of eliminating what didn't work. Where I failed in my editing during the shooting, where I missed the feeling, the rhythm of the scene, where I didn't get to the essence, at least as I feel it when I'm looking at it later, then I cut it out. I cut out the badly written "paragraphs." But I don't usually touch what I leave in. Thus, my editing technique is different from the classical, the traditional idea of editing. But this is only because our ideas of what editing is have been based until now on the narrative film requirements and practices only. Nonnarrative forms require a much more personal, intuitive and automatic kind of editing, and this can be done only during the shooting. This is not to say that there is no editing of any kind during the shooting of a conventional narrative film. Besides the editing in the editing rooms, there is also the editing or structuring within the shot, during the shooting. The shot is structured by how the actors move within the frame, by the placement of the lights, by how the sound travels, by the pacing and the movements of the camera. All of this takes place during the shooting. Narrative directors have to be concerned with that: Antonioni, Hitchcock, Rossellini. So, there is always that kind of structuring during the shooting. So that the conception and practices of editing differ in the different forms of the same art: how you organize the smallest elements into the total structure.

GB: So, critics such as Macdonald, Kael, Simon, and Kauffmann are unable to properly evaluate new narrative and nonnarrative films because they're using invalid criteria.

JM: Really, what they're saying is: "Why does Blake write those fourteener lines? Can't he write a novel? Can't he write something serious?" They wouldn't, of course, say that about literature, because they know that there are certain conventions in poetry that differ from those in the novel. But in cinema, the differing traditions of narrative and nonnarrative films do not exist for 99 percent of the reviewers. To them, cinema is what comes from Hollywood or from the European "art film" centers. This is even the case with Andrew Sarris. If you ask Sarris to define cinema, he comes up with something like this: "Cinema is that thing which people refer to when they say 'Let's go to movies.'" If we would take that kind of attitude with respect to literature, we would end up with nothing but "bestsellers." No art other than cinema is so lacking in valid methods of evaluating work in various forms. But things are beginning to change; mostly, I think, through universities and other learning institutions. We're beginning to develop an acceptance of different forms in cinema.

GB: Is *Reminiscences of a Journey to Lithuania* an example of a different cinematic form?

JM: Yes, it's like most of my work of the last ten years: it's created in the form of a diary, or an autobiography. It's a comparatively new form. Cinema has been going into various directions in the last fifteen or twenty years. Even within the existing forms of narrative films various forms of diary began to appear. First, there were films that were quite fictitious, like Stanton Kaye's *Georg*. He created a fictional diary. The script was written out and the seemingly real events were actually staged. Of course, you could consider Bresson's *Diary of a Country Priest* as another example: an adaptation of a novelistic diary-notebook by Georges Bernanos. Such forms were in existence prior to the work of the last decade. More recently, filmmakers began directly shooting material dealing with their actual lives, their day-to-day lives, their friends; and after they shot the footage, the material was structured, organized, and issued in the form of film notebooks. I have here in mind work of Warren Sonbert, Andrew Noren, Gerard Malanga, Michael Stewart,

Bob Branaman, Taylor Mead, Stan Brakhage (particularly in *Songs*), and of a good number of others. The diary, of course, is a variety of the narrative film: there are protagonists, the filmmaker himself, his friends. My first completed work in this form was *Diaries, Notes & Sketches*, and it contained day-to-day footage taken with my Bolex during the years 1965–68. The three-hour-long "volume" consisted of my daily camera "notes." Regarding *Reminiscences of a Journey to Lithuania*, in August of 1971, I went to Lithuania where I come from and I visited there my brothers, my mother, and I kept a camera notebook as I was staying there for two weeks. When I brought the material back to this country, I structured it into a film of three parts. In the first part, I used some of the material shot when I first came to this country in the early fifties. Then, I have the Lithuania footage. Part three consists of my visit to Austria, to my friend, Peter Kubelka. And each part serves a different function; each part touches on a different aspect of the ideas of "home," "culture," "displaced person," "roots," "homelessness."

GB: Did you feel that the particular film genre you were working in was considered by those who viewed it at the New York Film Festival?

JM: Well, Professor Gerald O'Grady presented the film to the audience as a film made in the form of a diary, an autobiography, and there were objections: "What are you talking about? A film is a film. What is this division . . . diary . . . autobiography?" It's like saying, "Anything that has two wings and two legs and flies is a bird. A bird is a bird. But we know there are differences. Everything that flies and has two wings and two legs is not a pigeon. Those interested in birds have to go into categories to make meaningful distinctions, and it's the same with cinema.

GB: Let's suppose that we have a critic who has made the proper distinctions in his mind and sets out to criticize a particular contemporary American avant-garde film. . . .

JM: That is only developing. That is only beginning. Proper criticism, during the beginning years, was very difficult. In the beginning, and, of course, I am speaking here about the early sixties, the period of NAC—with so many good films being made in such a short period of time, I could not act as critic. I was really a midwife. I was excited and wanted everyone to see the work of people such as Brakhage, Jack Smith, Markopoulos, and the others. But periods of great creativity do not last forever. Now, things are slowing down. Now, we have a body of works and the beginnings of an avant-garde film tradition.

GB: Which brings me to your writing in the *Village Voice*. What will happen when you switch from your role as midwife to a more critical posture? Will your critical views be accepted by those who believe that some of your previous comments exaggerated the worth of certain films? You didn't criticize the films, you simply praised them.

JM: That was enough, at the time.

GB: But you seldom offered the viewer a method of evaluating the films or of validating your praises.

JM: That cannot be helped. First, there is only the artist and his work. Then, there are his friends. The work, at first, grows through and with the artist alone, and his close friends. It cannot start from the other end, from the museum. Furthermore, the artist doesn't have to explain: it's enough that he did it. Explanations and analyses begin when the work goes to the people. No new art movement begins with a history; new art movements *make* history. The stage of serious criticism in cinema is only coming now. Again, I am speaking not about cinema in general but about the avant-garde film specifically. There are three or four people who are beginning to write, to discuss, to organize a critical position. Some very intelligent writers on the avant-garde film are beginning to come out of universities. The first really serious book on the avant-garde film will be coming out next spring. P. Adams Sitney's *The Visionary Film-Makers* (Praeger), a monumental work.[1] My own book, *Movie Journal* (Macmillan), just serves to introduce it. It's not really a book of criticism; it's just a history of the period. The histories, dialogues, and various viewpoints that are common to an understanding of literature and the literary tradition are only beginning in the avant-garde film. But there is progress. In the early sixties the only critical source was *Film Culture* magazine. Certain films were discussed there, and you would have some criteria for evaluation. The next stage came about through the anthologies. Gregory Battcock's anthology of writings, *The New American Cinema* (Dutton). Then, Sheldon Rensan's book, *An Introduction to the American Underground Film* (Dutton). Limited as it was, it did give an overview of the history of the movement. Then, there was P. Adams Sitney's *Film Culture Reader* (Praeger). Now, it's becoming more complicated. With Parker Tyler's book *Underground Film* (Grove Press), we have an alternate stand; a different view of the same films is presented, and now we can see a number of the early films from two sides. And then, there is *Artforum* magazine, which, under the editorship of Annette Michelson, has become a source of some of the most intelligent writing on film. A dialogue is beginning.

In literature, of course, dialogues have been going on for centuries. So, now, all of these writers are discussing the avant-garde film, and they have certain disagreements. Anyone who is intelligent enough can begin to guide himself. New books on the subject are being written and published in England and on the mainland Europe. If one still rents avant-garde films blindly today, all that I can say is that he is a fool.

GB: In your 17 August column in the *Village Voice*, you write that you avoid commenting upon commercial films because your critical standards cannot be applied to them because they are not serious enough.
JM: Sometimes I go to catch up on those that are discussed in the press. I sit and I relax and I have a nice evening. But also, I find myself forgiving so many things, relaxing all my standards. I would never approach any of the avant-garde films that I respect in this way. When I look at an avant-garde film, I measure it from the very beginning, moment by moment. And when a film begins to fail, even for a moment, how can we excuse it? One asks for a certain totality, a certain level of achievement throughout. The level of achievement in the commercial narrative film during the last decade has been very, very low when compared with the achievement in the nonnarrative or the new narrative film (for example, *The Chelsea Girls*).

GB: But there are some films that are not avant-garde and are not commercial, there are some fiction feature films that have reached a high level of achievement. For example, at your theater in New York, at Anthology Film Archives, you show films by Renoir, Ozu, Bresson, and other non-avant-garde moderns. You wouldn't term Bresson avant-garde, would you?
JM: To tell the truth, we don't divide that much; at Anthology, we don't use those terms. There is a great danger in dividing films in terms of avant-garde and non-avant-garde, of commercial and noncommercial. Is there a set number, how many people must see a film before it becomes "commercial"? Brakhage has told me that his *Dog Star Man* has been seen by over one million people. Does that make *Dog Star Man* a commercial film? I'm willing to dismiss that kind of terminology. The only distinction I can accept is nonnarrative and narrative. Even there, there are complications. So that, at the very end, we can speak only about the individual artists.

GB: Can we say that there are good films and bad films?
JM: That I can accept. One can speak in those terms. That's legitimate. Or in terms of different forms, or genres.

GB: Well, what kinds of distinctions can be made about the difference between a good film and a bad film?
JM: It finally comes down to the passion of the critic towards a particular film. But, of course on what is that passion based? First, he should see many, many films and be passionate about cinema in general. Then, all of the critic's background comes into play: that is, all of the aspects of cinema come into play: the history of cinema, the theory of cinema, the techniques of cinema, the forms of cinema, the contemporary examples of cinematic works, the individual creators. Think of a film as a chair. How does one decide if a particular chair is well made? By comparing it

with other chairs, by memories of all the chairs in which you sat. And even so, you may discover that you are wrong about that particular chair unless you sat in it for a few weeks. Only many, many viewings of a particular film can finally establish its superiority to others. However you live, whatever you do, you make choices, you make decisions. So, in cinema if you are in a position to show your friends some films, you choose the films you show to them; you don't pick them at random. You want them to see the most beautiful films, those that gave you pleasure and continue to give you pleasure. And you want to share that experience. So you begin to compare films in order to show your friends the best.

GB: I agree. An evaluation of a particular film is based upon the critic's intimate and extensive knowledge of all the aspects of cinematic art as well as his unique tastes and predilections. Do you think that such an evaluation can be validated in the space of a short column? Say, your column in the *Village Voice*?
JM: If I trust somebody's judgment, he doesn't have to go into lengthy backings of his recommendations. One word is enough. In other words: either one trusts my taste or not. Of course, my space doesn't permit me any lengthy analyses. I can express my feelings about a film, that's about all. That's why I write only about films I like. When I like them, I can express my enthusiasm in that one short column. But to be negative, to put something down, to attack some bad film that my colleagues are raving about—that's something else. To seriously attack something, you have to prove, you have to discuss. The next stage after passion is analysis. You have to discuss the film on aesthetic grounds, on social grounds, on technical grounds, on historical grounds; you have to place the film in a proper perspective and explain yourself. I have done this in a few cases, but I have done very little of that. It's the people like P. Adams Sitney, Ken Kelman, or Annette Michelson who can write ninety pages on *Dog Star Man*, whom you must look to.

GB: Of course, analytic criticism would take time away from your filmmaking.
JM: That's true. I'm involved with the Film-Makers' Cooperative, the Anthology Film Archives, *Film Culture*, my own films. So, I don't feel guilty about my nonanalytic writing. I'm not a critic! Really, I'm not a critic! The furthest I can go is to say that I'm a midwife. And that's about it. Or, if thought of as a critic, I'm as much a critic as Baudelaire was, or Apollinaire; that is, those artists who have written on art and artists in a way similar to mine. None of them wrote studies, analyses. They were practicing a very personal kind of criticism.

GB: Since the form of your films in the last ten years, the diary form, is a literary convention, I wonder if you have any thoughts about the subject of films derived

from specific literary works? Do you ever look at a film in that way; how well it cinematically accomplishes what has previously been accomplished in words?
JM: I saw Gregory Markopoulos's *Psyche*, and for years after I was not aware of the source, the novel by Pierre Louÿs. It was Gregory's film, and it had no relation to literature. And then I saw *Himself as Herself*, his film based on Balzac's *Seraphita*, and it didn't look at all like it was based on a literary work. These are the true adaptations.

Actually, they're not adaptations, they're something else. Gregory used the literary works for inspiration. And then he completely transformed the sources to turn his films into something else. But as far as direct adaptations are concerned, are there any successful adaptations? Of course, Bresson's *Diary of a Country Priest*. Actually, I'm against adaptations of plays and novels. I'm for original film sources.

GB: Why is that?
JM: Well, I should say that I'm not against adaptations if the film is based on a bad novel or play. Then it's simply material to be used; you can be very free with it. But if you are working from a great literary work? It's legitimate to take some aspect of, say, *Moby Dick*, for your inspiration, but to make an adaptation of it? What can you add to it? What insights can you add to a book like that? What other new angle can you reveal? It's all there. You can only simplify, banalize, distort. But, of course, when you deal with a bad novel, which is like a script to begin with, you know that the film can be better.

GB: Why do you think so many directors do it? Russell's *Women in Love*, Richardson's *Tom Jones*. Visconti's *Death in Venice*?
JM: Because the producers want it. The director has to play the game to assure the producer of his built-in financial returns.

GB: Can you conceive of a good director seriously setting out to cinematically reproduce a great literary work?
JM: Eisenstein considered filming Joyce's *Ulysses*.

GB: He even wrote a script for *An American Tragedy*. Murnau, of course, did *Faust* and *Tartuffe*.
JM: Of course, I haven't resolved for myself the contradictions involved in the subject of adaptations. For instance, I find it different with silent films. One thing that's legitimate is to illustrate books. Illustrations are decorative, and a filmmaker can add something to *Faust*, like Doré did with his illustrations of *Paradise Lost*. There is that tradition.

That doesn't insult me at all. Silent films based on great literary works could be looked at in that way. The characters don't open their mouths to vulgarize authors' lines. And, of course, in painting, every line of the Bible has been painted over and over all over the walls of the Western Civilization and, of course, some of these works are as great as the Bible itself.

GB: What about Dreyer's *Gertrude*?

JM: Dreyer always comes in as an example. But, there, he's dealing with a classic on the level, say, of Arthur Miller. It's a classic that is local, so I don't know how Danes look at it. To us, the literary source doesn't exist in *Gertrude*. We don't know the play. And with Dreyer, I would bet and swear that Dreyer is a ten-times better artist than the man who wrote the play.

GB: One reason I asked you about your feelings on the subject is that when you describe your editing practices you sometimes use literary analogies.

JM: There was a time when cinema was young that filmmakers tried to avoid any terms or analogies that would suggest relationships with other forms of art. They wanted to emphasize their individuality, their originality, and the uniqueness of their cinema art. But I think that cinema does not have to have that kind of inferiority complex anymore. We know what it can do. We know that it can do something original and unique. So now, at this point, we can begin to see the comparative area. To understand what cinema is, it is sometimes very useful to make use of the terminology, the means of expression, even the techniques found in other arts. All arts overlap. In all arts, you find similar forms. We have an arabesque in music; we have an arabesque in art and sculpture; we have an arabesque in cinema. Very often, I invite those who are seeing avant-garde films for the first time and object to certain aspects to think about other art forms they are more familiar with and find points of similarity. It helps.

GB: Talking about points of similarity, I'm surprised that so few avant-garde filmmakers have tried to do anything with transforming personal lyrical poems to film. There seems to be a meaningful overlap there.

JM: The problem here is the same as with the adaptations of novels: you just can't add anything to a good poem. And if a poem is bad, why bother with it? On the other hand, as the nonnarrative forms developed, they began on their own, and in their own terms (that is, in terms of cinema) to touch and draw inspiration from the same inner sources from which the greatest of the written poems have emerged. So that very naturally, and very organically, a form or, rather, forms of cinema have developed that correspond to those of poetry in literature. And it's here that we find some of the true glories of the American cinema of the last two decades. I have in mind works such as Brakhage's *The Dead, Sirius Remembered,* or *Prelude*; Anger's *Eaux D'Artifice* and *Fireworks*; Broughton's *Mother's Day* and *This Is it*; Baillie's *Castro Street, Mass,* and *All My Life*; Bruce Conner's *A Movie* and *Report*; Belson's *Samadhi* and *Chakra*; Jack Smith's *Flaming Creatures*; Robert Breer's *Eyewash* and *Fist Fight*; and etc., etc.—all works without any recourse to any literary sources; works ecstatically rich with poetic feeling and form. These works are expanding the medium of cinema or the expression of the poetic content in cinema.

Notes

1. Editor's Note: This book was published under the title *Visionary Film*. It has gone through three editions and become the classic study of American avant-garde cinema.

Tenants of the House:
A Conversation with Jonas Mekas

Jonathan Rosenbaum / 1982

From *Film: The Front Line 1983* (Denver: Arden Press, 1983). Reprinted by permission.

> Tenants of the house,
> Thoughts of a dry brain in a dry season.
> —T. S. Eliot, "Gerontion"

Preface: When I was approached last year about inaugurating a series of volumes surveying recent avant-garde film, I immediately started to wonder about how this could be done. Having lived nearly eight years in Paris and London and about as long in New York, I've had several opportunities to note the relative degree of information flow between these and other centers of avant-garde film activity, and the growing isolation of New York from these other centers made my own fixed vantage point less than ideal in some ways. When a colleague told me that Jonas Mekas had recently said that it was no longer possible to know what was happening in experimental film as a whole, a bell of recognition rang in my head, and I knew at once that Mekas was the only available oracle I could turn to. The Lithuanian patron saint of the American avant-garde film, now sixty, has been an American filmmaker for at least half of his life, and a chronicler of the avant-garde film in New York—mainly in the *Village Voice* and (more briefly) *Soho News*—for at least fifteen years. If he no longer knew with confidence where we were, a consideration of the nature of the very problem of our ignorance was clearly in order.

Out of this need and curiosity, the two following conversations took shape, with Mekas's kind consent, at the temporary headquarters of Anthology Film Archives on Broadway in Lower Manhattan, in late July and early November 1982. Robert Haller, executive director of Anthology, was present at both discussions, and some of his remarks are also included. The second dialogue, longer and somewhat more polemical than the first, occurred during a two-week season at the Public Theater devoted to Jean-Marie Straub and Danièle Huillet and filmmakers they admire (about two dozen films in all) that I was involved in curating at the time, and which became a logical reference point for part of our discussion. The results have been edited by Mekas as well as myself.

I.

Jonathan Rosenbaum: If someone were writing a survey of recent avant-garde film ten or twenty years ago, he'd have a much easier task. Things were much more centralized then. If someone came to New York from, say, Kansas with an avant-garde film and he or she wanted it to be shown, that person would have gone to see you, probably.

Jonas Mekas: Yes, between about 1960 and 1970. Before that, between 1950 and 1960, they went to see Amos Vogel[1] or the Museum of Modern Art. In a few other big cities, like San Francisco, you could count on one place where you could go.

JR: But if someone came from Kansas with an avant-garde film today, he or she would be likelier to search out an institution, not an individual. And the person in charge at the institution might think, "Do I like this?" But he or she would be just as likely to think, "Would the audience for the Collective for Living Cinema go for this?" "Would the audience for Film Forum like this?"

JM: Today, New York is split into a dozen showcases. Why did these different showcases develop? Because, beginning with the seventies, there were no longer twenty or thirty filmmakers to deal with, but literally thousands, making thousands of films. No one showcase could deal with that; so different showcases developed with preferences for different filmmakers. Actually, some of the showcases were started by filmmakers who felt excluded from other showcases. And, of course, filmgoing people as well as filmmakers became familiar with the preferences of the different showcases. Like somebody who is making abstract, personal films wouldn't necessarily go to see Karen Cooper at Film Forum—unless they were cutely animated.

The field is too big now; no one can cover it all. Amos Vogel could cover all the varieties of avant-garde, experimental, and documentary. In the sixties, the Film-Makers' Cinematheque was already neglecting a lot of documentaries. Today, it's impossible for any single showcase to show everything—unless you had three or four different programs every day. It's not only that you have to catch up so constantly; you also have to give some background and show what went before, which is harder and harder. That's why the Museum of Modern Art introduced their series "What's Happening?," to show the documentaries that no one was showing. And of course the feminist groups also have a purpose—to cover a certain area more in depth than any other. At Anthology the direction became more academically avant-garde because we felt that that part was neglected. We felt that once a film is shown at any of the showcases—no matter how good the film was, it had no chance of being re-seen. Until just a few years ago it was mainly just new work that the showcases were interested in.

There are certain historical necessities that determine these developments: the volume of the production, the number of different directions in cinema, the size of audiences. Before, the audiences could all fit into one theater; now, if you put all the audiences together, they make big numbers, even for the independent films.

JR: What I find disturbing about this is how everything has become consumer-oriented and service-oriented. Consequently, there isn't much of a sense of *mystery* about the avant-garde anymore: people aren't curious about what they can't see the way that they used to be.

JM: I wouldn't say consumer-oriented. Millennium, for example, in the first place serves its own members, then serves all the others, so that it's a semiclosed group. What do you mean by consumer-oriented—that it brings money? Millennium programs don't make money.

JR: I mean much more the kind of money and attitudes that come from outside funding. I'm thinking that the success of certain points of view become institutionalized, that certain categories of films now pre-exist in people's minds.

I'm also thinking of the differences between film magazines now and then. In *Film Culture* in the sixties—compared to what you'd find in *Millennium Film Journal* or *October* now—there was an amazing range of people coexisting, a real pluralism. In one issue—Winter 1962/63—it's actually possible to see Sarris, Farber, Kael, Markopoulos, Weinberg, Smith, and Stern, all cheek by jowl.

JM: Yes, that *was* a classical period.

JR: What seems so depressing is how relatively little opportunity there is now for exchange and cross-fertilization and people listening to other ideas.

JM: No, each one is interested only in their own thing and there isn't much variety, no.

JR: So if this same filmmaker from Kansas had to go to a film magazine today, he or she might have to choose one at the exclusion of another. It's all feudal strongholds now; one can no longer introduce a film into a single community.

JM: The only thing is, I don't know whether this is a negative or positive thing. What has developed is the phenomenon of the regional art centers. There are one or two hundred of these. And they very often try to show examples of all the varieties of film—some very new and "emerging" filmmakers, some classical avant-garde, some old Hollywood, and some new European work. Some of them import films directly from Germany, or France, and other countries. You can see European and South American films in Houston at the Fine Arts Museum today that you can't see in New York, for instance. Without these regional art centers, we would miss a lot of the European avant-garde. They come only because they have engagements at six or eight places and travel from one to the other. So while the New York and San Francisco showcases may be restricted to single directions, across the country that is not true—unless some center is run by some kind of fanatic of one kind of film.

JR: Well, you would certainly have a better notion than me of how much Americans are exposed on a national level to European avant-garde. But it seems to me that in a New York context, the situation of the European avant-garde is vastly inferior to what it once was.

JM: For the last five or six years there's been a drop, that is true. Not that the European avant-garde is necessarily all that active. The Italian avant-garde died out. The British and German avant-gardes slowed down, relaxed. Only the French avant-garde is still active. But we don't see any of it.

JR: One thing I want to do in my book is include certain films that, in one sense, are avant-garde precisely because they're overlooked and ignored. For instance, I know of very few Americans who know about even the existence of Jacques Tati's last feature, *Parade*, a circus film made in video.

JM: I didn't know he made a film in video! But not knowing that a certain film exists doesn't necessarily make that film avant-garde. . . .

JR: True enough. Although sometimes it's tempting to give preference to actual films over categories, regardless of the academic havoc this might create—there are so many homeless films of interest floating around, and so many standard avant-garde films of no interest whatsoever. I've seen *Parade* in both Paris and London; Tati made it in 1973. It was shot in video and transferred to 35mm film— an earlier version of the technique used on the Richard Pryor concert films. It's an experimental film not only in that respect, but also in its attitude towards the spectator. A lot of the film consists of a circus show that includes many of Tati's famous mime routines from his music hall days, but the audience consists of both real and artificial (i.e., flat and painted) spectators, and the camera is often positioned in such a way that this audience becomes just as prominent as the performers. Then there's an epilogue when a little girl steps down onto the stage after all the performers have left and plays with all the props that are left behind. Jean-Marie Straub has said that what's exciting about the film is that it's about all the degrees of "nervous flux—beginning with the child which cannot yet make a gesture, who cannot yet coordinate her hand with her brain, and going up to the most accomplished acrobats."

Parade, of course, represents only one example of an important work that is almost totally unknown in this country. Even when certain things get shown here, they often remain unknown. For instance, I just spoke to a graduate student who's taking a summer course in Rivette, Rohmer, and Chabrol and asked his teacher about Rivette's 1980 feature Merry-Go-Round—which he'd seen at the Museum of Modern Art in February 1980—only to discover that his teacher knew nothing about the film's existence!

JM: One of the reasons, maybe, for the new situation is that for the last five or seven years, the political avant-garde—at least the avant-garde that calls itself political—has dominated: the Screen group, Jump Cut, Cineaste, Camera Obscura. To tell you the truth, the way I really feel about these films, they are neither political nor avant-garde. Only the talking and writing about these films, in Screen, Jump Cut, etc., has a political tint or style. It's not politics—it's, rather, politics as a fashion, or style. It has nothing to do with changing the status quo of society.

Nobody writes about Klaus Wyborny in those places, although Wyborny is more interesting and more political. Chris Welsby is mentioned, but he's not given the credit he deserves because all these politically minded writers like Peter Wollen[2] are wallowing in certain semipolitical and semifeminist ideas. And semiotics is part of it. Fashionable politics. They can really make a film sound very interesting. They are all writers. They say, "A man is crossing the street"—and you think, "That sounds very interesting," but you look at the film and it's got nothing, it's just a man crossing a street—you could get a child to do it. There is no more qualitative, historical, comparative criticism. From the standpoint of semiotics and structuralism, you can analyze any image; any and every image is illuminating. You can talk about any frame for hours: it has nothing to do with cinema and nothing to do with anything. But it has to do with semiotics and analyzing of lines and shapes and light and how they all relate to history and masculine and feminine. We had a lot of that kind of writing here. Daryl Chin's[3] writing, for instance, started out as perceptive and sensitive. But no matter what he sees, he can write three or four or five single-spaced pages about it, and if one asks, "Should I go to see this film?" one gets only a description. You wind up knowing nothing. Everyone gets a lot of space, and that's it.

JR: One problem is, when critics do tell you what films to go to, they generally aren't writing about the avant-garde. Whereas people who do write about avant-garde often argue that there's something outdated about assigning grades to works. What bothers me even more is that critics in this country who are widely thought to be intellectuals of some sort—I'm thinking of people like Kael, Sarris, Simon, and Kauffmann—don't deal with intellectual films or subjects at all, as a rule.

JM: Yes, but I cannot reproach them for not treating avant-garde films any more than I can reproach certain musicians for preferring certain instruments, or certain painters for preferring certain subjects or techniques. I mean, they are very deep in their own areas and doing well, and I think we have that in independent cinema as well, and in art criticism. There are no universal minds who can cover all the periods and styles. I think Andrew [Sarris] is doing very well in illuminating a certain type of film, and that's it.

JR: Sure. But in the public mind, he and the others are perceived somehow as writing about and representing the whole of cinema. That isn't entirely their fault, of course—but it does lead to an enormous amount of omission and even repression. Five years ago, in London, Andrew was insisting to me that nobody but nobody was interested in Godard anymore—but, of course, his idea of "somebody" now excludes the avant-garde. It's a vicious circle that becomes all the more exclusive when avant-garde critics ignore many of Godard's works as well.

JM: l don't think Sarris was so wrong about that. The avant-garde, especially the American avant-garde, was never really interested in Godard. There was nothing in Godard for the American avant-garde, politically or formally. The only thing about Andrew is that he should just keep his mouth shut when it comes to avant-garde films in general. But he feels some time he has to open his mouth and say, "Maya Deren stinks," or "Stan Brakhage stinks." By the same token, I wouldn't presume to pass judgment on Hollywood films anymore.

JR: But you used to, and I found it very interesting when you did.

JM: Well, I saw absolutely every film that opened until maybe 1970. Now my work doesn't permit me to catch up with everything, so I feel I have no right to speak about it. I cannot compare.

JR: This may be because of all my years in Europe, but it seems to me that a lot of my European friends tend to see all kinds of films, and see them in relation to each other.

JM: I don't know who your friends are, but some of them are publishing film magazines, and if you look at the magazines like *Cahiers du Cinéma* or *Chaplin*, none of them write about the avant-garde except for *Cahiers*, once in a blue moon. You need to have a blockbuster like Michael Snow or Nam June Paik in order to get attention. These magazines are not balanced.

JR: What about the *Monthly Film Bulletin* in England?

JM: I'll have to look at that one. For the others, I don't think those writers or magazines see *all* films. They do not see the avant-garde. I have been there with shows of American avant-garde, and they never came to see the films.

Robert Haller: Lucy Fischer[4] is someone who writes about both commercial and avant-garde film.

JR: Sure, and there are others. I find, as a freelancer, that the most interesting films nowadays are quite often the ones that I can't write about, because they're not available or prominent enough. This is part of what I meant earlier about service- and consumer-oriented criticism.

JM: Dreyer's *Gertrud* has no distributor in the US!

RH: There's been a collapse of the 16mm distributors in this country. Films, Inc. have bought out virtually everybody. It's a giant, and there are a couple of pygmies, and that's it.

JR: What makes me angry is that people keep saying that everything will become available on cassette soon—all of Brakhage, for example. It's not true.

JM: At the Film-Makers' Cooperative in 1962 or '63 we discussed that—almost twenty years ago. Now it seems like it's already here. I don't know if it's really here. All I see is past enthusiasms and hopes. We get all these schedules from across the country of what gets shown—and there are certain constants, like Brakhage and Snow and local people. What understanding there is about what's shown, I don't know. Some aspects are rather bothersome. They rent only certain works—you begin to see the same titles over and over. Take Ernie Gehr. You will see *Serene Velocity* again and again, while a major film like *Still* rents once every two years. And others aren't seen at all.

JR: Is this because of what's written?

JM: It's partly that. Another thing is they feel they can't devote more to Ernie Gehr than one program every two years or so, so they tend to choose what's shown the most often. It *is* a problem.

RH: The situation isn't the same as it was twenty years ago, in those places where museums and universities had bought collections and show their films on a regular basis. Apart from that, it *is* like it was twenty years ago.

JM: We were talking about places like New York, Chicago, and San Francisco, where people who were interested in the avant-garde film saw all of it, whatever was shown, so they had a wider understanding or knowledge. Now, if you are in Kansas and the regional art center will have, let's say, twenty film programs a year, maybe sixteen of these will be devoted to Hollywood and European art films. And of the remaining four, two will be local works and maybe one or two will be classic avant-garde films. . . . I don't know how much knowledge there is now. I know that we show Sidney Peterson's films every four months at Anthology, and we always have three or four people.

II.

JM: It has to do with terminology a lot, because terminology can sometimes turn people off from a whole segment of cinema. Like if we say, "These are experimental films" or "These are avant-garde films." This has never been discussed very much in the open, but maybe it's time to look into this matter of categories. I tend lately in my own thinking to come to an approach that's very similar to that of the Metropolitan Museum. That is, I don't see how we can discuss all the varieties of cinema without setting one group of people against another, unless we take it as a whole. The Metropolitan Museum may not be up to date with the latest trend or vogue in art, but there are rooms for Egyptian art, for Greek art, for Impressionist art. There are different rooms for different styles and periods, and one building houses them all.

So one has to recognize that certain styles and forms are related to a place or time, they may not be repeated later, and you have to take and respect them for what they are. Certain historians gravitate only to one style or school or period. That period could be very brief—ten years or fifteen. But in cinema we have the situation that either we have writers or historians who are interested only in commercial film—all the Hollywoods of the world—or else just the avant-garde or experimental film, or else some in-between area, like the European independents. Now we have already another group, the American independents, who are neither avant-garde nor Hollywood. And usually those who write about one group exclude the others. So books and histories keep coming out that present very, very distorted views of film history. With me, this has become a standard practice, as far as the new books on film history go: the first thing I do, I look through the name index. If the names of Kenneth Anger, Stan Brakhage, and Bruce Baillie are missing, I throw the book out as amateurish and not serious.

JR: So what you're saying, in effect, is that we have no film culture—only film cultures.

JM: There is still this division according to how much it cost to make the film, is it done with amateurs or professionals, is there a union involved, is the government sponsoring it, or a bank, or am I sponsoring it out of my own pocket? That has to go out the window. What has to be stressed are the different varieties of forms, styles, and content areas, such as autobiography, for example. It's very possible that when we all look back at the history of cinema twenty years from now, we may find that autobiographical film blossomed between 1965 and 1975 or 1980. Then there's a whole period like direct cinema or cinéma-verité which left its mark and is gone now. The British documentary is another room in itself, just like the social documentaries of a certain period made in this country—or the wartime documentary, which is something else. But when one begins to create one collection of cinema, and that collection is selected by people who are uninterested in so-called "movies" or the avant-garde or the social documentary, of course all other areas will be excluded.

JR: But you're talking about taxonomy and preservation, which is what a museum does. How does one discover or create the necessity of including a new room? Furthermore, given the existing turf consciousness that seems to rule discourse among many prominent New York film critics—the notion that certain areas and subjects are staked-out property belonging to a few appointed or self-appointed individuals—how can new ideas or approaches manifest themselves? Where can they go? Is there a way of creating or addressing a broad community, or does one have to build another fortress, like Anthology Film Archives, to protect one's own critical investments?

JM: When we have a film selection committee meeting for Anthology, the films that we review and discuss are those which one of us very passionately stands for and suggests we should see. Therefore, unless there are one or two people who feel very passionately about the film, nothing will work. So that I don't see "turf" division as you say. Like you just came out recently very passionately for Straub. That is the only way Straub will get roots in this country among the audience and critics—if somebody such as you or Susan Sontag, as she has done, stands very passionately for him. The movement of avant-garde film is where it is today because some of us in the sixties believed very strongly, and we screened those films, and we screened, and we screened. And now they are recognized. We managed to put them into the sensibilities and minds and eyes of the people. So if Amy Taubin[5] doesn't stand for anybody passionately, nobody is to blame. Or maybe she does—she stands very passionately for Marjorie Keller's *Misconception*. I happened to hate that film with as much passion.

I don't think one passionate supporter is enough to establish a filmmaker. Maybe there are others. That's how the turf develops: there must be passionate people defending certain films very passionately. Maybe the problem we have today is that nobody feels very passionately about *any* film.

JR: I don't know about that. I've been reflecting just recently on Straub and Huillet's last feature, *Too Early, Too Late*, which I regard as one of the most ethical and beautiful documentaries ever made—although it shares the problem of the Tati film in being truly homeless, rejected or ignored locally by documentary and avant-garde filmmakers alike. On the level of its composition, it's a film in which the customary relationship for Straub and Huillet between a physical setting and a written text becomes inverted. Here the landscapes are "the body of the text," while the text becomes the "setting" for those places in France and Egypt—a bit like jazz, where the passing human and animal traffic functions like improvisations on a fixed, given terrain. It's a film of endless activity supported by a sustained distance, a complete absence of characters, and a continual human presence.

I can understand many of the reasons for Anthology's selection and fortress strategy—especially now, when we're entering a time like the early sixties when people think about living in bomb shelters. But what happens to the avant-garde as a social force, the way it was when you were defending Genet's *Un Chant d'Amour* and Smith's *Flaming Creatures*? How do the policies of *October* or *Film Culture* or *Millennium Film Journal* encourage young filmmakers or critics to think new thoughts? If *October* is following the lead of Vincent Canby[6] now in putting Fassbinder at the head of the class, what do we do about people like Straub-Huillet or Wyborny or Ulrike Ottinger? Do we bury them, too, in order to protect our own safety? Finally, if safety and self-preservation become the primary factors in aesthetic decision-making, how does our work differ from that of bankers?

JM: There are many things in your question that I'm not sure are being stated correctly. "Social force," for instance: was the avant-garde a social force at any time? And "encourage young filmmakers or critics": *Film Culture* was never too encouraging. How do you encourage anybody? I have always argued against film schools and "encouragement"—there is no such thing. From the very beginning, Arlene Croce[7] came on her own to *Film Culture*; so did Andrew Sarris and Eugene Archer.[8]

JR: Because there was a place they could go to.

JM: They had passion and something to say. It wasn't because I was encouraging them. How do you encourage a writer?

JR: By allowing people with passions to exist there. By printing them. Where can we go to find that kind of passion today? That's what I mean by encouragement. It wasn't simply an old boy network.

JM: I see—a forum to express their ideas. Well, it was much easier at that time, maybe, because there were very few publications. Do we have many today? I don't know. (*Laughs*)

JR: (*Laughs*) I just named three.

JM: Not that many today. . . ."Social force"? Those were different times. The pressures, censorship, was much stronger then; it was imposed on us, and we had to defend ourselves—a clash was inevitable. But today that problem has been removed. It's more permissive now.

JR: Maybe so. But there's a way in which institutional acceptance and promotion can take the teeth out of certain kinds of art that have something to do with protest.

JM: What art do you have in mind? The avant-garde of the forties, fifties, and sixties had nothing to do with protest.

JR: You don't think *Flaming Creatures* had anything to do with protest—
JM: No, absolutely no. He [Jack Smith] was floating around in that kind of reality. He was obsessed with that reality; he had to do it, and he did it with his friends. It had nothing to do with any politics; it was his world, the life that he lived.

JR: Don't you think that world and life was formed in relation to something else?
JM: Later, once it was shown, it *became* political. But the creation of it did not come from any political necessity. On the other hand, if you listen to Jack's soundtrack in *Blonde Cobra*, you can see that he himself, as a human being, did not like the type of civilization he saw around him when he walked down the street, obviously. So he created his own world that had nothing to do with what was going on around him in the offices or stores or Park Avenues.

JR: Your own films are full of things about politics.
JM: Indirectly, everything is political; everything under the sun can be interpreted politically. But the motivations for making it are not political in that sense; they're personal.

JR: But don't you think that whatever uses art is put to have political consequences?
JM: Consequences, sure. With a knife you can cut bread or stab somebody in the heart.

JR: I'm disturbed about the way that an extreme right-winger like Paul Schrader can accommodate Michael Snow's films to his own social philosophy.
JM: Do you think you can make a film that can appeal only to Democrats or Republicans?

JR: Well, no. But I am saying that art conceived of as social and political protest is received less warmly here than it might have been at another time.
JM: That's because in this country, it is very difficult for us to understand what's going on in another country, oppressed by dictatorships or devastated by political confusions. It's very difficult to identify with and really have some feeling for it. It has nothing to do with this time; it's any time.

JR: And yet if you think of the sixties and the impact a film like *La Chinoise* had . . . I remember Columbia students who saw it over and over again in New York at the Kips Bay only a few weeks before they helped to take over the Columbia

campus—which happened, in turn, right before the May Events in Paris, which were inspired in part by what happened at Columbia. There was a way in which both news and certain feelings about things were able to travel very quickly.
JM: There was something very similar in the air then in Paris and New York. But if you bring in a film from some South American country today, you won't get the same response.

JR: I'm both intrigued and a little appalled by the local responses to Tarkovsky's *The Stalker*, which opened recently at Film Forum. Everyone who deals with the film, including everyone who likes it, says it's a film about the Soviet Union, and I certainly wouldn't quarrel with that. But nobody is saying or apparently even conceiving of the possibility that the film could be addressing what's happening now in America as well, the way that people are living and thinking at this moment. Nobody seems to want to make that connection, which is precisely what makes the film vital and meaningful. People assume it's "political" because it describes repression and cowardice elsewhere, not because it relates to their own lives. This is what I see as the problem: European work which could actually address the conditions of people's lives—and here again I include Straub-Huillet—is never being read as such; it's invariably translated into something else.
JM: Maybe it's the style and the sensibility of the Tarkovsky film. Godard had a style and sensibility that appealed to certain anarchistic and youthful minds here. He didn't appeal to the masses—let's face it. Masses do not know Godard's name. His form did it. It was his form, his style, his temperament—not the content of his films—that inspired the students of Columbia. But I don't think Tarkovsky has that kind of electricity that Godard has. No one has; Godard is unique. Tarkovsky's content is very noble—but it remains only content.

JR: Not for me. The really interesting aspect of *The Stalker* is how much it resembles a structural film—almost any random five minutes has the shape and structure of the whole—while describing the way that we all live and think and lie to ourselves. These two qualities actually support one another—one could even say that they make the film equally unbearable to confront, in a way.

What I'm basically objecting to is critics who write about both film and politics, but who avoid connecting them in any way that might be challenging—such as linking them up with their own lives, for example.
JM: When Amy Taubin writes about a film and interprets it politically, there is nothing sillier.

JR: Even when Peter Biskind[9] or J. Hoberman[10] or Annette Michelson[11] write about film or politics, they often tend to keep each category squeaky-clean, without any serious threat of mutual embrace. My criticism of *Millennium Film Journal* is that it's not a magazine that wants to change the world; it wants to keep the world exactly the way that it is.

JM: *My* objection is that it's not readable! Actually, I have two objections. The main one is, if you haven't seen the film about which someone in *Millennium* is writing, there is no way of knowing what it is—there is no perspective, no judgment, no comparison; it's all descriptive. Equal space and treatment is given to everything there. It's academic, but not on a high level—like a student's class assignment.

JR: How would you compare its film coverage to that of *October*?

JM: *October* is in a different class. It's one of the most important magazines that we have, because it brings the best in its own area of interest. You may reject the whole direction, but at least it *is* a direction. And the pieces are always of a high quality. When it devotes a special issue to Fassbinder after twenty issues, then it's strayed from that direction—but that's a real anomaly. And I hope that it won't happen again, because it destroys what that magazine has achieved.

JR: I couldn't agree more.

RH: May I ask a question? I wonder what the two of you think about why institutions and artists do things. Very specifically, Emile d'Antonio is someone you probably think is a political filmmaker, and someone who's even interested in social change. But I don't think Emile is interested in social change. I think he's interested in articulating his feelings and ideas about what is happening in society. But I don't think he's under any illusion that he's going to change society.

JR: Well, one criticism that's been made of a lot of New York work generally—including, say, Yvonne Rainer's, as well as Emile d'Antonio's—is that it's about politics without being political. And this differentiates it from some European work. One argument I make about Straub and Huillet is that they really want to change the world. Now you can say that's utopian, and maybe the only way they might change the world at all is if one person's consciousness gets changed in a certain direction, then that could lead to other changes. So it's not a plan for a whole social revolution. But it's a beginning.

JM: Do you really think that they want to change the world more than Brakhage or [Peter] Kubelka? Do you really believe so?

JR: I don't know. Maybe they want to change the world in reverse directions.

JM: Certainly Brakhage has affected things politically more through changing the vision of what and how one sees things.

JR: That's what Straub and Huillet do as well. But what kind of implications do you see in Brakhage's work and the effect it has on people?

JM: It's obvious that some believe at this point it's more important to restructure the government, the social system, and for them that's the political action. And there are others who feel that's very superficial, that won't work unless you change human beings some other ways—and that's their action, that we have to work on sensibilities and certain feelings and emotions, and that's a deeper change than just the system. Of course, if you change the system, you try to impose something—I think the Soviets are doing that from the other end. The Poland of politics. Disaster. And the other way, which Brakhage wants and many others, what some religious leaders try—*that* doesn't work so easily either.

But these are only two attitudes, and they're both political actions coming from a very deep engagement in how one sees the world, how one judges where things are weakest and how they should be strengthened. At this point, I support more Brakhage's direction than those who think of changing the system. From my observation of my short life, I think that Brakhage's direction at this point is more correct. Therefore, his politics are for me more vital to humanity than those of . . . I don't want to mention who.

JR: Where my formulation of the problem differs from yours is that I don't see it as an either/or proposition at all. To me, there's no way one can change a political structure without changing your own consciousness. Although I *do* understand that there's a way in which developing the self in a certain direction *can* be a movement away from trying to change social and political structures.

JM: I have no doubt that Straub and Brakhage would agree that the most important change is the inner change. From what I heard Straub say at the Collective last spring, I didn't hear anything which would imply that he's a political filmmaker in any other, different way. I think he just wants the same thing Brakhage wants.

JR: Let me approach this from a somewhat different angle. It's often been said that there's a certain religious atmosphere that's been created around the American avant-garde, particularly in New York. A friend of mine recently said that going to the Collective or Anthology is a little bit like going to church.

JM: You see the same one hundred or 150 people, the same tiny island or group surrounded by ten million people who are totally disinterested in what's going on there. So of course you get that impression—

JR: But why is the impression religious rather than political—transcendental rather than materialist? Why does it resemble a sect, and not a cell group?

JM: I don't see it as religion, I see only the limitation—the small audience, the small interest. When you go to see a commercial film, you know that there will be millions paying money. So you don't have to feel anything about it; you go home and forget. But here you sit there and know that only fifty or sixty people came to this film, so you feel a little bit friendly, almost, to all the other people who are there. It's not so much religion; you feel like it's a community. But that's natural. There is a certain beauty in it.

JR: It *is* natural. But I can remember, when I was in college in the mid-sixties, I was a bit belated in getting interested in avant-garde film. And I can recall a certain attitude I encountered when I *did* go to see certain things in New York—that if one was serious, one went to everything, or most things; but if one was not serious, one only went to an isolated film here and there. The attitude was a bit like: Why weren't you in church last Sunday, the way you were supposed to be?
JM: Only Ken Jacobs[12] would say that. He said, "I never notice those who go to my films. I only notice those who *don't* come to see my films." And that is a religious attitude.

JR: It's understandable, in a way, because you and P. Adams Sitney[13] and Ken Kelman[14] were all going out on limbs—making a commitment which wasn't just a commitment of careers, but a social and aesthetic commitment. And there was a way of relating to that in a dilettantish manner, and a way of relating to it much more existentially. To me, that's what created an aura, which was not necessarily willed at all, that made it like a religion.
JM: Maybe it's impossible in 1982 because of the number of films and videotapes being made today. That's one of the reasons why I quit *Soho News*—a situation that was already coming while I was writing for the *Village Voice*. One of the reasons was that I wanted to do some work of my own, editing my own films. And I could still work on my films and see *all* of what was being done around me until some point in the seventies. But it became more and more impossible as the seventies progressed to see everything and do my own work. Before, one could spend two or three evenings a week and see everything and still do one's work.

JR: How does being a filmmaker rather than a critic affect the way you look at films now?
JM: I don't think that I look at films differently. The difference is only that film-makers aren't calling me that often to see their films. And I feel freer when I go to see their films, because I know I don't have to write about them.

JR: A big problem I'm having right now is with those packages of films by several different filmmakers at the Collective's retrospective. I nearly always find them indigestible—there are too many gear changes I have to make between each film. For the purposes of a survey on recent avant-garde film, you'd think these programs would be very helpful, but there's a phenomenological problem. I recently went to a whole program because I was especially interested in seeing a Wyborny film at the end; but by the time I got to it, I didn't feel that I was able to watch it. **JM:** I don't believe in potpourri programs. I am for one filmmaker in a program, so I'd never do what they're doing.

JR: Have you ever found that there's any way to make it work?
JM: It works with some of the classics which we have seen many, many times, but not with new and unfamiliar works. *Ballet Mécanique* wouldn't fall apart with *Étoile de Mer*, because we know them so well.

JR: Sometimes, though, certain odd pairings can work surprisingly well. Last night, for instance, at the Straub-Huillet season, *Othon* and *Every Revolution Is a Throw of the Dice* and Chaplin's *A King in New York* were shown in swift succession, and there were all sorts of beautiful and unexpected continuities—such as the fact that Chaplin begins his film with a revolution. Unfortunately, it's precisely this aspect of the series that was masked out in the service listings of the *New Yorker* and the *Village Voice*, both of which pretend it's only a straight Straub-Huillet retrospective because their formats apparently can't even contemplate anything that's slightly out of the ordinary. It's here again that the crushing inertia of institutions becomes relevant.
JM: In 1961, we wrote this manifesto of the New American Cinema. Eugene Archer was working for the *New York Times* then, and I showed it to him and asked him if they could print it. He said, "No, we couldn't—maybe the *Village Voice* could run it." Then I understood, of course, that the only kind of manifesto that the *New York Times* would print would be a press release, not a manifesto at all. In the same way, for an idea to get into the *Village Voice* today, it has to become not an idea, but something else.
RH: (*to JR*) I think your notion that institutions are shelters and places of safety and protection is totally false. I don't think institutions do that; I think they try to fill voids and do what nobody else is doing.

JM: At some point Anthology came in to fill a demand and void, but it's conceivable that after it fulfills that function, then it becomes something else. This is new in my thinking. But I look back at certain people who were writing about experimental/avant-garde films like Parker Tyler[15] and Amos Vogel, who wasn't writing but was running the distribution and exhibition side. And the interest and passion of these people, on a very high level, lasted for about a decade, approximately. And then they more or less lost touch and lost interest. For years I would make snide remarks about that, because I thought *I* can bridge at least two or three generations. But on the other hand, I think now I was wrong to say that, because I think we should not ask from a critic, exhibitor, or disseminator to do anything for any other generation but his or her own. There's a certain period when one really gets involved for ten or fifteen years. And if that is really done deeply, so much energy goes into it that later it takes another decade or two just to consummate it. The same applies to institutions. If Anthology Film Archives will serve any other generation of independent filmmakers but that of the thirties to 1948, or even to 1968 or 1970, that would be perfect. It's a limited collection, it's there, you know what it is, it's perfect. There is so much just to serve that period, to protect those works in the collection—we know now what it involves, to collect all the reference materials, etc., so you can really serve in depth university scholars on those twenty or thirty filmmakers. That's a big job, and it would be terrific just to do that and nothing else. But we've expanded, and I don't really know myself how wise it is to continue to expand and do more than that—to add new works, be in touch, make a video collection. Either it's a closed museum that represents a certain period or it's open. When it's closed, you can't accuse it of just protecting its own interests, because it has a definite, real function. But if it's open, then there are different requirements, and one has a right to ask and demand it to really do the job of an open museum—to represent contemporary work that's being done right now. So I see what you are saying.

So we're living in an era that's blasé and pathetic, where people aren't even worried *(laughs)*—and they *should* worry! One day they elect Reagan without thinking, and the next, a couple of years later, again without thinking, they begin to turn against him.

Notes

1. Founder of the pioneering film society, Cinema 16, and cofounder of the New York Film Festival. (JR)

2. Author of Signs and Meaning in the Cinema. (JR)

3. The New York–based critic and performance artist. (JR)

4. Contributor to *Film Quarterly, Sight and Sound, Soho News*, and other publications. (JR)

5. Journalist and critic specializing in the avant-garde, contributor to *October, Soho News*, the *Village Voice*, etc. (JR)

6. First-string film critic for the *New York Times*. (JR)

7. Film and dance critic, founder of the *Ballet Review*, and presently dance critic for the *New Yorker*. (JR)

8. The late film reviewer and journalist for the *New York Times*, an early colleague and friend of Andrew Sarris. (JR)

9. Editor of *American Film*, contributor to *Jump Cut, Film Quarterly, Seven Days*, etc. (JR)

10. Contributor to the *Village Voice, American Film, Film Comment*, etc. (JR)

11. Film and art critic, teacher, editor of *October*, and former contributor to *Artforum*. (JR)

12. Avant-garde filmmaker whose best-known film is *Tom Tom the Piper's Son*. (JR)

13. Film critic and teacher, author of *Visionary Film*, editor of several collections of essays related to avant-garde film. (JR)

14. Playwright and film critic, contributor to *Film Culture*. (JR)

15. The late, prolific critic, author of many books, most of them about film, including *The Hollywood Hallucination, The Three Faces of Film, Underground Film*, and *Screening the Sexes*. (JR)

Interview with Jonas Mekas

Scott Macdonald / 1982–83

From *October*, Summer 1984, 82–116; edited for *A Critical Cinema 2* (Berkeley: University of California Press, 1992), 77–108. Reprinted by permission.

This interview was recorded in two sessions in December 1982 and January 1983. It was transcribed and edited the following summer and fall. Early in 1984 Mekas checked it for accuracy, and I made final revisions.

From the beginning, my goal was to talk to Mekas about his own films, rather than about his well-known activities as an organizer and polemicist for the New American Cinema.

Scott Macdonald: Though *Lost Lost Lost* wasn't finished until 1975, it has the earliest footage I've seen in any of your films.

Jonas Mekas: The earliest footage in that film comes from late 1949. *Lost Lost Lost* was edited in 1975 because I couldn't deal with it until then. I couldn't figure out how to edit the early footage.

SM: When you were recording that material, were you just putting it onto reels and storing it?

JM: I had prepared a short film from that footage in late 1950. It was about twenty minutes long, and it was called *Grand Street*. It's one of the main streets in Williamsburg, Brooklyn, populated mainly by immigrants, where we spent a lot of time. Around 1960 I took that film apart. It doesn't exist anymore. Otherwise, I didn't do anything with that footage. Occasionally I looked at it, thinking how I would edit it. I could not make up my mind what to eliminate and what to leave in. But in 1975 it was much easier.

SM: Is that opening passage in *Lost Lost Lost*, where you and Adolfas are fooling around with the Bolex, really your first experience with a camera?

JM: What you see there is our very first footage, shot on Lorimer Street, in Williamsburg, Brooklyn.

SM: Were you involved at all with film before you got to this country?

JM: The end of the war found us in Germany. Two shabby, naive Lithuanian boys, just out of forced labor camp. We spent four years in various displaced persons camps—Flensburg, Hamburg, Wiesbaden, Kassel, etc.—first in the British zone, then in the American zone. There was nothing to do and a lot of time. What we could do was read, write, and go to movies. Movies were shown in the camps free, by the American army. Whatever money we could get we spent on books, or we went into town and saw the postwar German productions. Later, when we went to study at the University of Mainz, which was in the French zone—we commuted from Wiesbaden—we saw a lot of French films.

The movies that really got us interested in film were not the French productions, but the postwar, neorealistic German films. They are not known here—films by Käutner, Josef V. Baky, Liebeneiner, and others. The only way they could make films after the war in Germany was by shooting on actual locations. The war had ended, but the realities were still all around. Though the stories were fictional and melodramatic, their visual texture was drab reality, the same as in the postwar Italian films.

Then we started reading the literature on film, and we began writing scripts. What caused us to write our first script was a film—I do not remember the title or who made it, but it was about displaced persons. We thought it was so melodramatic and had so little understanding of what life in postwar Europe was like that we got very mad and decided we should make a film. My brother wrote a script. Nothing ever was done with it. We had no means, we had no contacts, we were two zeroes.

SM: When you were first starting to shoot here did you feel that you were primarily a recorder of displaced persons and their struggle, or were you already thinking about becoming a filmmaker of another sort?

JM: The very first script that we wrote when we arrived in late 1949, and which was called *Lost Lost Lost Lost* (i.e., four *Losts* as opposed to the three of the 1975 version), was for a documentary on the life of displaced persons here. We wanted to bring some facts to people's attention. It did not have to do so much with the fact that we were displaced persons, or that there were displaced persons. It had more to do with the fact that the Baltic republics—Estonia, Latvia, Lithuania—were sacrificed by the West to the Soviet Union at Yalta just before the end of the war and ended up as occupied countries to which we could not return. We were taking a stand for the three Baltic countries that the West had betrayed. Our script was an angry outcry. It was our first English script. We sent it to Flaherty, thinking he could help us produce it, but he wrote back that though he liked the script and found it full of passion, he could not help us. This was at a time when he couldn't find money to produce even his own films.

We did start shooting nevertheless. Actually, two or three shots at the beginning of *Lost Lost Lost* are from the original footage we shot for that film. A slow-motion shot of a soldier (actually, Adolfas) and one or two others (a family reading a newspaper, a skating rink, a tree in Central Park) were meant for that film. But my brother was drafted and so we abandoned the project. When he came back from the army a year or so later, things had changed.

SM: During all the intervening time you were recording other material?
JM: Yes, I was collecting, documenting, without a clear plan or purpose, the activities of displaced persons—mainly Lithuanians. I shot footage of New York immigrant communities, and I did some weekend traveling to record communities in Chicago, Toronto, Philadelphia, Boston. I worked in Brooklyn factories and spent all my money on film.

SM: A lot of the footage that ended up in the first reel of *Lost Lost Lost* is compositionally and texturally very beautiful. When you were shooting originally, were you thinking about the camera as a potential poetic instrument?
JM: The intention was to capture the situations very directly, with the simple means that we had at our disposal. All the indoor footage was taken with just one or two flood lamps. We made no attempt to light the "scenes" "correctly" or "artistically." Sometimes we were at meetings actually, most of the time—where we couldn't interfere, or we were too shy to interfere.

During the first weeks after our arrival here, we had read Pudovkin and Eisenstein, so in the back of our minds there was probably something else, a different ambition, but I don't think that that footage reveals much. In Germany we had bought a still camera and had taken a lot of stills. Maybe that affected how we saw and the look of some of the footage. We also looked at a lot of still photography. In 1953 or so I began working at a place called Graphic Studios, a commercial photography studio, where I stayed for five or six years. The studio was run by Lenard Perskie, from whom I learned a great deal. All the great photographers used to drop in, and some artists, like Archipenko.

In 1950 we began attending Cinema 16 screenings. By this I mean absolutely every screening of the so-called experimental films. We also attended every screening of the Theodore Huff Society, which was run at that time by the young Bill Everson. He showed mostly early Hollywood and European films which were unavailable commercially. I think it's still going on, but I haven't been there for years. It's one of the noble, dedicated undertakings—a University of Cinema—of William Everson, who has performed a great educational role for nearly three decades.

SM: I asked the question about your using the camera as a poetic device because by the second reel there are shots in which it's clear that more is happening than documentation. I'm thinking of the beautiful sequence of the woman pruning trees, and the shot of Adolfas in front of the merry-go-round.

JM: That shot of Adolfas was intended for our first "poetic" film. It had a title: *A Silent Journey*. We never finished it, and some of the footage appears in reel three of *Lost Lost Lost*—the film within the film about the car crash.

SM: Were you collecting sound at this time too?

JM: We were collecting sound, but between 1950 and 1955 this amounted to very little. After 1955 I collected more and more sounds from the situations I filmed.

SM: The early reels are punctuated by images of typed pages. Were you writing a record of your feelings during that time?

JM: Those pages are from my written diaries which I kept regularly between the time I left Lithuania (1944) until maybe 1960. Later I got too involved in other activities—the Film-Makers' Cooperative, *Film Culture*, the Cinematheque, etc.—and the written diaries become more and more infrequent.

SM: Did you know English when you arrived here?

JM: I could read. I remember reading Hemingway's *A Farewell to Arms* on the boat as we came over. Hemingway is one of the easiest writers to read because of the simplicity and directness of his language. He is still one of my favorite writers. So I could read and communicate, but writing took another few years. To write in an acquired language is more difficult than to read, as you know, and I am still learning. Until the mid-fifties I kept all my notes in Lithuanian. For another two to three years there is a slow dissolve: on some days my notes were taken in Lithuanian and on other days I wrote in English. By 1957 all the diaries and notes are in English.

My poetry remains in Lithuanian. I have tried—mostly fooling around—to write "poetry" in English, but I do not believe that one can write poetry in any language but the one in which one grew up as a child. One can never master all the nuances of words and groupings of words that are necessary for poetry. Certain kinds of prose can be written, though, as Nabokov has shown.

SM: Conrad's prose often has the suggestiveness and density of poetry.

JM: Conrad was much younger when he left his home and he was immediately cut off from all the other Poles. I think it helped very much that he had all those years on the ship. My brother mastered English much faster than I because he found himself in the army with no Lithuanians around. Of course, I am not talking about our accents. The Eastern European pronunciation requires a completely different mouth muscle structure than that of the English language. And it takes a lot of time for the mouth muscles to rearrange themselves.

SM: When you came to put *Lost Lost Lost* together in its present form, did you then go back to the journals and film pages with that film in mind or had those pages been filmed much earlier?

JM: I filmed the pages during the editing. When I felt that some aspect of that period was missing from the images, I would go through the audio tapes and the written diaries. They often contained what my footage did not.

Also, as it developed into its final form, *Lost Lost Lost* became autobiographical: I became the center. The immigrant community is there, but it's shown through my eyes. Not unconsciously, but consciously, formally. When I originally filmed that footage, I did not make myself the center. I tried to film in a way that would make the community central. I thought of myself only as the recording eye. My attitude was still that of an old-fashioned documentary filmmaker of the forties or fifties and so I purposely kept the personal element out as much as I could. By the time of the editing, in 1975, however, I was preoccupied by the autobiographical. The written diaries allowed me to add a personal dimension to an otherwise routine, documentary recording.

SM: Your detachment from the Lithuanian community in reels one and two seems to go beyond the documentarian's "objective" stance.

JM: I was already detached from the Lithuanian community—not from Lithuania, but from the immigrant community, which had written us off probably as early as 1948 or even earlier, when we were still in Germany, in the DP camps. The nationalists—there were many military people among the displaced persons—thought that we were communists and that we should be thrown out of the displaced persons camp. The main reason for that, I think, was that we always hated the army. We were very antimilitaristic. We always laughed and made jokes about the military. Another thing that seemed to separate us from the Lithuanian community was that we did not follow the accepted literary styles of that time. We were publishing a literary magazine in Lithuanian, which was, as far as they were concerned, an extreme, modernist manifestation. So we were outcasts; we were not in the mainstream of the Lithuanian community. That was one of the reasons why we moved out of Brooklyn into Manhattan. I was recording the Lithuanian community, but I was already seeing it as an outsider. I was still sympathetic to its plight, but my strongest interests already were film and literature. We'd finish our work in a factory in Long Island City at 5:00 p.m. and without washing our faces, we'd rush to the subway to catch the 5:30 screening at the Museum of Modern Art. To the other Lithuanians we were totally crazy.

SM: You begin *Lost Lost Lost* with your buying the camera, which does end up recording the Lithuanian community, but the camera is also suggestive of an interest which has come *between* you and that community.

JM: Yes, recording the community was part of mastering new tools. It was practice. If one has a camera and wants to master it, then one begins to film in the street or in the apartment. We figured, if we were going to film the streets, why not collect some useful material about the lives of the Lithuanian immigrants. We had several scripts that called for documentary material. One of them required footage from many countries. My brother took a lot of footage for that film in Europe, while he was in the army.

But, basically, at that time our dream was Hollywood. Fictional, theatrical film—not documentary. We thought in terms of making movies for everybody. In those days if one thought about making films for neighborhood theaters, one thought in terms of Hollywood. We dreamed we would earn some money, and borrow some from friends, and would be able to make our films, our "Hollywood" films. Very soon we discovered that nobody wanted to lend us any money. So we began to send our scripts to Hollywood. I remember sending one to Fred Zinnemann and another to Stanley Kramer. We got them back; I don't know whether they were ever read. Now one can see that our first scripts were not Hollywood scripts at all; they were avant-garde scripts. But we naively thought we could get backing for the films we were dreaming of.

Luckily, just around that time, in New York, there were some people, like Morris Engel and Sidney Meyers, who were beginning to make a different kind of cinema, who began breaking away from Hollywood. We saw *The Little Fugitive* and it made us aware of different possibilities. Before we arrived here, we were completely unaware of avant-garde film, of anything other than commercial film. As we were entering adolescence, when we might have become interested in such things, the war came, and the occupations by the Soviets, then the Germans, then the Soviets again. There was no information, no possibility at all for us to become aware of the other kind of cinema. The Russians came with their official cinema; then the Germans with theirs. After the war the United States army came with *Tarzan* and melodrama. Our film education was very slow. In late 1947, and in 1948, when we were studying at the University of Mainz, we were very excited by *Beauty and the Beast* and a few other French films. But that's about it.

SM: Is there some reason why you included almost no explicit information about your film interest in those first two reels—other than the obvious fact of your making the footage were seeing? When I originally saw reel three and the intertitle, "FILM CULTURE IS ROLLING ON LAFAYETTE STREET," I was surprised: it seemed to come out of nowhere.

JM: I have no real explanation for that. I figure, the professional life, even if it's a filmmaker's, is not photogenic. There are certain crafts, professions that are photogenic—to me—such as, for instance, bread making, farming, fishing, street works, cutting wood, coal mining, etc. Technological crafts and professions are not photogenic. Another reason is that until 1960 or so, no filmmaker was really filming his or her own life. Whatever one was filming was always outside of one's life—in my case, the Lithuanian community or New York streets. The diaristic, autobiographical preoccupations did not really exist. The personal lives of the whole first wave of American experimental filmmakers are not recorded on film. There is a little bit of Dwinell Grant, fooling in front of the camera. Francis Lee has footage of himself and some of his friends. But the personal had not yet become a concern. As a result, in *Lost Lost Lost* you do not see much of my own life until later. One didn't go to parties with the camera. If I had taken my Bolex to any of Maya Deren's parties and started filming, they would have laughed. Serious filmmaking was still scripted filmmaking.

SM: Who were the first people you ran into who were using film in more personal ways?

JM: My first contacts with the New York film-viewing community began very early. The second or third evening after I arrived here, I went to a screening of *The Cabinet of Dr. Caligari* and Epstein's *The Fall of the House of Usher* sponsored by the New York Film Society, which was run at that time by Rudolf Arnheim. Then we went to Cinema 16, but we did not meet any filmmakers there: we were just two shabby DPs watching films. When I heard that Hans Richter was in New York, running the film department at City College, I wrote him a letter saying that I had no money but would like to attend some classes. He wrote back, "Sure, come!" So I did and I met Hans Richter. I did not take any of his classes—actually, he did not teach any classes that winter—but I met many people: Shirley Clarke, Gideon Bachmann, Frank Kuenstler, the poet, and others. I continued seeing Gideon, and we decided—it was his idea—to start our own film group. It was called The Film Group. Beginning in 1991 we had screenings once a month, sometimes more often. We rented films, mostly experimental, avant-garde films. I wrote many of the program notes. Through those screenings we met other people interested in filmmaking. Another person very active during those years (between 1950 and 1955) was Perry Miller, who has lately made several important documentaries—one on Gertrude Stein, *When This You See, Remember Me*. She was running an international festival of films on art, a very big event, at Hunter College. She held at least three of these events, in 1952, 1953, and, I think, in 1954. I saw Resnais's early films there, and some films by local filmmakers. I remember a pattern film by John Arvonio, who filmed reflections in the rain in Times Square. Nobody knows that film anymore.

I don't know if it still exists. Also, no one seems to hear any longer of Wheaton Gelantine or Joe Slavin, or Peter Hollander, who distributed early films by Jordan Belson and others through a distribution center called Kinesis.

We undertook two or three documentary film projects with Gideon Bachmann. One was a documentary about modern architecture in a community not very far outside of New York called Usonia. I shot two or three rolls on the Frank Lloyd Wright buildings there. I think Gideon has that footage; I don't. In 1953 I ran a short film series at the Gallery East, on First Street and Avenue B, a Gallery run by Joel Baxter and Louis Brigante. In 1954 my brother and I started our own film society called Film Forum. George Capsis was the third member. We had screenings for two years. At one of our first shows—a Jordan Belson show, with Belson present—we clashed with the projectionists' union. They came and cut off the electricity. When we wanted to continue, they threatened to beat us up, so we had to stop the screening.

SM: Returning to *Lost Lost Lost*, the color in the first two reels is gorgeous.
JM: Much of it is time's effect on the early Kodachrome. I didn't like it in the original color. As it began aging, I liked it much more and decided to use it. I remember having a similar experience with Gregory Markopoulos's trilogy, *Psyche, Charmides, Lysis*. It seemed to me to become more and more wonderful as time went on. When some people looked at it later, they said, "It's horrible. what's happened to the color?" But I found the later color superior to the original.

SM: I assume that that process will continue.
JM: Yes. Even though I have a master now, on Ektachrome, the Ektachrome itself changes rapidly. The print stocks keep changing. And, of course, the color changed in the transfer from the original Kodachrome into the Ektachrome master. So there is no such thing as original color anymore. Every stage is original, in a way.

SM: It seems to me that your varied use of intertitles has always been a strong formal element in your films.
JM: I was always faced with the problem of how to structure, how to formalize the personal material, which seems just to run on and on. It's so close to me that I have to use abstract devices, numbers, or descriptive intertitles, to make it more distant, easier for me to deal with, to make the footage seem more as if someone else—maybe Lumière—were recording it.

SM: You mentioned that you feel that you can't be a poet in English, and yet both in the spoken narrative passages (in *Lost Lost Lost* especially, but also as early as *Walden* [1968]) and also in the printed intertitles, your spoken or visual phrasing evokes several American poets—William Carlos Williams, for example, and Walt Whitman.

JM: But those passages are not poetry. They are poetic, yes, which is a different thing. By the way, I wanted to make a documentary about William Carlos Williams. In 1954 or 1955 I made some notes, visited Williams in Paterson, and discussed the film with him. I wanted to make a film about his life there in Paterson. He was supposed to prepare some notes about what he wanted to have in the film. I lost my notes; probably his estate would know if his still exist, if, that is, he made any. I took LeRoi Jones (Baraka) with me. He may remember more about that trip.

SM: Had you read Whitman by this time?

JM: I had read Whitman in German translation in 1946 or 1947. Later I read some in English. By 1950 I had read it all. I had even translated some of his poems, or rather, had tried to translate them into Lithuanian. During those periods Whitman *was* important to me, along with Sandburg and Auden. Later I gravitated toward other preferences. I haven't read Sandburg for decades, but there's a lot in him that is very appealing.

SM: *Lost Lost Lost* seems to be divided not only into six reels but into three pairs of two reels, each of which has the same general organization: the first tends to be about personal and family life, the second about the political context of that personal and family life.

JM: That footage is largely in chronological order, though I took some liberties here and there. I worked with it as one huge piece. I kept looking at it, eliminating bits and dividing it up in one way and another. I didn't plan on six reels originally, in fact I had seven or eight at one point, but figured that that was too much to view in one sitting. I considered three hours the maximum for a single sitting.

SM: When the unfinished film-within-the-film that you show at the beginning of reel three was originally made, did you conceive of it as a sort of parable of your own experience as a DP?

JM: No. That film was very much influenced by my viewing experimental films at Cinema 16. I wanted to make my first consciously "poetic" little film. At that point I thought it was totally invented and outside of me. All I wanted was that it be very, very simple, just one moment from somebody's life, a memory.

SM: In that passage, as it appears in *Lost Lost Lost*, you seem to be developing a parallel between yourself and the protagonist. Both of you go to the woods to walk off the pain of your losses.

JM: Now, from the perspective of years, I can see that connection.

SM: In reel three you begin to develop the more gestural camera style with which, after *Walden*, many people identified you. In later reels the gestural camera becomes increasingly evident, so that the film as a whole seems, in part, about the emergence of that style.

JM: It's more complicated than that. My first major work in Lithuanian, which to some of my Lithuanian friends is still the best thing I've done, was a cycle of twenty-odd idylls I wrote in 1946. I used long lines and an epic pace to portray my childhood in the village. I described the people in the village and their various activities during the four seasons, as factually and prosaically as I could. I avoided what was accepted as poetic Lithuanian language. My aim at that time—I talk about this in my written diaries—was to achieve "a documentary poetry." When I began filming, that interest did not leave me, but it was pushed aside as I got caught up in the documentary film traditions. I was reading Grierson and Rotha and looking at the British and American documentary films of the thirties and forties. I feel now that their influence detoured me from my own inclination. Later, I had to shake this influence in order to return to the approach with which I began.

Now that I am transcribing all my written diaries, I notice that already in the forties there are pages and pages of observations of what I've seen through windows, what I've heard in the street—a series of disconnected, collaged impressions. If one compares my camera work with those pages, one sees that they are almost identical. I only changed my tools.

SM: That's interesting. I had assumed that your gestural camera represented the development of an American film style, growing out of your progressive acculturation.

JM: [Looks through his diaries.] Here's an example, written when I was in the Schwaebisch Gmuend DP camp, about three months before I came to this country:

May 17, 1949
8PM
Two drunks are walking along the Street.
"Let's go, let's go . . ."
"Where do you want to go?"
"What? It's raining."
"Let's go to the Truman street, joptvaimat (a Russian curse)."
They have a silent exchange. I can't hear it.
"You told me that you have it, you prick."
They both walk away.
A woman comes through rain, pressing a large empty plate to her side.
Down the corners of buildings noisily run streams of rain water. At the
other end of the street—music, boyan. A man in green pants, his hands in

pockets, runs by, his head pulled into his shoulders, wet. A girl runs by. A voice from the window:

"Where are you running? Lost your key?"

The man in the window is whistling, the girl keeps running without acknowledging him and without turning back.

A man, all wet, slowly walks by, I know him, it's Grazys. Another man, in grey suit, black hat, his hands in trouser pockets, lifting them up so that the bottoms wouldn't get too soaked. Through the window I can hear a man's voice singing:

"O, Zuzana, sirdis mana,

koks gyvenimas grazus"

(Oh, Susanne, my sweetheart,

how wonderful is life—).

_____

No change in the sky, but it looks like it's raining less. The puddles in the street, little streams, brooks of rain water rush along the edges of the street, down. Camp policeman with a new MP uniform. In the window—heads. Women, children.

SM: In reels two and three of *Lost Lost Lost*, you seem very lonely, and yet you were obviously very busy with many people—which emphasizes the fact that there's a sizeable gap between yourself as maker and as protagonist.

JM: When I read my written diaries, I see that I was very, very lonely during those early years, more so than, say, the average Italian immigrant. There's an established Italian community here which one can become part of. It's lonely, but not that lonely. Italian immigrants know they can go back to Italy if things don't work out. Once we left what Lithuanian community there was in New York and moved to Orchard Street, we were very much alone. One of the reasons why I went to City College for a few months was to meet new people. I could not stand just walking the streets by myself. My brother was in the army. For two years I had no friends, nobody. If I had been a communicative, friendly person, it might have been different. But I was never that kind of person. I was always very closed and extremely shy. Actually, I still am, but I have learned techniques to cover it. At thirteen or fourteen I was so shy that when finally, for some reason, I began speaking to people—other than members of my family—everybody was amazed: "He speaks! He speaks! Really, he speaks!" This shyness did not disappear all at once. Even though we started publishing *Film Culture* and went to film screenings, we'd go home and be alone. We were still thinking about Lithuania. Our mother was there, our father, and all our brothers. Until Stalin died we could not even correspond.

I did a lot of walking in this new country, but as yet I had no memories from it. It takes years and years to build and collect new memories. After a while the streets begin to talk back to you, and you are not a stranger any longer, but this takes years. That experience is not pleasant to go through, and so it's not always reflected in my footage, though it's in the diaries. I put it into the film later, by means of my "narration, or, more correctly, my "talking."

SM: Some of it comes through in the mood of those images.
JM: Some, yes.

SM: I showed Marie Menken's *Notebook* recently and noticed not only a feeling similar to the one in your work, but a similar use of tiny passages of text as a means of contextualizing and distancing personal footage.
JM: Oh, yes. I liked what she did, and I thought it worked. She helped me make up my mind about how to structure my films. Besides, Marie Menken was Lithuanian. Her mother and father were Lithuanian immigrants, and she still spoke some Lithuanian. We used to get together and sing Lithuanian folk songs. When she'd sing them, she'd go back to the old country completely. So there might also be some similarities in our sensibilities because of that. But definitely Marie Menken helped me to be at peace enough to leave much of the original material just as it was.

And John Cage. From him I learned that chance is one of the great editors. You shoot something one day, forget it, shoot something the next day and forget the details of that. . . . When you finally string it all together and watch for ten minutes, you discover all sorts of connections. I thought at first that I should do more editing and not rely on chance. But I came to realize that, of course, there is no chance: whenever you film, you make certain decisions, even when you don't know that you do. The most essential, the most important editing—frame by frame editing—takes place during the shooting as a result of these decisions.

Before 1960 I tried to edit the material from 1949 to 1955. But I practically destroyed it by tampering with it too much. Later, in 1960 or 1961, I spent a long time putting it back to the way it was originally. After that I was afraid to touch it, and I didn't touch it until 1979.

SM: It's in the fifth reel of *Lost Lost Lost* that you seem, for the first time, to be back in touch with rural life and with the land.
JM: Yes, that's where the "lost lost lost" ends. I'm beginning to feel at home again. By reel six one cannot say that I feel lost anymore; paradise has been regained through cinema.

SM: It's the paradise of having a place where you can work and struggle for something that you care about?

JM: When you enter a whole world where you feel at home. A world for which you care. Or, a world which takes you over, possesses you, obsesses you, and pushes all the other worlds into the shadow. Still, I don't think that I'll ever be able, really and completely, to detach myself from what I really am, somewhere very deep: a Lithuanian.

SM: Did you live in Vermont for a while?
JM: We lived in Vermont for two seasons, during the filming of *Hallelujah the Hills* (1963).

SM: Reel five is exhilarating in its use of light and texture. And you take some chances by allowing yourself to be very vulnerable: you allow yourself to look foolish.
JM: I realized I was taking chances. I have to give credit here again—one is always taking lessons—to Gregory Markopoulos. Gregory had taken chances that I thought wouldn't work, but he always managed to pull through. I don't know how familiar you are with Markopoulos's work; it's practically impossible to see it these days—he doesn't show it in America. I learned from Gregory that what seems embarrassingly personal soon after a film is made, later comes to be part of the content, and not embarrassing at all.

Another lesson came from Dostoevsky, from a statement of his that I read when I was fifteen or sixteen and which I have never forgotten. A young writer complained to Dostoevsky that his own writing was too subjective, too personal and that he would give anything to learn to write more objectively. Dostoevsky replied—this is my memory; I may have adapted it totally to my own purpose, it's not a quotation: "The main problem of the writer is not how to escape subjectivity, but rather how to be subjective, how really to write from one's self, to be oneself in language, form, and content. I challenge you to be subjective!" It is very difficult to be openly subjective. One has to keep it within formal limits, of course; one must not wallow in subjectivity. Perhaps I come very close to that sometimes. . . .

SM: Did the fact that 1976 was the American Bicentennial year have any impact on the making of *Lost Lost Lost*? It does tell a quintessentially American story.
JM: *Lost Lost Lost* was completed because the New York State Council on the Arts (maybe because of the Bicentennial) decided to give four very special $20,000 grants. Harry Smith got one too. Suddenly I had enough money and I said, "This is my chance."

It's amazing, when one thinks about it: everybody says   and it's quite true—that this country is made of immigrants, that America is a melting pot, etc. But it's not reflected very often in American literature. There is no major work that really documents the immigrant experience. Sinclair's *The Jungle* is the closest we have that I know of. *Lost Lost Lost* is a record of certain immigrant realities that have been largely ignored in art.

SM: *Guns of the Trees* (1961) is probably the closest of your films to a recognizably commercial narrative. What was the background of that project?

JM: First I wrote a sketchy, poetic script that consisted of thirty sequences. I wanted to improvise around those sketches, and that's what we set out to do. "We" means Adolfas and I. We had agreed to assist each other on our own productions: first I'd make a film, and he'd help; next he'd make a film, and I'd help. He helped me on *Guns*, and I helped him on *Hallelujah*. The only thing that went wrong, and really very badly wrong, was that at that time we had a friend, Edouard de Laurot, who wanted very much to be involved in the film as well. From solidarity and friendship, we decided to invite him to work with us. He was a brilliant person, but very self-centered and very dictatorial. Edouard's position was that absolutely every movement, every word, every thing that appeared in the film should be totally controlled and politically meaningful. I tended, even at that time, to be much more open; I was interested in improvisation, chance, accidents. I was too inexperienced and unsure of myself to push through with my own shy vision. So often I did things Edouard's way. It came to the point, finally, that we had to part, to end the friendship. This was an important lesson for me: it was clear that I had to work alone in the future. I was never happy with that film.

SM: How did you come to make *The Brig* (1964)?

JM: I wanted to make a film in which sound was about as important as the image. I was attracted by the sounds of *The Brig*—the stamping and running and shouting. It was a staged reality that was very much like life itself. I thought I could go into it the way a news cameraman would go into a situation in real life. Cinéma vérité was very much in the air at that time. People connected truth to cinéma vérité camera technique: style produced an illusion of truth. I made the film, in a sense, as a critique of cinéma vérité.

At that time the most widely used newsreel camera was the single system Auricon. You could record the sound in the camera during the shooting on magnetic sound-striped film stock. I rented three cameras and shot the film in one session, in ten-minute takes. Two days earlier, when I went to see the play on stage, the idea of making the film shot through my mind so fast that I decided not to see the play through to the end. That way, when I filmed I would not know what was coming next: the opposite of the usual situation in which the filmmaker studies and maps the action in an attempt to catch the essence of the play. I went to Julian Beck and told him that I wanted to film the play. He said this would be impossible since it was being closed the next day. The police had ordered it closed on the pretext that the taxes had not been paid. I decided that I wanted to do it anyway; I only needed a day to collect the equipment. We concocted a plan to sneak into the building after the play had been closed and begin shooting.

It was so sudden, an obsession. The cast got into the building at night, through the coal chute. So did we, my little crew—Ed Emshwiller, Louis Brigante, with our equipment. Shooting was very intense. I had to film and watch the play at the same time. Most of the time I did not even look through the camera. I'd finish with one camera, grab the next one, and continue. I'd have to yell out to the actors to stop while I changed cameras. Ed and Louis loaded the cameras while I shot.

SM: Did you assume that people who saw the film would not know the play?

JM: No. Some of the people who later saw the film had seen the play. But among the people who were not familiar with the play some were actually fooled by the "amateur" style. They thought that the United States Army had permitted me to go into a real brig and make the film. This was the case with some Italian newspapers.

SM: The credits say that you shot the film and Adolfas edited it. How much was edited out? Was the play just an hour long?

JM: The editing involved was technical work. When I would run out of film and grab another camera, the actors would stop and overlap a little bit. I liked the film with the overlaps, and actually the first screening included them. The Living Theater liked it that way too. But David and Barbara Stone, who were at that point beginning to get involved in distribution, agreed to distribute it, and for distribution's sake, we decided to eliminate the overlappings. My brother took care of this. He had just come back from Chicago, where he did the editing and salvaging of *Goldstein*. Also, though I shot the sound on film, I had a separate tape recorder running independently, for safety's sake. We decided to intensify the sound in certain places by merging the two soundtracks. My brother did that. Also, one camera was always slowing down towards the end of a roll, so we had to replace those parts of sound with the separate recording, or resplice it practically frame by frame. There was a lot of that kind of subtle technical work, which my brother does very well.

As far as the play itself is concerned, I filmed the whole thing. There were parts, however, which worked on stage, but didn't work so well on film. As in real life—some of it was just too boring to film. As documentary as the play is, towards the end it becomes more theatrical: acting and melodramatic lines I couldn't do anything with. I decided to cut those parts out. The people from the Living Theater were not too happy about this decision at first, but eventually they accepted the changes, and now they're very happy with the film. The play ran approximately ninety minutes. I cut out about twenty minutes.

SM: There's a weird dimension to the play: it has to be as rigorously unrelenting in its production as a real brig would be. The people who "play" the marines were, I assume, as demanding on themselves and each other as real marines would be—maybe more so, depending on how long the play ran.

JM: I think the play ran for about a year. All those punches were real; they were rehearsed, but real. Every actor had to know the parts of all the other actors so that they could rotate roles. I'll be punched tonight, and you'll be punched tomorrow. They were incredibly dedicated to their theater.

SM: What's interesting to me is that it's the same performance as the real thing. It's just in a different context.

JM: That's why I wanted to film it. It could be treated as reality, though actually the play was not as intense as the film. I intensified it by picking out certain details, by cutting out dead spaces, and by the movements of the camera. Still, for the theatergoer of that period, *The Brig* was a very intense experience. In 1967 or 1968 I was invited to the University of Delaware to see their production of *The Brig*. Kenneth Brown, the author of the play, was there too. The production, from all I remember was pretty intense. But it didn't have the same impact on the audience as the original performances did. To have the same effect in 1968 you had to be two or three times more shocking. Society had become more brutalized.

I should add another footnote here. In the late sixties, a TV station in Berlin did their own version of the play. They planned it all very carefully, spent a lot of money on it, took a month to make it—and it was a total dud. It didn't work.

SM: The sound in the film is somewhat rhythmic. Over and over it starts relatively quietly and then builds, finally going past the point of audibility. Was the distortion done on purpose?

JM: In one track there was distortion because I was too close to the sound with my camera mike. Also, one camera distorted the sound when it slowed down. But I decided to keep the distortions. More than that: I combined the tracks to intensify the sound even more. That was one of the major objections at the time I made the film, and I had to overrule it. Noise is very much part of that film. The noise is more important than what's being said.

SM: It's like some kind of horrible music.

JM: It's not a pleasant film to see. You don't want to see it twice. You might say, "Oh, I liked it," but you don't want to see it twice.

SM: I have a somewhat personal response to it. My life certainly seems robotized at times. I get up at a certain hour, hurry through breakfast, run to school to teach, and when the bell rings, I walk to the next class. On one level the film is about the military, but it also seems potentially to contain a comment on the discipline we impose on ourselves during much of everyday life.

. . . To turn to another film now, what was the nature of your collaboration with Markopoulos on *Award Presentation to Andy Warhol* (1964)?

JM: I wanted to give that year's Independent Film Award to Andy Warhol. I had arranged a series of screenings, including Warhol films, at the New Yorker Theater. But he said he didn't want to be on stage or do anything as public as that, so I suggested that we make the award in his studio and that I'd film it. He said that would be okay. We collected some of his superstars of that period and two rolls of film and set it all up. On my way to the studio, I suddenly remembered that I would actually have to award him with something, so I bought a basket of fruit at the corner store. During the actual presentation, I needed someone to operate the camera, which was a motorized Bolex. Gregory happened to be there and said he'd do it. Much of the time he's actually in the film, on the set; the rest of the time he was operating the camera. I slowed down the film in the printing as a form of tribute to Andy: most of his films—actually all the films from that period—were projected at sixteen frames per second, though they were shot at twenty-four. I did the same thing, but I had to do it by means of optical reprinting because I wanted to have the sound on the film.

SM: How did you get involved with *Show Magazine*, and *Film Magazine of the Arts* (1963)?

JM: Did you see that one?

SM: Yes, it's a nice little film.

JM: *Show Magazine* needed a promotional film, and somebody suggested to them that I make it. I agreed to do it. They paid well. I conceived the film as a serial film magazine that would come out once a month, or once every three months. We shot a lot of footage, with *Show Magazine* people always present, taking us to various places. When I was shooting, I noticed that they were always dropping issues of *Show Magazine* on the floor everywhere. When I screened the first draft of the film for them, they were shocked to see that I had eliminated all those magazines and much of the footage of fashion models they had me shoot (although you see some of that at the very end of the film). So that was the end of that project. I think that the concept of a film magazine, had they really supported me, was a good one and would have received much better publicity than the kind of thing they wanted.

SM: I think that's the first film of yours I saw.

JM: There are some parts I like very much; I like the whole thing, really. They seized the original right after the screening. They were planning to hire their own editor to reedit the film their way. They also took all the outtakes, but decided finally not to do anything with it. All my prints are from the work print.

SM: Was the greenish tone of the black-and-white imagery caused by printing black-and-white footage on color stock?
JM: That particular tint was my choice.

SM: You used some interesting music by Storm De Hirsch and others.
JM: The section with Lucia Dilugoszewski is unique. I think she's an exceptional composer and performer, but she's never been recorded on film.

SM: *Walden* is the film of yours I've seen most often. It's also been around the longest. When I first saw it, I was conscious primarily of the diaristic aspects. But, more recently I've been just as aware of the changing film stocks and the different tintings of the black-and-white footage. It now seems simultaneously an exploration of your personal environment *and* of film materials.
JM: Those are all controlled accidents. Some of the stock was used because it was available when I ran out of film. When I was filming the part now entitled "A Visit to Brakhages," I ran out of film, and Stan found some outdated Kodachrome under his bed. It was a very different texture than the surrounding material. Sometimes I ran out of color, so I used black-and-white. I had no plan to explore film stocks. But once you have all those different stocks, then you begin to structure with color; you pay attention to their qualities. The aspect you notice had also to do with my whole approach to film laboratories. You know how paranoid and careful some filmmakers are about labs. Usually the filmmaker tries to supervise the lab work closely, checking one print and another, refusing prints, switching labs. . . . I don't do that. I consider that whatever happens at the lab is what I want. I don't indicate that they should make this part lighter and that darker. I do my work in the camera, and all I ask from the lab is to make a straight, what's known as "one light" print, with no special timing, no anything. Usually I get results that I like. I have never rejected a print. If something goes really wrong, then of course I indicate on the next print that it should be corrected. I think that I have complete control over my materials; I don't leave anything for the labs to do or undo.

SM: You must have had a tremendous amount of diary footage by the time you made *Walden*. How did you come to make that particular film?
JM: The Albright-Knox Gallery in Buffalo had a special celebration—I don't remember the occasion—and they commissioned new works in the fields of music, dance, and film, and maybe some other arts. Film was included at Gerald O'Grady's

request; he was the adviser there. I was invited to make a film and given ten months to work on it. I used the material that was easiest for me to put together. The gallery helped to make a print and paid the expenses. The version I screened in Buffalo had sound on tape; it was also slightly shorter than the present version. Later I decided to finish the film and to include some other material.

SM: For me the strongest reel of the four has always been the first. Several sections from that reel are distributed separately.
JM: Yes, *Cassis, Notes on the Circus, Report from Millbrook*, and *Hare Krishna*, all filmed in 1966.

SM: It led me to wonder whether you edited it reel by reel or . . .
JM: I worked on the thing as a whole. I put those particular parts into distribution, however, before the rest was finished and before the invitation from Buffalo. Eventually I think I will pull them out of distribution, except for *Cassis*—which is different from the version you see in *Walden*—and *Report from Millbrook*, which is also different.

SM: When did you become familiar with Thoreau's *Walden*?
JM: It's one of the books that Peter Beard is obsessed with. During the shooting of *Hallelujah the Hills* he gave me a copy, and when I was editing *Walden*, I always had it around. For a long time I thought that that was the first time I read it. But recently, while retyping my early diaries from 1948, I discovered that I was reading *Walden* then, in German.

SM: It's sometimes thought of as a book about country living, but Thoreau was living just outside of town. In that sense your use of Central Park as your "Walden Pond" strikes me as particularly appropriate.
JM: Not only Central Park. To me Walden exists throughout the city. You can reduce the city to your own very small world which others may never see. The usual reaction after seeing *Walden* is a question: "Is this New York?" Their New York is ugly buildings and depressing, morbid blocks of concrete and glass. That is not my New York. In my New York there is a lot of nature. *Walden* is made up of bits of memories of what I wanted to see. I eliminated what I didn't want to see.

SM: Is New York the first big city you've spent a lot of time in?
JM: Yes, the first big *modern* city. All other cities I had been in before coming here—cities like Hamburg or Frankfurt or Kassel—had been destroyed in the war. There wasn't very much of the city left.

SM: By the time you made *Walden* you'd been filming for a long time. Had it gotten to the point where you were deciding in advance that you wanted to go film this or that for a specific film? It's clear that you decided to go to the circus several times for *Notes on the Circus*.

JM: No, I didn't plan. I just recorded my reactions to what was happening around me. *Notes on the Circus*—originally I thought I'd get it all the first time. But I got involved in the circus and went three or four times. I decided in advance to film Peter Beard's wedding, but when I arrived, I discovered that my Bolex wasn't working. Peter happened to have a Baulieux camera, so I used that. I had never used it before, so it was very risky.

SM: What is your connection with Peter Beard? He's very prominent in the diaries.

JM: I had met him before *Hallelujah the Hills*. He was the cousin of Jerome Hill, whom I knew by that time. We became friends during the shooting of *Hallelujah the Hills*, and the friendship has continued.

SM: In the first reel you say, "I make home movies, therefore I live," a line that's quoted a lot. Had you seen much home movie making?

JM: No. I hadn't seen much 8mm until the Kuchars came on the scene. They brought a few others out into the open. Many millions of cameras were floating around in the country for home movie making, but no one saw the footage. We did attend amateur club screenings in the late fifties.

SM: All your films are involved with social rituals, but *Walden* seems particularly involved with the specific social rituals that are often the material of home movies: weddings especially.

JM: There are a lot of weddings in my diaries. A wedding is a big event in anybody's life; it's colorful and there's always a lot of celebration. As a child, I remembered for years my sister's wedding. Where I come from, weddings go on for a week or two. Occasions like that attract me. There are, of course, no such weddings here. . . . But I film them anyway, hoping to find the wedding of my memory. There are also places to which I keep coming back. One is the Metropolitan Museum. On Saturday and Sunday lots of people sit on its front steps. There is something unique about this and for years I've kept going back, trying to capture the mood which pervades it. I think I finally decided I've gotten what I wanted and I'm not going back again. The autumn in Central Park is also something unique and for years I kept going back to it, but now I think I've gotten that. Winter in Central Park also. . . . And I've filmed a lot of New York rains.

During the period when I was shooting the *Walden* material, I wanted to make a diary film of a teenage girl just leaving childhood and entering adolescence. I was collecting diaries and letters of girls of that age, and making many notes. I wanted to make a film—actually, a series of three or four films, one of a girl fifteen, one of a woman and a man twenty-five; then forty-five; then sixty-five. I never progressed beyond the notes. But on several occasions I took some shots with three or four girls whom I thought I would use in that film. I always filmed them in the park. Some of the young women were friends of friends. I don't even know some of their names. But that's the reason for the repeated shots or sequences of young women in the park.

SM: During the making of *Walden* did you try different types of music with different imagery?

JM: By then I was carrying my Nagra or my Sony and picking up sounds from the situations I filmed. There is a long stretch where I did not have any sounds, so I had John Cale play some background music. It's a very insistent, constant sound that goes on for fifteen or twenty minutes. There is no climax; it's continuous, with some small variations.

SM: It works very intricately with the imagery. There are all sorts of subtle connections. Even within the slight variations, a slight motion in the sound may be matched by a parallel motion in the imagery.

JM: I should add, or rather reveal a secret: that John Cale sound is tampered with. . . . I doubled the speed. . . . It didn't work as it was. I tried different sounds for different parts. I made many different attempts. Sometimes I had two or three televisions going simultaneously, plus phonograph records and a radio. As I was editing, I was listening and trying to hit on chance connections. The tape recorder was always ready, so I could immediately record what might come up.

SM: *Walden* begins with the sound of the subway.

JM: There's a lot of subway noise, subway and street noise, in *Walden*. It's a general background in which all the other sounds are planted.

SM: The opening subway sound goes on for a very long time and suggests a rush through time. Then it stops abruptly and the doors open, just as you're waking up and as spring is waking out of winter.

JM: I like that noise. It has continued through all the volumes of my film diaries. Also, that was a period when I did a lot of walking, and the street noise was always present.

SM: I assume that, as was true in *Lost Lost Lost*, the material is more or less chronological, though not completely.

JM: Yes. I had to shift some parts for simple structural reasons. I did not want two long stretches like *Notes on the Circus* and *Trip to Millbrook* right next to each other. That would be too much; it would throw the structure out of balance. There had to be some separations. I shifted those longer passages around, but in most cases I didn't touch the shorter scenes; they are in chronological order.

SM: The last reel has the John Lennon/Yoko Ono passage. Did you know them?
JM: Yes, I knew Lennon. I'd known Yoko since 1959 or 1960 perhaps. Around 1962 she left for Japan, then decided to come back to New York. But she needed a job, for immigration, so *Film Culture* gave her her first official job in this country. We have been friends ever since. I met John after he married Yoko. When they came back from London to settle in New York, they were quite lonely. On their first night I took them for coffee, very late. We could find nothing that was open until eventually we came to Emilio's on Sixth Avenue. We sat and drank Irish coffee. John was very happy that nobody knew him there, nobody bothered him. But just as we were about to leave, a shy, young waitress gave John a scrap of paper and asked for his autograph. She had known all along who he was.

SM: Am I correct in saying that at the time of *Walden* you had a sense that there's always less and less of the basic things that are most valuable in life?
JM: There is a very pessimistic passage of "narration" or "talking" in the Central Park sequence where I say that perhaps before too long there won't be any trees or flowers. But I don't mean for that attitude to dominate the entire film. In general I would say that I feel there will always be Walden for those who really want it. Each of us lives on a small island, in a very small circle of reality which is our own reality. I made up a joke about a Zen monk standing in Times Square with people asking, "So what do you think about New York—the noise, the traffic?" The monk says, "What noise? What traffic?" You *can* cut it all out. No, it's not that we can have all this today, but tomorrow it will be gone. It *is* threatened, but in the end it's up to us to keep those little bits of paradise alive and defend them and see that they survive and grow.

Of course, there is another side to this, another danger. Even in concentration camps, in forced labor camps, people could still find enjoyment in certain things. Not everybody in the forced labor camps sat with his or her nose to the floor, saying, "How dreadful! How dreadful!" There are moments of feeling, happiness, friendships, and even beauty, no matter where you are. So what I said before could be seen as a justification and acceptance of any status quo. I wouldn't want what I say interpreted that way. Somewhere I would put a limit to what I, or a human being in general, would or should accept. As Gandhi did.

The question is how one is to counteract the destruction. Should one walk around with posters and placards or should one retreat and grow natural food in Vermont and hope that by producing something good, and sharing it with others, one can persuade those others to see the value of what you are doing and to move in a similar direction?

Change can't come from the top. The top, which is occupied by various governments, is totally rotten. This civilization cannot be revolutionized, changed: it has to be *replaced*.

SM: The title of *Walden*, and the titles of other films, I believe, have changed.
JM: Yes. *Walden* was originally titled *Diaries, Notes & Sketches* (also known as *Walden*). But now, since I have many other reels of diary material, there is a confusion—at least for the labs. When I was using the title *Diaries, Notes & Sketches: Lost Lost Lost*, they kept writing on the cans *Diaries, Notes & Sketches* and skipping the rest. I had no choice but to rethink the titles. All of my film diaries are *Diaries, Notes & Sketches*, but I now call the individual parts only by their specific names: *Walden*, *Lost Lost Lost*, *In Between*, *Notes for Jerome*, etc.

SM: How does what we see in *In Between* (1978) relate to *Walden* in terms of time period?
JM: The *In Between* material is from "in between" *Lost Lost Lost* and *Walden*.

SM: I had thought of the title as a reference to your situation of being partially rooted here, but still Lithuanian. . . .
JM: Yes, that may be true. It's amazing how much one can hide, unconsciously. A cover-up.

SM: *Walden* is very involved with traveling, whereas in *In Between* there's more home life. And there's a sense of a relationship with a woman.
JM: I did not want to make *Walden* too long, and there was a certain pace established there. Several of the sequences in *In Between* are much slower. They're not single framed. I did not want to put that material into *Walden*. After finishing *Walden*, I still thought that I would like to use that footage so I collected it and put it into *In Between*.

I made several versions of *In Between*, one of which I put into distribution, then reedited. It was a difficult film to structure because of the Salvador Dalí footage, which was very different from the other material. I decided finally to separate that part; I put Dalí in his place, so to speak, and I used numbering to break it up a bit. It's now one of my favorite films.

SM: You mentioned last time that there was a tremendous amount of material collected in the fifties, only a small portion of which was used in *Lost Lost Lost*. Is the same thing true for the sixties?

JM: Maybe a little bit less. In *Lost Lost Lost* I used about one-seventh of the footage I had; in *Walden* and *In Between* I used perhaps a third. *Reminiscences of a Journey to Lithuania* was shot about one-to-one. I used everything in the film.

SM: You still have the unused material?
JM: I have it all. I may go back some day and make something else with some of it. Some material is not at all bad. But so far it hasn't belonged anywhere. Much of what was not used in the early reels of *Lost Lost Lost* is not so interesting, though it's material of historical importance about immigrant life. It should not be destroyed. Though it's slowly rotting away. . . .

SM: My first experience with *Reminiscences of a Journey to Lithuania* (1972) was at Hampshire College in 1973. After the screening some guy in the back row screamed at you, "Why can't you leave anything alone!" At the time it was sort of jolting. I'd watched the same film and to me it seemed quite lovely, but it had produced this violent response from this other person. Was that especially unusual?
JM: Until ten years ago, that was a very common reaction to single-frame shooting and to short takes, to the use of overexposures or underexposures, and in general to the work of independent filmmakers. There is less and less of that now, since people have gotten used to this type of film language.

SM: *Reminiscences of a Journey to Lithuania* is the earliest edited film in which you seem primarily involved with time, in which your return to the past is one of the major themes. There are mentions of the past in *Walden*, but not a direct concentrated involvement with it. Was it that you were going to be able to go back to Lithuania, so the whole issue became more frontal for you?
JM: You may be correct. I don't know. It's complicated. The official reaction in the Soviet Union, and all the republics there, is to have no contact with any refugee, exile, DP who left during the war—for no matter what reasons—unless that person is potentially useful to them. I had written already for *Isskustvo Kino*, a film journal in Moscow. Some Soviets had seen *The Brig* in Venice, and the editor of *Pravda*, who saw it in New York, wrote a glowing review. The film was invited to the Moscow Film Festival and presented there as an important antimilitary, anticapitalist work. They sent correspondents from Moscow to interview me here, and interviewed my mother in Lithuania. Suddenly I felt I had enough clout to apply for a visa to visit Lithuania. Since I had been invited to the Moscow Film Festival, I thought I would ask to be permitted to go to Lithuania also, to visit my mother.

For over a decade I had not been allowed even to correspond with my mother. I had written some poems against Stalin, so I was a criminal. My brothers were thrown into jail because of me, and my father died earlier than he would have, because of that. My mother's house was being watched for years, really, by the secret police. They hoped that one day I'd come home and they'd get me. My mother told me that in 1971. There was not a night, during my visit home, when I wasn't prepared to jump out the window, to run from the police if they decided to come after me. And this in 1971, many years after Stalin's death.

The Lithuanian government, that part which deals with the arts, saw that I had been favorably received by Moscow, from *Pravda* to *Literaturnaya Gazeta*. So they figured it was okay for them to permit me not only to visit my mother, but, as it turned out, to publish my collected poems. Until then I did not exist for them, officially, that is. Actually, they had mocked me in some articles in the official party paper. They had presented me as an example of a sick and corrupt mind, printing some paragraphs from my writings with words omitted, sentences turned around. That was around 1965. But once Moscow became favorable to me, Lithuania immediately followed suit. Suddenly I could film whatever I wanted. Usually visitors are not permitted to go into the villages; they stay around their hotels. I was offered an official film crew to do whatever I wanted, but I said, "I will be using my Bolex; I don't want any film crews." They found it strange, but they gave in. They had their own crews around much of the time, making their own film about me and my mother—in Cinemascope. They sent me a print, which I have.

I also shot some Moscow footage on that trip, but I haven't used it so far.

SM: When you came to Utica in 1974 or 1975 to show *Reminiscences*, a woman of Lithuanian background came to the film and seemed very upset about it.
JM: In general, the attitude among the older generation of immigrants is that if you go to visit one of those countries, you are a member of the communist party, or at best you are a spiritual communist, you are betraying the cause of those who are fighting for the liberation of Baltic countries. The younger generation, however, go for cultural exchange, on the assumption that the only way to help Lithuania is to go there and inform the people. Otherwise they know nothing, they live in controlled ignorance. So you send books, whatever you can, and when something you send gets there—which is a miracle—somebody sees it and something happens. The older generation of immigrants is for a complete cut-off, which doesn't help either side.

SM: In *Reminiscences* Lithuania under Soviet domination seems relatively comfortable. There are a couple of instances where your brothers joke about what Americans will think; their mood seems to be, "We're doing pretty well; things are okay."
JM: Yes. Lithuania is an agricultural republic which produces a lot of food for the rest of the Soviet Union. So it's in a privileged position. To a degree, that is. As long as we do not confuse food with liberty. . . . There, they do not confuse the two. They eat, but they also want liberty. Only Moscow and Washington confuse bread and economic prosperity with liberty.

When the Soviet film representative here in New York insisted on seeing the film, I showed it to him; he hit the ceiling. "How do you dare to make and show a film like this to the world! Why didn't you show the factories? Why didn't you show the progress? I said, "In this film I'm interested only in my mother and my childhood memories, that's all. This is my past." But he couldn't understand it. He thought it was outrageous and an insult. Even a bottle of vodka didn't improve his mood. The star of *Solaris*, Donatas Banionis, saw the film with him, and he thought it was great. The two of them almost got into a fist fight over the film. Only another bottle of vodka and a few songs calmed things down.

SM: Did you have a time restriction? How long were you allowed to stay in Lithuania?
JM: There was no limit. I could stay as long as I wanted. They said, "Why don't you stay here forever?" And so did my mother; she was already looking for a wife for me there. But I had to come back.

SM: At one point during the second half of the film, you say, "the morning of the fourth day." It comes as a shock because it seems as if we've been there a very long time. By the way, an intertitle at the beginning promises "100 GLIMPSES OF LITHUANIA." Why do you stop after the ninety-first section?
JM: Only ninety-one? I thought I went up to ninety-four or ninety-six. Anyway, I decided to take pity on the audience, to give them only ninety-one. On the other hand, what is "one hundred"? It's just an idea; the film shows one hundred glimpses in a loose sense.

SM: There's also one missing, No. 71.
JM: I did not like that segment. I cut it out, never replaced it with other footage, and never corrected the number. Too much work involved. I figured most people wouldn't notice. Maybe eventually I'll put something there.

SM: The time structure of that film is very complex. The first part opens with the end of your period of uprootedness. Then it goes back to the earliest part of your American experience. In the second part a similar thing happens: by visiting Lithuania, you're simultaneously moving forward in terms of your personal development, and going back to the time, or at least the place, where you were before the 1950 material. In the third part your life with your American cultural family—Ken and Flo Jacobs, Annette Michelson—continues, and you visit Kremsmuenster, a centuries-old center for the maintenance of culture.
JM: That developed organically. It's not that I sat and thought about time or about the past. I went directly to Austria from Lithuania; that's the way the footage was

shot also. Originally I thought I would just use the Lithuanian material, but as I thought more about it, I liked the way the Austrian material complicated everything. Then I decided to complicate it further, give it more angles, more directions, by adding the Brooklyn section. Later I added some Hamburg footage. It just developed as I worked on it. Time became very integral, time and culture. Culture, as represented by Kubelka, Jacobs, Annette, Nitsch, had become my home. It was clear already at that time that there was no going back to Lithuania for me.

SM: Your mother is really spectacular in that film.
JM: She's still in very good shape. She's ninety-six now.[1]

SM: *Notes for Jerome* has a very different kind of organization than the other films. It's more involved with a specific place, Jerome Hill's environment in Cassis. Was that material made intermittently during this period?
JM: The whole film is about forty-five minutes long. Thirty eight minutes or so are from the 1966 trip. There's also about three minutes from the trip the following year. Ten years later, in 1977, I made another visit. I used about two minutes of that footage.

SM: There's a very different use of intertitles. Sometimes they're repeated and become motifs.
JM: They are not always descriptive. In all the other diary volumes most of the titles are used very factually to describe what will be coming up. In this film many of the titles are not descriptive. They make statements which are not connected with any image. I was experimenting with a different use of titles.

SM: The sound is different too. There's no narration.
JM: There's very little of my voice, maybe because I did a lot of taping there and had enough other sounds.

SM: Were you drawn to Cassis just because of the friendship with Jerome Hill?
JM: Jerome Hill had a little outdoor theater there on the shore of the Mediterranean. Usually he brought over some musicians, like the Julliard Quartet. But in 1966 he persuaded the city of Cassis to cosponsor—he sponsored part of it himself—the Living Theater's production of *Frankenstein*. A special theater was built outdoors for the performance. Jerome wanted somebody to record the event; I agreed to help him. I filmed *Frankenstein* and *The Mysteries*. They are still sitting in the cans. Someday I'll screen them—for the interest of theater students   I don't think they work as films. But as theater, *Frankenstein* was the greatest performance I have ever seen. Not the one that was brought to New York, but the one in Cassis.

SM: Was the Cassis section in *Walden* done at another time?
JM: That was done in 1966.

SM: Is *Paradise Not Yet Lost* (1979) finished, or is it part of a larger film?
JM: I am not sure. I have been thinking of changing it. I may make it into a two-screen film.

SM: Is the amount of material that you have for all the other years similar to what you had for *Paradise Not Yet Lost*? That's a pretty big film.
JM: I have as much material from every year. There is a whole Cincinnati film.

SM: Cincinnati?
JM: Yes. I stayed there for a while. Also, I spent a lot of time around Jackie Kennedy's and Lee Radziwill's children. I have a lot of footage from that period.

SM: How did that come about?
JM: After Kennedy's death Jackie went through some difficult years during which she was concerned about the children. She wanted to give them something to do, involve them with something. Peter Beard was tutoring them in art history at the time. He suggested that I teach them some filmmaking. I got them simple cameras and made up some basic exercises, which they had great fun executing. It proved to be just the thing they needed. Caroline has since turned to photography and cinema, as you may know. John, by the way, when he was still in school, made some very exciting four-screen 8mm films—actually, one of the most exciting four-screen films I've ever seen, almost as good as Harry Smith's.

SM: Are you to the point where the footage feels like a weight you carry, or is getting back to it something you look forward to?
JM: I really live only in my editing room. Or when I film. The rest of my life is slavery. But I am afraid that most of my early material—and my early films too—are fading, going. It would take about forty thousand dollars to preserve my films. That's a lot of money. Money—or dust. Money against the dust of time into which all our works eventually disappear.

Notes

1. Elzbieta Mekas died on January 12, 1983, at the age of ninety-seven.

Just like a Shadow . . .

Jérome Sans / 2000

From *Just Like a Shadow* (Göttingen: Steidl Publishers, 2000). Reprinted by permission.

Jérome Sans: I know that you don't take yourself seriously, but you are considered as a cult figure and you have influenced different generations of filmmakers and other artists. What do you think of that?

Jonas Mekas: To begin with, I have to say that I am not a thinking person. People think too much. And they take themselves too seriously. I live without any plan. My greatest discovery was when I understood that I don't have to do anything; all I have to do is to permit things to happen, not to be in their way. I am not sure I have influenced other filmmakers or artists. My function has been that of a midwife who helps fragile, newborn things to survive the first steps in this world. My function has been that of a guardian who tries to protect helpless newborn young things from attacks by the Establishment. To take oneself too seriously in the arts, or life, is foolish. Art or life without humor is not worth living.

JS: You became a film theoretician, writing day-by-day history of the underground. Minister of propaganda of the New American Cinema. What does it mean being a critic for you?

JM: It's like this: a critic, as it's known in film magazines and the daily and weekly press, is a person who passes judgments on films. This one is bad, this one is good, etc. I never really passed judgments on films. From the very beginning of my *Village Voice* Movie Journal column in 1958, I wrote only about films that I liked. I was a film enthusiast, not a critic. I am not a film critic, I never was.

I always felt that my function was to relate to the readers some of my enthusiasm about the films that I liked. When I see a film and I like it, I want to share my enthusiasm for it with others. There is so little in this modern commercial world that is really and truly exciting, I mean something that reaches deep into your soul, that it's very important for me that those little fragments of beauty, of Paradise, are brought to the attention of friends and strangers equally. That's why I began writing for the *Village Voice*.

JS: Why did you create in 1967 the first cooperative building for artists at 80 Wooster Street, a cooperative which began Soho?

JM: The real creator of Soho was George Maciunas, the Fluxus guy. I only helped him. We were friends since childhood, practically. When in 1967 he came up with the idea of creating the first Soho cooperative building on Wooster Street, he needed an eight-thousand-dollar deposit on the building, so I said I'll try to get the money. It was Jerome Hill, to whom I devoted my film "Notes for Jerome," who came up with the money. He wanted to help the Film-Makers' Cinematheque; he wanted us to have our own place. So I got the eight thousand dollars, and George's sister Nicole pitched in with a few more thousand, and we took the building. The rest is history. That's how Soho was born. Why did we do it? That was the only thing to do if you wanted to have a cheap place to live and work in those days. Of course, later it became one of the most expensive places to live or work. But not in 1967. In 1967 the area was totally dilapidated. It was the genius of George Maciunas to see the possibilities the area offered. I have to add one more thing. And that is the crucial contribution to many key art organizations of the sixties by Jerome Hill. I have to tell you frankly that without Jerome, *Film Culture* magazine would have closed by 1960. Without Jerome, neither the Film-Makers' Cooperative nor the Film-Makers' Cinematheque would have survived. Without Jerome there would be no Anthology Film Archives. And no Soho. Jerome was an incredible, visionary person. And he trusted me totally.

JS: Since 1950 you have always carried your Bolex camera, all day long and everywhere. Why this desire to record everything?

JM: I have no real answer. All answers that I have given to this question in the past could be wrong, they are all inventions. One of the answers, usually, is that as an exile, as a displaced person, I felt that I had lost so much, my country, my family, even my early written diaries, ten years of them, that I developed the need to try to retain everything I was passing through, by means of my Bolex camera. It became an obsession, a passion, a sickness. So now I have these images to cling to. . . . It's all ridiculous, I think. Because what I have, after all, is already fading, it's all just like a shadow of the real reality which I do not really understand. When you go through what I went through, the wars, occupations, genocides, forced labor camps, displaced person camps, and lying in a blooming potato field—I'll never forget the whiteness of the flowers, my face down to the earth, after jumping out the window, while German soldiers held my father against the wall, a gun in his back—then you don't understand human beings anymore. I have never understood them since then, and I just film, record everything, with no judgment, that I see. Not exactly "everything," only the brief moments that I feel like filming. And what are those moments? What makes me choose those moments? I don't know. It's my whole past memory that makes me choose the moments that I film.

JS: Why this single-frame technique, and not some other newer, "advanced" technology?

JM: It took me approximately fifteen years to really master my Bolex so that it could really and automatically and spontaneously do what I wanted it to do. I always compare it with what a saxophonist, a jazz musician does: he practices for many years—until the instrument begins to follow the most subtle movements of his fingers. It would be destructive, even stupid to suddenly change your instrument only because somebody invented a new instrument. I am a very busy man. I have no time and no need or desire to change my tools, my Bolex. Especially since Bolex is a very precise camera, very suitable for my kind of filming.

JS: You have been recording everything around you, in your film diary, your personal life and your cultural life, the New York avant-garde of the fifties and the sixties and seventies as the center of your life of that period. Why?

JM: I usually film my friends, or my family. As it happened, all the people who played a central role in the life of the arts in New York during those decades, they were all my friends. And, of course, most of them were not yet famous at all. We were all involved in the same thing. We were like a large family. We knew each other, we helped each other. And of course, sometimes we argued. It was an incredible period. Why did I film it all? I have no real answer. I think I did it because I was a very shy person. My camera allowed me to participate in the life that took place around me. My film diaries are not like the diaries of Anais Nin. Anais, whom I knew, she organized about her psychological adventures. In my case, the opposite, whatever that opposite may be, may be the case. My Bolex protected me, while at the same time giving me a peek and a focus on what was happening around me. Still, at the very end, I don't think my film diaries are about the others or what I saw: it's all about myself, conversations with myself.

JS: Your day-by-day chronicle in the *Village Voice* Movie Journal is a fantastic series of texts and statements which are actual and radical and with no mistakes. But do you have any regrets or corrections to make?

JM: No, I have no regrets and no important corrections to make. The films which I praised in my Movie Journal have all become classics. My only regret is that on one or two occasions—I do not remember what it was—but I remember that I became, regretfully, a "critic," and criticized some films. I should have never done it. One should write only about films one likes and stay away from films one doesn't like.

JS: From Allen Ginsberg to John Cassavetes, Kenneth Anger, Stan Brakhage, through Norman Mailer, Salvador Dali, Hermann Nitsch, Yoko Ono, and John

Lennon . . . to whom you were very close; to Surrealism, Fluxus, Beat, Pop, Action-
ism, New York cinema . . . all very different personalities but they all shared new
attitudes based on a poetry of freedom and spontaneity.

JM: It all comes down to something like this: Here I am, a shy thin boy whom
everybody in my village, when I was seven or eight, they all thought, ah, poor boy,
he's about to die. So, years later I come to New York, and here I am, a farmer boy,
and I do not want anything but to write my poetry and make my films. But Fate
had other plans for me. All these people kept coming my way, George Maciunas,
Salvador Dali, Jackie Kennedy, Yoko Ono and John Lennon, and everybody else; I
didn't need them and didn't know them and was not looking for them. As I said, I
just wanted to write my poetry. But we were all brought together: Allen Ginsberg,
Robert Frank, Stan Brakhage, Kenneth Anger. No, I was not looking for Salvador
Dali: he was a legend, I would have never dared to bother him. But he became curious about me and came to visit me unannounced, with Ultra Violet, to my 414 Park
Avenue South loft, and we became friends. Andy Warhol sat on the floor of my loft
for months, watching movies, before I found out who he was. The point I am trying
to make here is that it all happened by itself. I had neither time nor desire to meet
any of these people, I was always too busy, as I still am, not even having time to
eat, and my stomach has shrunk from not eating; living just on Italian sausage and
goat cheese and garlic and wine, so that now I can barely eat anything. Anyway,
once a psychic woman looked at me and told me that my incarnation lineage has
gone through Giordano Bruno, some feisty Spanish Lieutenant, and George Washington. When she told me that once I had been George Washington, it explained
to me everything: why I was in America and why all these people circled, gathered
around me and why it all happened by itself, very easily . . .

But back to your question. I think that my acceptance and enthusiasm for what
was happening during that period in America came from my cultural starvation
in the Soviet Union and Nazi Germany. I was now very excitable and sensitive
to anything that was new in art. Actually, I have to tell you, that my life in New
York has been even more complicated by the fact that, according to my Japanese
horoscope done for me by Yoko Ono on a napkin at the Paradox Café on the Lower
East Side, in 1967, I was here on this planet Earth as a very young, inexperienced
soul whom everybody was supposed to help. . . . I am not sure how this goes with
the George Washington story. . . . Anyway, the paradox of this Paradox Café story
is that I ended up by helping others, and not in reverse. . . .

Freedom? Spontaneity? It's very interesting how one's deep personal obses-
sions or needs can color and even twist one's perception, of others. I am rereading
some of my early diaries, my writings on Bill Burroughs, and John Cassavetes,
the controversy about the first and the second versions of *Shadows*, and I begin

to understand that my criticism of Cassavetes's second version of *Shadows* was not based on what Cassavetes wanted to do but on what I wanted to do and was doing. . . . The spontaneity was more important to my life than to Cassavetes's life.

JS: When they first appeared, you were the only one to understand the importance of Andy Warhol films (*Sleep*" *Eat*) and write positively about them. Why so, and how do you consider his films in the context of his other work?

JM: I get very excited when I see something new coming into the world. Andy's films had a monumental newness about them. So I had to tell about them to the people, I had to write about them. There is something in my character that if I see something that I like I have to share that experience with others. I cannot enjoy even a sunset by myself: somebody else has to see it with me. Why didn't others immediately see the importance of Andy's films? It's difficult to tell. New York intellectuals and artists, they liked Hollywood, or else they liked classic avant-garde cinema. But *Sleep* didn't fit into it. It takes a sense of adventure to see it for what it is. Let's face it, even today, all the people and museums that buy Andy's paintings have very little interest in his films. There are entire areas of his cinema, such as the hundreds of film portraits taken at the Factory that are totally unknown and neglected even by the museums that own and handle Andy's work. But I consider that even those portraits constitute one of the most important undertakings in portraiture in twentieth-century art. But when are we going to see them? Museums don't care about them. And, of course, *Chelsea Girls*—it's a monumental, fantastic work. But who shows it? So things haven't changed that much since the sixties.

JS: What did Andy Warhol think about your films?

JM: He liked especially *Walden* and saw it several times. He also liked *The Brig*. It was after seeing *The Brig*, and learning about my filming techniques which were very simple, that he decided to begin to film with sound. What I did, I used a newsreel style Auricon camera that records image and sound on the same strip of film, simultaneously. He liked that idea and began filming with an Auricon camera. That's how we shot *Empire*; I was the cameraman. There was a funny discussion: should we film the Empire State Building with sound or silent. . . . We decided to film it silent. And yes, he liked *Notes on the Circus* very much.

JS: Is *film d'art* for you a pejorative term?

JM: It's a very confusing term; besides its pretentiousness. In America, beginning with the fifties, movie theaters that showed films made in Europe or anywhere else outside Hollywood, were called art theaters. Even today, anything that is shown in America in subtitled versions, is called art films. But we know that neither Lumiere Brothers nor Mélies nor D. W. Griffith nor Rossellini nor Eisenstein made *films d'art*.

Even Godard didn't make them. Brakhage doesn't make them. We make films. So what kind of animal is this *film d'art*? I don't know. Do you know what eight million people in America answered in 1966 when they were asked if they thought they were artists? They said yes, they thought they were artists. When George Maciunas began creating cooperative buildings in Soho, in 1967, he used to ask the people who wanted to join the cooperatives, "What do you do, what's your profession?" If someone answered that he or she was an artist, George used to say, "You say you are an artist? So you pay double." He hated people who considered themselves artists and not just painters or filmmakers or musicians.

JS: You were the only one to fight for new forms in cinema. Is that why you were so close to all other "underground" artists, poets, musicians, etc.?
JM: Somehow we were all together, one family. And there was a great intensity in the air. Poetry readings, jazz places, cafés, where we would gather attracted me because of the energy, intensity. We were one intense, ecstatic family. Maybe not in body, but in spirit. This doesn't mean at all that we all agreed with one another. Some of us didn't speak with one another for months, even years. Still, we were together.

Besides writing, after 1953, you organized screenings of avant-garde films in various places in New York before opening Anthology Film Archives.

In the spring of 1953, I escaped Brooklyn and moved to the Lower East Side of Manhattan, to 95 Orchard Street. Very soon after that, I began my first avant-garde film screenings at the Gallery East, corner of Avenue A and Second Street. That was the beginning. Gallery East was an offshoot of the Tenth Street crowd, De Kooning and all. That's how it all began. The Gallery East series was followed by at least ten other showcases, including Film-Makers' Showcase, where Warhol's *Sleep* opened, and Jack Smith's *Flaming Creatures* was premiered, and Kenneth Anger's *Scorpio Rising*; and then there was Film-Makers' Cinematheque on Forty-First Street where most of Andy's later work, including *Chelsea Girls*, was presented. All this happened before Anthology Film Archives were opened in late 1970.

JS: Why did you create Anthology Film Archives?
JM: In 1968, I received a call from Jerome Hill, a filmmaker and friend who spent half of his life in Cassis, France, and the other half in New York and Big Sur, California. He said his friend Martinson, who was then chairman of the Public Theater, one of the most important theaters in New York, called him and offered space in his building on 425 Lafayette Street, for a film theater. Jerome asked me if I wanted to do something there. I said yes. So I invited P. Adams Sitney to run the new project, which we decided to call Anthology Film Archives. We invited Peter Kubelka, Stan Brakhage, Ken Kelman, and James Broughton to help us to set up a

new kind of film museum for the avant-garde and classic cinema. One of the most controversial aspects of it was our creation of what became known as Essential Cinema Repertory Collection. It consisted of some 310 titles, mostly avant-garde, but also some classics, such as Renoir, Rossellini, Eisenstein, Vigo, etc. These films that made up some 110 different programs were the basic repertory of Anthology Film Archives, a repertory that reflected the most exciting achievements in cinema. The basic reason for having such a repertory was this: The period between 1957 and 1967 was the most productive, the most inspiring period in the arts in America. During the same time, if we take, for instance, the year 1960, we had in the United States only a dozen universities and colleges teaching film; by 1967, according to the American Film Institute's survey, there were twelve hundred universities and colleges teaching film. Each of those twelve hundred film departments, besides teaching Hollywood film or commercial cinema, they had to show to their students some programs of the independent, "underground" cinema. But since they hadn't seen much, because they were not in New York or San Francisco, they kept calling me or P. Adams Sitney for advice, what to show. I had to do all the work for them: select films, write notes on the films, locate the distributors, etc. I did it once, I did it twice, I did it ten times, twenty times and more, but I had enough of it. Why don't we get a little committee of people who know avant-garde film and prepare a list of films that we approve and send that list to all the schools that call us for help? Every film on the list is important for one or another good reason. That's how the Essential Cinema Repertory Collection was born. We had many meetings, our little committee of five, during 1970–1974, and we selected 310 titles. We intended to continue, but meanwhile our main sponsor, Jerome Hill, died, and our work was interrupted and never completed. Still, what we voted in, during the 1970–1974 sessions, into the Repertory, constitutes the basis of American and international avant-garde cinema until the year 1970.

JS: What is the present activity of Anthology Film Archives?
JM: Anthology remains the most active showcase of independent avant-garde cinema in the United States. At the same time, I have to say that the field of independent cinema has become so wide, during the past thirty years, that no single institution can cover the entire field. Where we differ from all other film showcases and museums or archives in America is that we are the only institution that is also very deeply involved in the preservation of avant-garde cinema, and we run the largest library in the world of paper materials, information on the avant-garde. Our film holdings presently comprise over twelve thousand titles, most of them independent productions. We have very little money for the preservation of films we hold, but we don't give up searching for money.

JS: Critic, archivist of the works of others, why are you simply not just making your own films?

JM: Several complicated reasons contribute to this complicated situation. First, if I see a film that gives me aesthetic pleasure, if I see that a film is endangered, I have to do everything I can to get money to preserve it so that others can see it and have the same ecstatic experience ten, thirty years later. Reason two: I am not a rational person, I never know why I do what I do. Reason three: I have no money to complete my own films or preserve them. None of my films are preserved. And most of my footage filmed during the last twenty-five years sits on the shelf unfinished because I have no money. I don't even have money to eat, telling the truth. I dream of eating. . . . I don't have to tell you that I get no salary from Anthology Film Archives: there is no money for salaries at Anthology. But this problem of food or eating is not exactly new in my life. In the early sixties, when I had to put all the money I could find into *Film Culture* and Film-Makers' Cooperative, Jerome Hill had made an arrangement for me to eat at one West Sixty-First Street restaurant on his account. That saved me. In the mid-sixties, it was David and Barbara Stone who fed me when I was really desperate. Brakhage told me once that when he came to New York in 1955 he was so poor, he used to pick up leftovers of sandwiches from street garbage cans. Naomi Levine used to get very angry with me when I refused to take her to restaurants. No, I never go to restaurants to eat. I have no money, I used to say. She didn't believe me. Because she thought I was a millionaire incognito. . . .

Please do not misunderstand me. I am not complaining. I am telling you this only because I want posterity to know how the American avant-garde cinema came into existence. Our films were more important to us than our own lives, health, anything. I am perfectly happy with my Italian sausage, and goat cheese, and garlic, and wine, and I only wish others could be as happy. Imagine, running one of the most important film museums in the world and doing it without any salary? Crazy, of course it's crazy. But we are very happy, all of us at Anthology. Crazy and happy.

JS: Do you think avant-garde films have to stay where they are and not try to jump into the big distribution system?

JM: The truth is very simple: nobody wants us. You can jump as much as you want, but you'll fall back to where you are. You know the story of the frog that wanted to be as big as a bull? . . . By the way, a bull is a Wall Street symbol. . . . The truth is that cinema which used to be called underground or, now, independent/avant-garde, is by its very essence more complex, more demanding than what the "big distribution" systems are selling. We don't fit into the airport bookstore class. Same as in literature: poetry is being printed in two or three thousand editions, but novels, even the worst ones, are printed in millions. It's not realistic, not a good thinking to expect that Brakhage or Isidore Isou will suddenly be sold in the airport racks by millions. . . . Humanity is not there and I don't even think it should be there. . . . There was a time, in the sixties, when Brakhage and Markopoulos wrote scripts for which they tried to find Hollywood producers, and I used to laugh and tell them, good luck. I knew Hollywood because I had spent some time there, and I knew most of the Hollywood people. I knew that Stan and Gregory were dreaming, they were idealistic, they were poets. Later, Shirley Clarke flirted with Hollywood. It also ended in zero. All of the new so-called New York school filmmakers such as Morris Engel, Lionel Rogosin, Emile De Antonio, and Shirley Clarke, had Hollywood dreams.

JS: How many films have you made and to how many hours would it all amount to?
JM: Film-Makers' Cooperative, in New York, a cooperative that distributes films by some five hundred independent filmmakers, distributes twenty-five of my films. They all add up to about twenty-five hours. The film which I am editing now will be about six hours long. In addition to the films, I have issued five videos that add up to ten hours. In reality, all my film work is one long film which is still continuing. I don't really make films: I only keep filming. I am a filmer not a filmmaker. And I am not a film "director" because I direct nothing. I just keep filming.

JS: Why is cinema so important to you? What does cinema mean to you?
JM: I am not too sure if cinema is really important to me. My obsession with filming has nothing to do with what I think about cinema. I just have to film. I have no choice. If I don't film, I get sick. It's madness. I am being pulled into it by an irresistible force. That's about all I can say about it.

JS: What is the future of cinema? Godard said, "Cinema is dead."
JM: To say that cinema is dead means as much as saying Piero della Francesca is dead. Or Cézanne is dead. Godard likes to say things like that for effect. He likes effects. As for myself, cinema is not restricted to celluloid: to me cinema is the art of moving images, no matter on what material it's created: video, computers, or anything else. Godard should spend some time with the new, eighteen-year-old generation who have revived the Super 8 cinema. Then Godard would say, "Ah, cinema is only beginning."

JS: Why are commercial and experimental films always opposed to each other?
JM: They are not opposed. The idea of opposition has been planted in people's minds by people who know neither cinema nor the laws of life. Is poetry opposed to prose, to the novel? Of course not: these are two different forms of literature, and they run parallel. Is an étude or song in music opposed to a symphony? Of

course not: these are different forms of music. The same in cinema. Or life on a farm: is a cow opposed to the sheep? The sheep gives wool and the cow gives milk, but they are not opposed to each other. They eat from the same meadow and sleep in the same barn. Same with the avant-garde and commercial forms of cinema. None of them are opposed to each other. Anthropological film. Educational film. Narrative film. Films on art. Poetic, avant-garde film. Essayistic film, etc. These are all different forms of cinema. None of them is opposed to another.

JS: What do you think about professionalism in cinema?

JM: A good professional is a good craftsman who knows how to build a house exactly like his father used to build it; or make a wheel, or bake good bread, or make good wine, cheeses, or anything else. I admire craftspeople, they are true professionals. But I hate experimenters who destroy our bread and dwelling places and wine and yogurt and everything they touch because they want to improve on what has been tested by hundreds of generations. But, of course, what I say here about professionals has nothing to do with art. Artists are never professional craftsmen, because gods have propelled them and possessed them in order to ex-pand the human possibilities, of what they now call human potential. They are in the front line where they meet all the bullets and bayonets. And no past lessons, no professionalism will save them: they have to invent new technologies and new forms in order to record new sensibilities and new emerging content and help to form that content. The craftspeople, the professionals, the more they remain faith-ful to the past, the more useful they are to humanity. But imagine Stan Brakhage or Kenneth Anger or myself hiring a professional to shoot our films. It's my heart and my nerves that control my fingers and the rhythms of my films. Avant-garde cinema is totally "unprofessional" in that regard.

JS: You use all the technical imperfections in your film.

JM: In a diary form of cinema, technical imperfections are part of the content and part of the form. They reveal aspects of inner and outer reality that could not be caught through technical "perfection." Technical perfection, in truth, does not exist. Any perfection, any technique has to be measured by the content it attempts to capture. An overexposure, a clumsy movement can be more "perfect," as far as the content goes, than any "steady" or "properly exposed" footage. So it's all rela-tive. Like Einstein's curve of time and space.

JS: You never use any story boards, never reshoot and never use crews. . . . Isn't that some kind of adventure?

JM: My filming techniques are determined by my reactions to what I am filming. I am not filming reactions; these are my reactions. Therefore, nobody else, no team or crew, no advance "story board" can help me—this is real life that cannot be put on any board because it's totally unpredictable. And what's more, I usually film only those moments where there is a celebration of life, excitement, joy. And, of course, it's a sort of adventure, because everything is unpredictable. Adventure of the camera, what I can do with the immediate moment, how much and in what way I can capture the essence and the ecstasy of the moment, will I get it or not? So I work frantically with my Bolex. And when I work with my Sony, it's not that much different—I mean, as far as the concentration goes—as I am desperately trying to get to the heart of the moment. So, of course I have to do it all by myself, because it's me who is excited about it all. No teams, no hired cameramen, no sound people. It's just me, my camera and life around me.

JS: Can we then speak about a spontaneous creation, as the real "cinéma vérité"?
JM: Here you have touched one of my sensitive spots, with the word "creation." You see, I do not really believe in creation. I have always insisted that what I do, I do from necessity. When I film something, I don't film it because I want to create something. I do it because I want to capture the essence there in front of me. When I film, I try to go directly to the essence, to what I feel is the essence, and this has absolutely nothing to do with "creation." I just film it. That's all. As far as sponta- neity goes, I am not sure if there is any other "creation" other than a spontaneous one, or improvised, be it me, or Stan Brakhage, Kenneth Anger, D. W. Griffith, or Adam Mickiewicz, or Renoir. Cinéma vérité? That was a term used to describe a certain style, a certain way of filming "real life," films usually concerned with certain themes that society was interested in. Cinéma vérité grew out of the excitement caused by the coming into existence of light portable cameras with sound. So we had Jean Rouch and Richard Leacock and many others. They made films of either social or anthropological interest, some great films. But I am somewhere else. My films are totally of no interest to society. They are totally useless to society.

JS: You have said that your editing is done during the filming.
JM: Another word for editing is structuring. Structuring in art takes place on many different levels: it's the rhythm of your heart, it's light, movement, color—it's something that gives life to your film. And of course, it can be done only during the moment of filming—or painting, or composing, or writing—when one is totally and completely lost in what one is doing, making, "creating." And I am not talking only about my own style of filming. I am also taking about Alfred Hitchcock and Jean-Luc Godard and Preminger. Preminger told me once that when he films he shoots so that later the "editors" would have no choice but to leave his footage as it is: he didn't give them any other choices, he hated studio editors.

JS: You said that, in your cinema, you are going back to the Lumière Brothers, to the beginning. Does this mean that you think that between then and now almost nothing has happened?

JM: No, I don't mean that. A lot has happened. The whole history of cinema happened. But in every art there are periods when a lull comes in, everybody somehow gets tired and decadent, when we forget what cinema is all about. Then it's time to go to the beginning and refresh our senses and our imagination, to clean it out from all the junk, and start afresh. Just the camera, a roll of film, and you. Rediscover cinema anew.

JS: Don't you think there are today other moving image technologies, maybe easier than motion picture cameras?

JM: In every art, there are constantly new tools being added, new colors, new sound instruments, new film/video/computer technologies. But just because a new instrument was invented to make sounds, we cannot expect Yehudi Menuhin to drop his violin and jump into, say, electronic sound; or me leave my Bolex which does for me what I want and which I have been using for forty years, and jump into computers, which I know nothing about. I would have to spend ten years before a computer would follow my fingers. Of course, that is impossible. Eight millimeters, 16mm, 35mm, 70mm, etc.—and each of these film formats uses different film stocks, different lenses, and produces images of very different texture and density, color quality, etc., etc. Same as a painter, he can choose colors he needs for a specific work, watercolors or oils or inks or pastels or anything else, and the choices are not taken at random but by exact intuitive knowledge. Same in cinema. Each tool or format does a different thing. And it's not a question of it being easier or more difficult. That never comes into play.

JS: The camera gives you the possibility to show everything.

JM: It depends what one means by "everything." Each of us grows with certain preferences, we love this or we love that, and in our films we usually exclude "everything" and we work only with a reality which is our own preferred private reality. "Everything" doesn't exist in art. Or life.

JS: In your writing and in your films the form of a journal or diary is the central form. Why?

JM: My theory regarding the emergence of the diaristic forms in the arts, in all of the arts, after the Second World War, is that we all got tired of invented stories. The gruesome realities of 1933–1944 have destroyed all our stories, or, as Adorno said, poetry. All that we could still try to do was to turn to real life, and look around us, and try to understand what was going on, what was real in our own story. Everything else seemed senseless, escapist, unreal. That's at least my personal interpretation of why I choose the diary form. My own story was even more complicated by the fact that very soon after my arrival in New York, I got totally involved in so many activities related to the avant-garde/independent film that I had left only little fragments of time for myself. The diary form suits perfectly when you have no time. You just make little notes, that's all. And that's what I've been doing.

JS: Do you consider yourself an artist?

JM: I consider myself a filmmaker and a poet. I make films, or, more correctly, film, and I occasionally write poems in Lithuanian. What do I think about people who call themselves artists instead of filmmakers or musicians or painters? As I already said earlier, some twenty-five years ago, there was a survey done by some newspapers, I read in the papers, they asked people all over the States if they felt they were artists. You know what? There were eight million people in the States who said yes, they were artists. So that's great. . . .

JS: What does it mean to you to add more pictures to an already image-saturated world?

JM: In this world, everything is transitory. All those pictures will be gone in twenty, thirty years. With the exception of those few that will contain something essential. People will want to preserve them because they'll want to resee them, exchange them with others. It always comes down to intensity, how intense is this precious stone, this pearl, this piece of music, or this painting, or this film. And even if the images are transitory, the making of images is a very innocent activity—so let the people make them and be happy; just watch people when they are taking polaroids—they laugh, they are happy.

JS: When and why did you start making photograms, stills extracted from your films?

JM: It all began very innocently from a very simple down-to-earth necessity. In 1983, I needed money for the renovation of the Anthology Film Archives building. Tetsuo Kinoshita, my Tokyo friend, suggested I choose a dozen images from my films and he and his friends would produce silk-screen prints from them, sell them, and Anthology would be saved. So I did that. The first series was exhibited at the Hara Museum in Tokyo in 1983. They didn't sell, but my Japanese friends helped Anthology in other ways. Some of these prints were exhibited in Paris at the Jeu de Paume in 1994 during the retrospective of my films. In 1995, Anthology was going through another money crisis. Again, my faithful Japanese friends suggested that

I choose some new images, and they would try again. So I began selecting images. Suddenly, I got obsessed with it. Meanwhile, my Japanese friends informed me that the guy who was planning to finance the project had gone bankrupt. But I couldn't stop. I produced little polaroids from the slides and kept looking at them and carrying hundreds of them in my pockets. While in Paris in 1995, I showed them to Agnès B and Yann Beauvais, who was at that time running the American Center. They liked the idea of *images immobiles*, and they gave me my first big show in Paris, at the Galerie du Jour. The American Center closed just before my show opened there. The Galerie du Jour show was crucial to me. Tetsuo Kinoshita came to see the show and his review helped to set up the Tokyo Metropolitan Museum of Photography. Here the help of Ikkan Sanada was also crucial. In any case, my Frozen Film Frames were on their way into the world.

Now why am I making them? Not for money of course, because very few of them have sold. . . . I am making them because I am obsessed with the possibilities of having two, three frames/images together, detaching them from the context, and letting them be by themselves. I am not collaging them now, of course, they were collaged by my single-frame filming technique during the moment of filming. Thus they are not calculated collagins but spontaneous collagins done during intense moments of filming. They do one thing when they are in the film and they become completely something else when they are detached and enlarged and framed and presented in a gallery situation. The fact that these are film frames remains always present in the viewer's mind and eye, since I keep the film and the soundtracks and anything else that could be in the strip of the film from which the print was made. How do these images relate to photography? I am not sure how. They are like cousins. One difference is that none of my individual images, or frames, have been consciously composed. However, we can also find the same "anticomposition" preoccupations today in photography. In any case, it's not my business to figure out the relationships or differences, I am not a photography historian. All I know is that I am obsessed with making these images, and it's up to the others to see where it all fits. These images are a fact, and critics will have to deal with them whether they like it or not. Especially since I have more images than most photographers have . . .

JS: How do you choose each of them?

JM: There are several things that determine the choice of the images. One is the visual dynamic between the frames determined by light, color or shapes. Another is the clashings by content—be it a face or abstraction. The faces, the possibilities of portraiture in motion. And also what the image means to me, personally. The rarity of the images also comes into play, for instance, the images of Carl Theodor Dreyer—I like them as images, but at the same time these are very rare images.

JS: How many images have you done? In editions of how many?

JM: The Tokyo edition of 1983 consisted of some twelve images. Silk-screen prints were made in editions of two hundred each. The series of 1995 and 1998 were in editions of twenty-five, cibachrome, some one hundred images. So far I have produced slides of seven hundred different frozen film frames.

JS: Is there a logic or a system in it all?

JM: Maybe there is, but I don't see one, not yet. It's all a search, accident, chance, luck, good friends, and Saint Teresa of Avila, my friendly saint.

JS: You have said that you are a regionalist. What do you mean by that?

JM: I mean that I am limited, that I don't represent "everything" or "all"; that I have a small world of my own, and I work within it. Anyone who claims to be international or global, is a fool. The whole idea of globality is silly. Or maybe even evil. The only way to reach everybody, this I learned from Dostoyevsky, is to be yourself as much as you can, as personal as you can. In other words: totally regional.

JS: What are your future projects?

JM: It's difficult to tell because it's mind-boggling. I still have to put together all my film diaries of the last twenty-five years, because if I don't do that within the next two, three years, they will be gone, color faded. But I have neither the time nor the money to do that. Then there are piles and piles, thousands of pages of my written diaries, the dust is falling on them. But I have no time to edit them together because Anthology Films Archives needs me. Ideally, I would need a three-year leave to complete all this work. But I need a sponsor for that, and I do not have one, not yet. But Saint Teresa is working on that. She will see that it's all done, in due time, if it's good for the soul. Because there is nothing more important, in life, or art, as the soul.

Conversation between Jonas Mekas and Stan Brakhage

Stan Brakhage / 2000

Full interview previously unpublished. Printed by permission of the Estate of Jonas Mekas.

Editor's Introduction: The following conversation took place at Anthology Film Archives, New York, on November 3, 2000. It was originally prepared for Vogue, *but only appeared in a heavily edited form.*

Stan Brakage: So, Jonas, what shall we talk about?
Jonas Mekas: We are supposed to have a serious conversation . . . and keep in mind that *Vogue* is not a journal of film criticism. . . . It's *Vogue*, a magazine of and for the people. . . . So we should never forget that. . . . So here we are, two, as far as *Vogue* readership goes, two totally unknown people. . . .

SB: Yes . . .
JM: Because, here you are, Stan Brakhage, whom not only myself, but most of those, who write serious film criticism, or make movies, consider as probably the number one living filmmaker. And this is not only in America, but everywhere. In short, you are one of the most important people working in cinema today, in the importance of the body of your work, and the influence on other filmmakers, what others have picked up or inherited from you. But how many *Vogue* readers have even heard your name, I wonder. . . . So there we are.

SB: And here is what you are to me: In addition to being a great filmmaker who has forged ahead in an area where you are practically unique in, that is, the diary, journal film. How can I say, you are the Madame de Sévigné of film, you are the only one, really, for me who has created a believable, meaningful, extended journal across most of your adult life. In addition to this, you have found somehow, which is overwhelming to me, you have found a way to sponsor films that you love and to create cooperatives through which they could be distributed; to create the Anthology Film Archives so that they could be preserved and shown in a repertoire and continue today to be certainly the only solid place for this whole area we want to call Poetic Film.

So you've done not only these two things—but you also nave this rich life as a poet, which, not knowing Lithuanian, I can just read the translations into English, but those are very moving to me. I respect you also as a poet. So I am overwhelmed with your largesse. I don't know how you keep all this going.

JM: Anyway, we both have been in it all for fifty years now. You have been making films since 1953. And me, in the spring of 1953 I moved into the Lower East Side of New York and opened my first showcase for the avant-garde films at the Gallery East, Avenue A, and First Street, only two blocks from where we are now. I showed Kenneth Anger, Gregory Markopoulos, Maya Deren, Sidney Peterson. So you see I didn't move very far. . . .

SB: Well, the man who really gets something done is the one who can stay at home. Of course, ironically, you are an exile, exiled from your home.

JM: We lived in a century where for maybe half of the world was made impossible to remain, to live at home. So now, very often I say that cinema is my home. I used to say culture was my home. But it got a little bit confused, culture, nobody knows any longer what it is. So I stick to cinema.

SB: That's where you and I first got into trouble with what culture was, and art. I was so frightened that the social concerns of the sixties would overwhelm the long range, as I viewed them, aesthetic possibilities. I quarreled a lot with you, in the sixties. As I look back on it now, I think that you were largely right, that I needn't have been afraid for the arts in the ways in which I was. Let's say, many of the films that came out were very stupid from a standpoint of art, or aesthetics or even craftsmanship. Still, they were crucial to the moment. You were treating the world, very much the way I was treating my children: I mean, I would never make my children suffer so that I could make another film. And you had that attitude. . . .

JM: You know, we are celebrating Anthology Film Archives' thirtieth anniversary. So the other day some of us, P. Adams Sitney, Ken Kelman, myself, we got together and talked about the early days, about the creation what we called Essential Cinema Repertory . . . which for the readers of *Vogue*, I should tell, consisted of some 330 titles of very carefully selected films that we felt indicated the perimeters of the art of cinema. So we sat and talked, and we came to the conclusion that we did not make any bad mistakes in our choices. And then I looked at what I was showing in the sixties at the Film-Makers' Cinematheque, the films that upset so much some of my friends, and I discovered that what I showed, what I promoted, all those films later ended up in the Essential Cinema Repertory. . . . What's now considered the classics of the sixties, that's what I was showing at the Film-Maker's Cinematheque. But some of my friends thought I was too permissive.

There were, of course, some that did not become classics. But it's like in cooking: can one eat and eat just steak? Myself, being a farmer—I grew up on a farm—I know that, sometimes some salad is needed. One cannot live on steak alone. . . . Important works are always surrounded by some that are not that important. But as time goes they fall off. In a sense it's almost like Darwin's law applied to the arts. Not the biggest, but the most essential survive.

SB: I was afraid that they'd sink the ship.

JM: They just evaporate. Your work, Snow, or that of Kenneth Anger, Maya Deren, they keep growing, they are here, and they will remain here.

SB: But I also wonder if that doesn't have more to do with you, what you provided.

JM: What came up, what P. Adams Sitney brought up during the conversation that I already mentioned, was that what's lacking today is the serious or passionate writing on the contemporary avant-garde film. And they are being made today. That, of course, was my function in the *Village Voice*, in the sixties, via my column Movie Journal. But where are the *Village Voices* of today?

SB: I don't know any. Is there any aesthetician or critic of any kind that regularly deals with the Poetic Cinema in the entire North American continent?

JM: There are some quarterlies, but there is no regular, weekly coverage. There are many, many alternative newspapers and monthlies, but none of them cover the Poetic Cinema. They are all about Hollywood kind of film only.

SB: Then, that much true now for poetry, architecture, or some of the performance arts; there is no regularity of coverage going on in on the North American continent.

JM: And then you walk into a newspaper store and you see twenty, thirty magazines on art. . . . And you look through them and see nothing but advertisements . . .

SB: In defense of myself, one of the ways that I got most laughed at, in the sixties and seventies, was when I was trying to defend the word "art." I finally had to give it up because it was taken away by everybody and applied to every kind of consideration, and it ceased to be a meaningful word.

JM: I think it was in 1966 or 1967 Peter Moore had a column in *Popular Photography* magazine, and he reported, I read, on a survey conducted across the United States, at that time, where people were asked whether they felt they were "artists." You know what? Six million people said they felt they were artists. Of course, when you have six million artists just in one country, then you give up using the word "art."

SB: And they keep producing through the colleges every year more and more of them; soon, someone said, half of the American nation will be teaching art to the other half.

JM: I will always remember, when I was a child, my father told me once, that after the First World War there was so much worthless money that when he used to drive to the market, he used to take a bag full of money, a bag, not a wallet. . . . So there are times when not only money loses its value, but also terms. Some terms get so overused that you have to forget them for a while until the times clean them up.

SB: We have other words that have suffered from this, words like "love," "God, "evil," even "evil" is used far too loosely. So I would say that isn't just film that suffered from these difficulties. All the arts, what we call traditionally the arts, have suffered very much from this breakdown of terminology, this lack of serious critique. In a way, here is a discipline far older than any other we know of human beings, we have a record that goes back older than any science, anything, but when it's taught in public schools, in fact in colleges, it's as a playground for finger painting and for expressing yourself.

JM: I would like to bring something else into this. When you began making films, in the early fifties, and when I turned to cinema, around the same time, there were several other very important developments on the way—action painting, improvisational theater of Strasberg, and the Happenings theater, conceptual art, and Fluxus, and video art—and it all somehow produced a thing called installation art. And nobody really knew what to call this new thing. It developed, and it grew, and it would be foolish to ignore the coming into existence of the installation art. You walk into the Tate Modern and there is a whole floor full of them. On the other hand, now when the installation art has swallowed video and film and sculpture and painting and everything else, I meet more and more, very young usually, people, in New York, Paris, and wherever I go, who are interested in returning to the very basis of their arts—canvas, paint, music with no electricity, and no mixing of any kind. . . . Dance, just pure movement, just body in movement, with no theatrics. . . . At some point you have to go back to the very essence: what is really music, what is really painting, what is really cinema, poetry, etc. Installation artists now are very happy, they have been recognized, they are in the center of practically every museum, they have no problems, nobody attacks them. So now other artists can return to the innocent essence of their arts. . . .

We have here, at Anthology, a young man, Gregory Zucker; he's seventeen. I just had a screening of his first five films. They are all black and white, and silent, very short film poems. Very beautiful. Very sensitive. Just playing with light and darkness. And he's not interested in DVD or video or TV. He's just using his 16mm camera that he found in his father's closet.[1] And there are many such young people everywhere. And they know each other, they exchange films. The avant-garde cinema today is no longer local: it's international. There used to be American avant-garde, French avant-garde. Now it's international. Not long ago we sent a program of avant-garde cinema to Moscow. On that program there were films by young Irish, Japanese, American, Lithuanian, Russian filmmakers. At one or other time, they all worked at Anthology, as interns, or students.

SB: This happens also in Colorado. At the University I get students from Korea, Ireland, and they are not interested in Hollywood, they come to study with me and Phil Solomon.

JM: And very young, they are all between seventeen and twenty-five. So the avant-garde is alive.

SB: But they have no outlets, essentially, except for Anthology here, and the Millennium, and the Monday night shows at MOMA. On the West Coast they have Pacific Film Archives and the cinematheque.

JM: I have one personal question. Now, when you look back at the fifty years of your filmmaking—say, you are being expelled to some godforsaken island and you have a choice to take with you some of your own films. Which ones would you take?

SB: I'd say, the *Book of Family*. Marie Nesthus helped me to define what actually are the chapters that would make up the *Book of Family*: *Scenes from Under Childhood*; *Sincerity* and the *Duplicity* series, the *Weir Falcon Saga*, and *Tortured Dust*. So there are fifteen hours or twenty hours of film. So that's one. And I have to take also a very short one because it's my very favorite, and it's the untitled film, and in parentheses it says "for Marilyn." Eight-minute film. Also the *Text of Light* and *Dog Star Man*. And then, I'd probably surprise a lot of people, with this, but I think I'd take the *Trilogy* which was the first real breakthrough of hand-painted film that wasn't related to music, and that includes three films, *I Take These Truths*, *We Hold This*, and *I* . . . and that permits me to include all the *Ellipses* films of which six now. But those are ones that are just scratched on film, film scratching and painting and printing. So that would be my list of the moment. But what about you?

JM: I would take *Walden*, *Reminiscences of a Journey to Lithuania*, and my very latest which you haven't seen yet, *As I Was Moving Ahead Occasionally I Saw Brief Glimpses of Beauty*.

SB: This has to be one of those archetypical titles of Jonas Mekas. I salute you for that one. [the sound of wine glasses clinked] Remember, when we were choosing the name Anthology Film Archives, we thought that it should be Anthology, without the article "The," because there will be other anthologies. It's such a sadness when I say that, because ours was the only one. No one else attempted to do this. And we assumed that there will be many, that they would contradict the list we were making and would set up a dialogue.

JM: No, that didn't happen.

SB: Didn't happen.

JM: You see, we were the only ones who were crazy. Same as Andy Warhol was making his films, *Sleep*, *Screen Tests*. I thought, and I wrote so in the *Village Voice*, that the time will come when everybody will be making film portraits, because it's so easy. But it did not happen. Nobody imitated Andy. They cannot imitate or repeat Warhol, they cannot repeat or imitate Dreyer, or you. If they try you immediately see that it's some kind of academic imitation. So all those things happen only once. And that's the beauty of it. All those things that you are doing, or others are doing, they happen only once.

SB: That's also the great truth. I have come to an age when mostly I say, "I don't know." That's what passes for wisdom. Some few things I do know. Not going into politics, I'll just say, one thing I know is that there's no two people on earth alike, who at any moment are going through anything that they have ever gone through before or ever could again; that all their cells are as unique as snowflakes are. One just with a piece of black velvet and the magnifying glass could give themselves a thrill of that because there are only about five forms of snowflakes, and I have never been able to find two that were alike. And I've done a lot of searching.

JM: But the interesting thing is, that despite the fact that every snowflake has its own shape, if you go beyond the shape, you'll find that beyond every snowflake there is water . . . H_2O. . . . Somewhere they all meet. . . . And somewhere we all meet. . . . When some people call me an independent, I usually say, no, no, I depend on so many things.

I depend on all my friends, I depend on all of my past, what I read, all the poets, living and dead, and I don't know what it means to be really independent. Is there such a thing?

SB: Gertrude Stein said that there are those who are independent dependents, and those who are dependent independents . . . [they laugh]

JM: Here is a place for a joke. Real life joke. Pip Chodorov told me this. His father had a TV program, and he was sent to film Ezra Pound. So he spent maybe three weeks in Rapollo with Ezra Pound, and filmed, but Ezra never said a single word the entire time. Last day, before Chodorov left, they all sat around a table loaded with food, ready for a last meal. And then Ezra Pound spoke: "If you don't feel like eating, you don't have to eat," he said. That was it. When Chodorov went back to New York and told this to his literary friends, they were amazed. "Man," they said, "he said to you more than to any of us."

Now, I want to talk to you, Dear Readers of *Vogue* magazine.

Dear readers: we have amongst us some of the greatest artists that this art, called cinema, motion pictures, kinema, has ever produced. Stan Brakhage. Or Ken Jacobs. Kenneth Anger. Nobody else will ever do what they are doing. So we better . . . we should love them and help them, and take care of them and cinema. I don't know how to put it but these are such unique achievements of the human spirit. These are fragments of paradise on earth.

SB: This is really that side of you that could not stand to see what you cared for and loved and respected just shuffled aside; that you deeply felt you needed to speak for and save them and preserve them, you know. It's true. Again, no one else will ever do a film journal like you do.

JM: Since some of this conversation will be printed in *Vogue* magazine, which is a very nice popular publication, a magazine for the people, I would like to say something, and Stan will also say something on this, and that is, that I think it's a very unfortunate mistake to think that what the avant-garde filmmakers are doing is something very far out, not for every day, something just for the very, very few, and absolutely not something for the *Vogue* magazine readers. Our lives, or the strangeness of our lives, may be of some interest: but not our work. But I think that our work, our films are universal. Poetry is universal. Not exception, but the rule, so to speak. It's not for some particular, special person: It's for everybody.

Sometimes, in the evening, someone, be it a reader of *Vogue* or some esoteric publication, I can imagine you sitting down by yourself. There is a silence, TV is off, you relax, you pick up a volume of poetry, and you read. And I believe that many readers of *Vogue* magazine do that. And there is no difference reading a Sylvia Plath volume and seeing a film by Stan Brakhage or Maya Deren or Bruce Conner.

SB: Of course, the film is more difficult to see, than just pick up a book. But I hope that the technology will eventually make it possible to bring film into the homes with the minimum of distortion, or close enough to what film is.

JM: I wonder sometimes where such ideas come from, I mean, that the avant-garde, or Poetic Cinema is difficult, that it ruins your eyes, etc., etc.

SB: College professors do it. Because I never had any trouble with Hollywood at all ever. I never had any meanness or misunderstanding. Most of them look at your work, look at my work, and appreciate it.

JM: In schools, they teach poetry, they teach Faulkner, or Proust, in the same classes where they teach Pound and Olson and Millay, or Trakl. In literature that kind of separation does not exist.

SB: But there is a kind of professor that knows that if he or she books Hollywood movies only, and praises them as the epitome of film, that they will be popular. They will have huge classes and they will be very popular and they'll secure their tenures.
JM: Now, our dear readers, it's time for another joke. Real life joke. P. Adams Sitney told me this. When he first began teaching at Princeton, some ten years ago or so, he walked into the auditorium of for his first class in film history. He was amazed to see some four hundred people. He was used only to see some twenty or thirty at Cooper Union. So he begins his class. And as he talks he begins to see a strange phenomenon: it seems as if all students are looking somewhere away from him, to some side corner. Eventually he focuses on the corner, and he notices, that Brooke Shields is one of his students. . . . He was sort of crushed by this event. But, he says, Brooke proved to be one of his best and most serious students. Four hundred students enlisted in his avant-garde film class to see Brooke Shields.

SB: I don't care anymore. I fought very hard for certain words. I was mean at times. And I was mean to you and other people. We were all mean to each other; at certain periods we fought so valiantly for our beliefs, like knights riding against each other, you know, with a lance of words. You used to accuse me of rolling big huge boulders down from Colorado mountains. . . .
JM: Hoping that they would reach us and crush us. [both laugh]

SB: So you were right in that sense, I didn't need to worry so much. I wish, if I could achieve the perfect, it would be that you could put fairly on my tombstone Tennessee Williams's theme that goes through all his plays: Nothing Human Disgusts Me Except Deliberate Cruelty. Several things still disgust me, besides deliberate cruelty, but I'd like to achieve that at the end. And I want that to imbue my work. Whatever it is, I still continue, I am mostly painting now on film, and that is really all what I can afford. I can afford only a few photographed films. Mostly I paint, and it takes a long time to make twenty-four individual frames for every second.
JM: My own diaristic style came very much from the fact that I had no time and money to make a scripted, "conventional" film. I had only bits of time and bits of film. So instead or making films, I just filmed. I sometimes joke, I say I am not really a filmmaker: I am only a filmer. To make a film, to be a filmmaker, you first have to have some idea what you want to do, to see a certain shape of your film. But that's not what I do. I film real life. I never know what will come next. There is never an a priori idea or shape to my films: the shape emerges from the accumulation

of material itself. I'm obsessed with filming. I go through my life with my Bolex camera. My Bolex and me. And I have to film. Here is a question for you. Let's take a film you did in Canada, *The God of Day Has Gone Upon Him.*

Did you see in your mind its shape when you began it, or did that shape develop as you went along?

SB: I knew from the beginning that that was the third part of a trilogy. Now I think it's a quartet, but it's the third part that goes with *Child's Garden* and the *Serious Sea*, and the *Mammals of Victoria*. The title comes from Charles Dickens's *David Copperfield*. This was the first summer we went back to this place on Vancouver Island where Marilyn, my wife, comes from and was raised, to the ocean. I still was hairless—most of my hair was gone from the chemotherapy, I had come very close to death. So I was in the mode to see that ocean in relationship to the end, or to the night, or to the darkness. My head was filled with things like Rothko's old age paintings, you know, like the Houston Chapel, or . . .

JM: They have a very beautiful Rothko room now at the Tate Modern in London. You go through all the clutter and then you lay down in that room and you rest your eyes and your body and your mind.

SB: That's true. That Houston Chapel, it saved my sanity. I was there for six weeks teaching, and I went almost every day to this Chapel. Also Braque, the old age Braque, the real brown period, with the wooden plow, and that whole series of Braque's very old age paintings. I felt old like that, I had expected to die, and I still expect to die any moment, because of chemotherapy.

JM: I just wanted to know for myself, if you had any idea, a feeling of the shape before you began filming it because to make a film, a filmmaker is one who already at the very beginning of making the film sees its shape more or less. But I never have that. Never. I am just a filmer. Because it's life. I don't know what the next moment will bring, or when I will want to film.

SB: But you're such a stylist. You know that it all hangs together. You know I called you the Samuel Pepys of film because you're a stylist in that sense.

JM: Yes, but the style and the techniques come from this procedure, that I am dealing with the real life from moment to moment and instantaneously. I keep telling, that the difference between Bolex and a video camera, say Sony, is that when I see something that I want to film, an expression, say, I can catch it with my Bolex within two seconds. But a video camera, you have to first connect the power, that takes two or three seconds; then you press the button, that takes another one or two—by that time the subtle moment that I wanted to catch is gone. All I get, on video, is after-events.

SB: Do you ever think about money?
JM: I never think about money.

SB: I knew you'd say that. [laughs]
JM: But I should tell you something that you may not yet know. You see that space next to this building? It belongs to Anthology Film Archives. That's where we are going to build a library for our paper materials; it will cost us three million and a half. But I am not worrying about it. In this building we have the largest collection of paper materials on avant-garde/independent cinema. So we have to make them available, and we have to protect them. So there is a necessity to build this library. And therefore, I know it will happen, it will be built. I do not have any doubts about it. All it takes is to believe in it, and work, work, work. . . .

Notes

1. Editor's Note: Mekas is speaking about the editor of this volume. The cameras actually belonged to my grandfather, Dr. Jan Jakob Smulewicz, a prominent New York–based radiologist.

Jonas Mekas in Conversation

Raimund Abraham / 2003

From *The Brooklyn Rail*, Winter 2003. Reprinted by permission of the Estate of Jonas Mekas.

Jonas Mekas: I think I need to make an introduction to this conversation. We are here on the roof of a building at 32 Second Avenue. Formerly a courthouse, now it is Anthology Film Archives' headquarters. The occasion for this conversation is our need to construct adjacent to this building—in a space that is twelve feet by one hundred feet—a library for our paper materials, of which we have a lot. The library would house fifty years of history, that part which is on paper, of independent/avant-garde film in the United States. Actually, one could say, internationally. We have engaged Raimund Abraham to design and supervise the construction of the library which we decided to call the "Heaven and Earth Library" in honor of Harry Smith because the library will house a large collection of Harry Smith's materials, the music records, the books, the paintings.

Raimund Abraham: We met in '65, when you were still up on Forty-Second or Forty-First Street?
JM: Forty-First Street.

RA: Then I witnessed that Anthology moved to different places. I always felt that moving from one place to another enforced the spirit of the Underground, which you represented. With the acquisition of the Courthouse that odyssey came to an end and it became more or less permanent. I think that the library would be morally enforcing that permanency.
JM: I agree with your perception of the development of our journey through various spaces.

RA: Despite the fact that you became permanent, you remained outside of the support system of cultural institutions. For example, the Museum of Moving Images, in Queens, gets heavy financial support from everywhere, and you were still struggling despite the decision that you were becoming permanent. It didn't really affect your continued struggle for survival.

JM: Anthology Film Archives deals with a very uncommercial aspect of cinema. The emphasis in what we show and what we preserve and what we support is cinema of avant-garde persuasion. There is no money in it. And the way I see it, the avant-garde film will remain outside of the commercial interests. No one is buying it, the screenings are limited, and the support is practically nonexistent. But I don't see this as something bad: I think it helps us to remain poets.

RA: My challenge as an architect is not only to respect your independence and your status of being outside of the whole cinema system. I would not be interested in just making an addition to that building. What intrigued me the most was the gap between the courthouse and the neighboring building. The gap is eleven feet wide, which would be considered by any professional architect unusable. In that context the metaphor of heaven and earth almost become literally implemented because you have the gap. You start out with a very compressed dark space, earthbound, and then you reach up to the sky to heaven. And then you start to embrace the buildings, so I don't see it as building an addition, but I see it as an independent element that embraces the old building. That is what really interests me in this respect. But I actually wanted to start out by asking you a question. When did you start wearing hats?

JM: Very, very early. When I was a child my uncle was studying in Switzerland and Germany, and every summer when he used to come back, and I was five or six, he used to always bring back hats as presents. They were white straw hats usually. The hat was always there in my childhood. Then somewhere in 1960, I began wearing hats myself—it's part of me now, and I like it.

RA: The first hat that I wore was the hat of my grandfather, which I remember was a black hat. I remember it more like an American hat. It was much bigger than hats are now. So hats became for me not only just wearing something, but became like an object of my own history. I have fifteen hats at home that I don't wear anymore, but I know at what time I was wearing them. The most traumatic experience that I had was a hat of my father's. When I was in the subway going to Brooklyn, I was reading, and I put it down on the bench, and then I left, and I realized that I left my hat. I turned around and saw my hat on the bench, and then the door closed, and the subway took the hat away.

JM: [*laughter*]

RA: When you wear a hat, it changes your perception. Brecht wrote this beautiful poem, "Above us are the clouds, the clouds belong to our world, above the clouds

is nothing." The hat is like the lowering of the heavens because the rim becomes your horizon of vision. It has a certain weight.
JM: Sometimes I feel strange when I am walking in a huge crowd and I am the only one who has a hat!

RA: If you go into a church, you have to take your hat down.
JM: Of course.

RA: In the Judaic tradition the worshipers have to wear their hats to protect the sacredness of the temple. I have a very funny story: Carlo Scarpa, an Italian architect and one of my heroes is an independent architect who built very little. He was always in debt, and he never had any money. And when the tax collectors for the fifth time removed the furniture from his house, he decided to cast it in concrete. Coming back to the hat story. During my first visit, I had to find the key-keeper, a local farmer in the nearby village. Entering the old cemetery, we both took our hats off. After he unlocked the gate to the Scarpa cemetery, he immediately puts his hat back on. This monumental, but simple gesture was a manifestation of a precise but subconscious critique of design versus architecture, beauty versus the tradition of burial.

So now we are stuck with the hat. . . . Did you know that Richard Serra always obsessively and in my opinion trivially claims that architecture is not an art because it has to be used? So now I think you and I are very similar in our rejection of the term "art" because you always say that you are a filmer and not a filmmaker, and I always say that I am a worker in the discipline of architecture and it's no concern of mine if I am an artist or not. And what about Hegel's definition of Architecture as the mother of the arts? What about "Baukunst"?
JM: I make films. My objection is to the overuse of the term "artist."

RA: We reject that because the term "art" has been abused in our time. On the other hand it does exist in our time like beauty, truth.
JM: I would ask Richard Serra to talk about what he means by function/use.

RA: He permits himself to be used when he puts sculptures in a gallery where he controls the space or he puts it in front of a stupid office building. He blames the stupidity of the office building made by a bad professional architect, so it generates his hatred of professional architects.
JM: I think that he defended his sculpture, downtown, called "Tilted Arc," that it performed a function there, that it was necessary in that space. So what does the term usage or function mean? Music also performs a certain function also in developing our sensibilities and keeping us together. Like various work songs, folk songs.

RA: It is very true that architecture in that sense is more difficult than any other discipline in the arts, to reach that level of abstraction because you have to think about a toilet and the most trivial functional supports. But you can also make a toilet that has sacredness; the toilet in my house in Mexico is a toilet that is a chapel.

JM: A Japanese writer, Tanizaki wrote a little book, a beautiful essay, *In Praise of Shadows*, exactly about Japanese toilets.

RA: Ah, yes I know this book, but I lost it!

JM: I bought a few of them and I am giving them to friends.

RA: You gave me the one I lost.

JM: Yes. But all this talk today about music as art, poetry, literature as art, fiction . . . I think this art business should temporarily be thrown out the window.

RA: I know!

JM: Then Richard Serra wouldn't have to attack architecture anymore. He will accept it as he accepts poetry, music, or sculpture.

RA: I said so many times that I was not only inspired by, but was lucky to have met Kubelka in Vienna in the sixties, who at the time was the most radical film-maker for rejecting almost anything that would be considered a deviation from the principles of cinema. I discovered that, got the strength to become independent, realizing that what I needed was a piece of paper and pencil to make architecture, as you needed a camera to make film without being a director or cutter. I am always amazed by looking at the end of a Hollywood film how many people are involved in making a film.

JM: It's the same as in music; you could be just one performer, a violinist, or part of an orchestra. There are different varieties of music. I don't deny a place for Spielberg in cinema. The same in architecture: you can build a house for one person, one family, or a cathedral.

RA: But on the other hand, if we reject this idea of art, the fact is that all the different languages and all the different disciplines of the arts are based on syntactic foundation. There is a principle that we all respect. You edit your film; you are fully aware of how you structure your film, as I am fully aware of how to translate an ideal geometrical condition into a building. The only interesting thing to me is when you take Peter Kubelka, let's say of the four films he made, in particular the first three, where he is preaching the principle, the essence of his films. It is so interesting to me that the same principle being used by Hollywood is what independent film discovered years ago. You pack in two thousand images into half a minute, which was rejected thirty years ago because people said they couldn't see it.

JM: But that was true, they couldn't see it. People have been completely trained to see it only in the last thirty years. Technology, computers, movements, speeds all around us. They are able to see it now; they were not able to see it thirty years ago.

RA: But because they didn't respect when it was shown as independent cinema. Now they believe Hollywood as they believe newspapers. In a way the Eskimos (who was this guy in the sixties that wrote *The Hidden Dimension*?) could not be deceived. They could see every single frame because their eyes are trained in a complete white world so any black dot becomes a sensational perception. What the eye can see is what you want to see.

JM: They've been trained. Their visual perception has changed and has been trained over the past thirty or so years. The children grow up with video games. It's completely changed their perception. It's very natural. As in literature what some of the poets did in the beginning of the century in poetry has come now into prose, into fiction. It is part of literature.

RA: It is very important that the principles of any discipline of the arts will have to disappear when your work is complete, that means that you are fully aware of those principles while you work but they cannot dominate.

JM: I am not so sure that I am aware of principles. When I was working on my last film, everything came out of the material I was working with. I didn't care about any principles. It developed its own principles. Principles are there to just leave them alone and go somewhere else. Nothing is there forever.

RA: I am always suspicious of work when the underlying principle becomes obvious. The famous Austrian writer Thomas Bernhard could have written only one book instead of ten. When the same principle is recognizable dominating the work it becomes style, but, according to George Kubler, "style" is like a rainbow. We can see it only briefly while we pause between the sun and the rain, and it vanishes when we go to the place where we thought we saw it.

JM: You can see the same principles in all of his works, same as you can see certain principles in mine, but that doesn't mean that those same principles can be applied to the work of anybody else.

RA: But in your work, your principles are much harder to identify. I think that is where work becomes mysterious. In a way, architecture is much more obvious because you have geometry and you have to deal with geometry; without dealing with geometry you cannot make architecture. But if geometry would start to dominate your work, it would lose all its power. It almost like the same as Gertrude Stein said, "A rose is a rose is a rose." And you can say, "A square is a square is a square." Only if you confront that square with material—steel, concrete, brick—then the challenge of that ideal determines its transformation into architecture.

JM: What is the basic principle of using this space (the library) and knowing that this will be a library?

RA: Any compressed space is at an advantage for me because I always want to reduce.

JM: You had a challenging space on Fifty-Second Street also.

RA: It was twenty-five feet. This is half the size. For me any idea that I have about architecture does not originate from an idea of buildings. I hate buildings. It originates from my reading of the place. Heidegger had a very beautiful term as an etymologist rather than as a philosopher; he discovered that "Ort" in German— there is no real actual equivalent word in English—it's neither site nor place. "Ort" originates from the tip of a lance. The tip of a lance, you can put it in the sun and it reflects the light or you can turn it around and mark a place, conquer a place by putting the lance in the ground. It is a new understanding of "Ort," of that place, that generates my ideas.

A library is also for me a book. The mystery of a book is not what's written in a book, it's that the pages touch each other. Mallarme had this idea about an infinite book where he could read in any direction. All the letters in the book touch each other, it's invisible, it's inside, it's folded inside. This for me is an ideal space, where there is compression like in a book. Only half of the space will actually be accessible, the rest of it will be a void where you can look all the way up and all the way down to the sky and the whole wall will have books, artworks. And then when it reaches the light, the heaven, it embraces the whole building and then you have there more generous spaces for exhibitions or readings. I wanted it to be reaching out like a hand over the old building, and from the street you can start to see it having useful projections, for lettering whatever you want to use. It is two stories up. There is not much more to say about the library. We should have actually brought the model. It's the way that you and I live; it is a spontaneous environment that we live in, and Anthology is more or less like that. It has a personal feeling that there is stuff all over the place. Now when you make architecture, architecture is more fragile than any other discipline; you can violate it really easily. For the user there has to be a certain respect for the architecture. There is a conflict between spontaneous use and architecture. Maybe not everything needs to be architecture.

JM: You are designing a structure that will have a very specific purpose.

RA: Exactly. It is going to be very specific; the more minimal a space becomes the more fragile it becomes. This is the last building I want to build.
JM: Like Chaplin would say after every film, "That is the last film that I am going to do."

RA: I always had the courage to say no to a project that didn't interest me. All my life, I never went after a job so to speak in professional terms. Right now after giving ten years to a building, I feel exhausted and don't want to get involved with a job of that magnitude. There is my own house in Mexico in construction and the library here. That is like building a house for friends, it's personal. You are not a client. You are my friend, a hero of mine in terms of what you make. That is intimate. I don't consider that part of my statement. If someone said, build a skyscraper uptown, I would say no, maybe [*laughs*]. The issue in our time is not what can be built but what should be built.
JM: I am running Anthology Film Archives and in order not to go crazy I make my films on the side because Anthology is a major museum. What we have at Anthology—imagine if you would have all the Picassos, all the Braques, all Giacomettis, all Brancusis in one place. At Anthology we have all that! Nobody realizes this.

RA: What Kulbelka always told me is that he was always so jealous about sculpture or architecture because it is physical, you can touch it, and somehow you can talk about permanency and eternity. But film is so fragile—you have a little celluloid that you have to protect against aging and so forth. So it is a very fragile art.
JM: Everything falls to dust.

RA: We have to both get involved in the professional world, you in the Anthology Film Archives and I when I build a building. But when I build, I depend on every bricklayer, ironworker, carpenter. When I draw, and only then, I can claim to be an independent architect. And this dependence on others to implement your work is maybe the most crucial difference between built architecture and any discipline of the arts. Palladio made woodcuts. He published four books where all these ideas where manifested. He did not have to make working drawings; he took some of the ideal prototypes and then built them. He just made drawings that showed the ideal geometric proportions. The builder knew how to build it, and on the side he would make adjustments. When you do that here you have a lawsuit. The circumstances have become so severe against architecture that that's why there are so few architects because there are so few who can resist those forces. That's politics.
JM: The idea to build a library became a necessity when we could not practically move through our basement filled with boxes of collections of paper materials that keep coming from film historians, from estates, etc. The scholars come and want

to see the papers, but they are not accessible. There are boxes and boxes of them in the basement, not available to visitors. We have to make those materials available before time begins to destroy them. They must be properly stored under proper conditions. We have the largest collection of paper materials on avant-garde film, and it's not available. It's rotting there in the basement.

RA: You have the richest country in the world, and they let it rot.

JM: So there is this urgent necessity. I don't know how much it will cost, and I have no idea how the money will come. But when there is a necessity someone will come, and will help, and the library will be built. Actually the idea of the library was always there, ever since we acquired the building in 1977.

RA: You had to overcome incredible obstacles just to acquire the building. Everybody said impossible, forget it.

JM: If I would begin to worry about what I do, I would never get anything done.

RA: There's hope, and hope and despair are inseparable.

JM: I don't have hope. In the past, my projects never failed because I never undertook any unnecessary projects. Never did anything that someone else could do. This is something that I know only I can do, or more correctly in this case: something that we can do together. Nobody else would ever do it. I know we have to do it, so it will be done.

"Fragments of Paradise . . .": A Conversation with Jonas Mekas

Michael J. Thompson / 2004

From *Logos: A Journal of Modern Society and Culture*, Spring 2019. Reprinted by permission.

Editor's Introduction: The following interview was conducted by the editor of Logos: A Journal of Modern Society and Culture *in 2004 at Anthology Film Archives in New York City. It was published online in spring 2019 following Mekas's death.*

Michael J. Thompson: As I was preparing for this interview, I was going through some of your older writings, some of your diaries, and I came across something that you wrote back in the 1960s and you wrote: "The official cinema all over the world is running out of breath, is morally corrupt, aesthetically obsolete, thematically superficial, temperamentally boring." Today, isn't it the same situation?

Jonas Mekas: One could use the same rhetoric, I guess, today. I mean, let's face it, it was, shall I say, not a clash but a rebellious attitude of those who were just coming in directed against those who were there and established, so those kinds of statements were the incoming powers and were never 100 percent rational or just. They're just in the context of the time, I mean, emotional, they're not necessarily rational. Today, well, you could say that about cinema but one could say that about all of the arts all over the world. You see, that's why one thing you could find in the New York of the 1960s in the world a very concentrated, very emotional, very, very intense groups of people that stood out and everybody noticed. If you look today, they were times when one would say, "This place is the capital of the arts," but New York really was in the sixties and seventies and everyone was looking at it from other continents also as the center of something exciting happening there, as the capital of the arts.

You cannot say that today, there is no visible, intense movement in any city in any country so in that sense one could apply what I said that the breath has run out of, the enthusiasm, there is no great temperament visible anywhere. But the reasons may be different. I think the reasons are that the world, because of the sciences, communication technologies have become more unified in a sense, so it's dissipated. Admittedly something happens here, something there, say in Tokyo, in Melbourne, in São Paulo. They begin to dress the same way, buy the same shoes, so it's this democratization. The negative, I'd say they're the negative effects of democratization. . . .

MJT: And globalization . . .
JM: And globalization, which we did not have then.

MJT: But you did have, if not a global kind of sensibility, you still had an avant-garde movement that had some kind of affinities with one another in places like Germany, France, New York, Japan. There were still painters and writers, even surrealism or abstract expressionism. . . .
JM: It was like, to us in 1960, that was history, that was past, not present. As far as the present was going, in New York, in America there was the avant-garde, or experimental film by some twenty people, not much more than twenty, and we knew everybody, and then there was Hollywood. Of course there was developing something else in between like thirty-five independents and feature lengths, so that's it. So, French realists, that was in Europe and long ago; Dadaism, that was maybe thirty-some years ago in 1960, maybe thirty-five—that was history. It's difficult for me to sometimes put—I mean, when I begin to think that what we did was thirty-five, forty years ago, that's history.

MJT: That's interesting, because it seems to me, when I look back at the twentieth century and I put New York avant-garde or underground film movement in some kind of context, what I think of is dates like 1908, 1916, Stravinsky's *Rite of Spring*, Schoenberg's music, the poetry of Celan in the 1950s, but in every case it seems to me the avant-garde was supposed to break with what you just described—conformity. The avant-garde was trying in some way to break through commodification. . . .
JM: That's what between 1955 and 1965, the artists, filmmakers, were doing and that's how we felt. That's why we started *Film Culture* magazine, and it's there that John Cage at the beginning comes in and the Happening theater and the music there, beginning '58, '59, and there you begin to see that and they were all doing something opposite, something completely different, not rebelling but you could call it rebellion. Or literature, I mean, when Allen called the poets of the first anthology "The New American Poets."

MJT: Allen Ginsberg?
JM: No, Allen is the last name, Donald Allen. Allen was the editor of the anthology

for "The New American Poets," and that's where I took the New American Cinema. As a guess, there is a new American poet, but there is also a new American cinema. The "new" meant they were really breaking out, there were all the others but "we are the new," these are the new and it was a really ground-breaking anthology.

MJT: So now there's nothing new because . . . ?
JM: There must be something new. . . .

MJT: Maybe there's something new, but there's no movement . . .
JM: No, there's no book that becomes suddenly or slowly visible, and they would speak for themselves, and everybody would write articles you know in all the papers like they did in the sixties, but there was Warhol, there was the underground. I mean, there were always headlines. . . .

MJT: So you mean there's nothing sensational?
JM: Now maybe they made it into sensation, but we did not do it for sensational reasons.

MJT: But it became sensational to the outside.
JM: Maybe rappers come closest to it. In painting there is nothing, there is nothing, nothing exciting. There was something happening in the installation art which of course goes back to the sixties, but there was nothing there exciting either. Now, is there any visible excitement in literature at this point? I haven't heard about it, maybe on the internet, maybe there is something. They would probably say we are now a different civilization, different technologies, and we are looking for excitement in the wrong places. I'd say that is a possibility. Even those who were not of the same generation made all those exciting things in the sixties; even the older generation noticed it, and they were looking into it, rejecting, accepting, or criticizing, but there was nothing of "okay, I'm in a different generation, I'm trying to search, I'm not a doctor, I don't see it." Maybe things are happening in the sciences and maybe in music. There's a lot of activity in music, I think.

MJT: What about, you mentioned before different civilizations . . . what about literature and film that's coming out of cultures that are outside of the West, say Asia or Africa, Latin America. I mean, this may not be anything formally experimental, but is there something new there?
JM: As far as I know it's not happening in South America. I think Africa in music, according to some people who I have been following, African music was very exciting twenty years ago. Now some of them became so successful that they became commercial. So in independent cinema, in the avant-garde, like when I go to Paris

as I've been for the last five years it's been much more exciting than New York, much more. And it was very close to the excitement that existed in the New York in the early sixties; they have their own lab developing, and all are not unimportant all over France. So, in publication there are many more books and various other publications that come out in Europe, France especially. But in New York, in the United States, there's not much published here at all.

MJT: What about some of the other things that you've written about that I've seen for decades, that I've noticed you've picked out time and time again. Is identifying Hollywood as this kind of institutional and cultural problem, because of the problem of commodification—now my question is, has the avant-garde maybe, or parts of the avant-garde been taken up into the machine, into the commodification machine? I mean, Greg and I were talking before, and he mentioned how you could have a shower curtain with Jackson Pollock on it, I mean you could have a Mondrian's work become . . .
JM: The closest that the avant-garde has come to is—I think that in principle it can never become a commodity. It's the same as poetry can never become as popular as prose. They cannot exploit it. It's unexploitable. Criterion Collection issued a package on DVD, so it's more accessible. They packaged Joseph Cornell, because Cornell is known as an artist. He has much wider appeal, but those are exceptions.

MJT: Okay, that's an exception, but does the whole phenomenon of DVDs for example, does that lead to the destruction of the experience of film?
JM: In the sixties when they came out with the original, they came out with Super 8; everybody thought that now we can make copies everyone will buy and that will be cheap and that included Warhol, it included everybody. We made some copies, nothing happened, there was just an excitement and after a few months we realized. . . . when video came then again some filmmakers thought that now we can put it all over the world. In a sense, some of these films cannot be put on video; they lose their color and entertainment. Now DVDs rectify this a little bit, they approximate the original.

MJT: Well, we're sitting here in Anthology Film Archives where people come to experience these films in a group setting. . . .
JM: If seven people come to see Brakhage's films, it's a big deal, and whenever I bring *Echoes of Silence*, there is always one person.

MJT: So is there any kind of social experience in seeing cinema anymore? Is that important?

JM: That is what is lacking. We can put Brakhage and some other films on DVD, but there is no network similar to that of commercial film/video network to disseminate these films. They won't put money into it. It's still expensive to produce a digital copy, and nobody wants to put that kind of money in because who will buy it? So there are limitations, very simple economic limitations. That's why the print quality is still in six hundred copies, twelve hundred copies, not twelve thousand because who will buy it? How do you promote poetry? I think that there are certain dramas, certain arts that are more limited in appeal because they appeal to more subtle aspects of our existence, being, mind, and they cannot be promoted. They resist promotion. Promotion would destroy them. Some forms of modern contemporary dance cannot be.

MJT: I think of the music of Luciano Berio, he combines music and theater and how listening to it on DVD is impossible, you actually have to be there and experience it in an attempt to prevent commodification. Is that the case too with avant-garde film, that it just resists inherently being sucked up into the machine of commercialism?

JM: I think the language, the content of the avant-garde film, creative film does not appeal to masses. It requires a certain kind of, not education, but familiarity. You have to learn the language of film.

It's like a little joke I have. I grew up in this little Lithuanian village. At home, we spoke a local dialect, but there was already the official written Lithuanian language. So I went to the primary school, and I had to learn the official accepted Lithuanian dialect. Then, at the same time at the gymnasium, high school I guess you would say, I had to learn Latin and French. Then the Russian army rolls in and they say Latin is totally unnecessary and French is unnecessary, now you learn Russian! So we all learned Russian. And then two years later Germany comes in and the Germans occupy Lithuania and now Russian is no good, the German is good. So we begin learning German. During the War, I end up in a forced labor camp near Hamburg. I lived together with Italian war prisoners and French war prisoners, and so I think it is a good occasion to improve my German. So I begin to learn local German and there I discovered that even some Germans don't understand local German, they speak Platdeutsch. Then I begin to learn Italian and discover from talking to other Italian colleagues that I'm really learning not Sicilian but Roma dialect of Italian. And so it went until the American army comes and now we are learning English. By the time I end up in New York, I had enough of all those languages because I learned a lot of languages. Now I will learn the language of cinema. That's what I did in Germany in the displaced persons camps. My brother and I got interested in cinema because now we can talk in a language that everybody will understand. So we come to New York, we get a Bolex, and we begin to film. We went to screenings and shows. Then we begin to show our work to others, and the others say, "What is this? We don't understand you. This is not cinema." So then I realized I learned the wrong language of cinema, so now I've written on cinema in whatever language I want. That's the end of the joke.

Modern poetry was one thing in the nineteenth century. It changed with poets like Ezra Pound. Different language, different content, different film. One can be educated into something, but one has to already desire it—have an inclination—a movement towards it, otherwise there will be a block. You cannot educate somebody to read well. One has to want, one has to desire movement, then you can begin to educate. Otherwise, it's empty.

MJT: Does this reflect—this gets into a couple of different issues—I mean, say the days of Beethoven or the way Beethoven was understood and appreciated or Mozart or say even in Greece with Greek theater, the way that it was art the entire community could understand and it engaged the entire community. Is the avant-garde the result of a kind of shattered culture, fragmented? People like Adorno talking about the culture industry, kind of dividing everyone up into different groups and segments—is the avant-garde the result of this kind of aesthetic elite that's keeping alive some kind of sensibility?

JM: Maybe in the Middle Ages the elite existed only on a social level; elites were those very educated, richness also meant availability of education. I mean, in the fourteenth, fifteenth, sixteenth centuries there was a prince but this prince could also write symphonies and now wealth and social class is only money and no education. So those were times where you'd meet someone else who was maybe writing poetry that you would like or making music that you would like, you would have to go by carriage, it would take weeks to meet them or across the ocean two months. I am just thinking of all those Americans who went to Paris by boat, so it was more difficult for those little groups to emerge. I think it's much easier now. I think it has something to do with advance of civilization, communication that some groups of, say, musicians, poets begin to communicate and get together. Little special groups emerge that differ very much from the general, wider group, the accepted culture. You can call those little groups elitist. They are concentrated, intense centers of advancement in various arts.

MJT: So in that case, has the avant-garde served a function only for those who participated in it?

JM: What is the avant-garde in cinema? People say Maya Deren was a mother of the avant-garde, but she was the close to the end. She was not the beginning, she was the end. She was educated in Switzerland, in Europe, and we don't even know yet what she has seen there but she brought the tradition of the European avant-garde and she knew them all and she closes the first European avant-garde. And after that comes Markopoulos and Brakhage and all the new American avant-garde come in not only—but with a different content, a different language. It was the same with painting. De Kooning and all those guys developed a different language for painting at around the same time.

In the sixties, some filmmakers got very, very angry. Markopoulos used to say that "Television is stealing some of our techniques; we should sue them." No, the changing language becomes intellectual property of the whole culture, for everybody, all the people. You cannot legislate it, so the avant-garde, those that are really interested in poetry and cinema in the avant-garde, of course we look at those films and look again and again, and you read poetry. For all the others, only some aspects appeal. Not only television but some of the techniques have been accepted in narrative cinema, the fast cuts and sort of shorter takes. That has become part of the new language of narrative cinema. If you look at Douglas Sirk and if you look at any contemporary narrative filmmaker, I mean there's a huge influence of the avant-garde.

MJT: So the avant-garde then only wanted to change the language?

JM: No, no, for the film avant-garde I think there is different content. Brakhage maybe was the most radical. We always say he really contributed most to changing the language of cinema. When he started making his *Songs* on 8mm film, they were very different from his 16mm films. He started them because his 16mm camera was stolen. He ended up with 8mm because he was thinking about what this camera could do. What can I do because it's more impressionistic, no detail there on 8mm. As opposed to let's say fifteen hundred dots per frame, you only have one hundred dots per frame so it had to be very personal. His films showed just little reactions, little songs about himself. The technology determines the content and the form. It's very difficult to determine what came first. I think that first Brakhage had something in his mind, some idea, and then comes the question of how to do it, the form. You cannot create Brakhage's *Songs* with a 35mm camera, it. You cannot move as freely. The image is different. So I think that at the very beginning there is the content, which is a very nebulous kind of thing, you can't even describe when *Dog Star Man* was finished, you can't tell exactly what the content of that film is. There's moving, climbing, struggle—it's still very poetic.

MJT: So the avant-garde equals simply experimentation?

JM: No. This is one of my heretical statements: the avant-garde, experimental film, has nothing to do with experimentation, absolutely nothing to do with it. There is much more experimentation in Hollywood. We go to the center. When Kenneth Anger made *Fireworks*, he was driven, he knew exactly what he wanted.

The film was done, I think, in one evening, something like that. He just had to do it, and he did it as he felt he had to do it. When Stan Brakhage does something, he knows exactly what he is doing. It's like the woodworm burrowing through. The only difference is if the woodworm finds some hotspots, he goes around them, that's Manny Farber's theory. It's very natural and there's no experimentation. In Hollywood, sometimes they try this, then that. Even when the film is finished, they show it to the audience and listen to what they have to say. If the audience says, "We don't like that," they cut it out. If you cut one millimeter of a Brakhage film, it will break. There is no experimentation, there is only execution. You don't experiment when you write a poem, you just write. There's no experimentation. These are all terms imposed on this area of cinema and they don't make much sense.

MJT: So then John Cage . . .
JM: Did not experiment. He executed certain ideas.

MJT: He just thought differently, experienced the world differently.
JM: Very radically and drastically so. Experienced it for first time in a new way. Again, the literal meaning of the avant-garde is the first line, those that are first hit by the bullets.

MJT: So with the fading of the avant-garde in terms of its energy, what happens now?
JM: That means there are no great, no drastic, no new ideas that come from the spheres of arts.

MJT: And when they don't come what happens?
JM: People have become very pragmatic. Just think of the growth of the film schools, all those thousands and thousands of students who just want to go and make something in the industry. All those grants that are being given, like the Jerome Hill foundation. Hill was a friend and helped us to really make avant-garde film visible. When he died, the Foundation was taken over by practical bureaucrats, and now the Foundation is giving grants every year. I just looked at who they gave grants to; they gave I think five grants in the spring session, and there was not a single avant-garde film. One was a social documentary, one was feminist, one was something for minorities. The films have to be practical, serve the community and not antagonize anyone. These choices, I thought, showed how Jerome was betrayed by those who followed. This money exists now just to help graduating film students to make films, but not for the avant-garde.

MJT: So it's interesting you say that these films were something that had to serve the community, don't antagonize, don't be radical, don't be different.

JM: It's like this: to apply for a grant for instance, you have to know what you're doing, what the film is called, this and that. How can one who is doing a poem with a camera submit it? So, they have the grants. Okay, I want a grant, but I cannot tell you myself what my film will be. It may just be a failure. Give me a grant because of my past achievements, trust me. That's how it should be. The Jerome Hill Foundation for instance should change their guidelines completely. They should give grants based on past achievement, not because someone is able to write an interesting presentation.

MJT: This gets into the issue of technology and how this impacts form. This impacts the artistic impulse. Wouldn't the inexpensive growth of digital film, editing equipment, and the fact that you can do all this work on the computer make it easier for those people who are up and coming?

JM: But it was always easy. It was always easy and difficult. The classic body of the American avant-garde between 1945 and 1970 was created without grants or support. The American avant-garde was created without the grant system establishment. The fact that something was easier makes no difference. It actually just makes it easier for all the bad work. It increases the production of bad cinema. It should be difficult. It should be a little bit difficult, that it takes an effort. You really have to want to make a film so that you put an effort. You slave to get some money, you go and steal the camera, steal the film and that's how it has been done. And when everything becomes easy then nothing is important.

MJT: There's a line that I picked out from Walter Benjamin, and it says "A magician and surgeon compare to painter and cameraman. The painter maintains in his work an actual distance from reality, a camera penetrates deeply into its web." There's something unique about cinema as opposed to other arts.

JM: But I don't see such a difference. The painter penetrates into reality and most of the filmmakers remain on the surface. I mean, I think he was too enthusiastic. He got carried away talking about cinema.

MJT: But isn't there something about movement, dynamism, isn't there something about that? You have centuries and centuries of painting, but there's something so dynamic about film itself.

JM: Yeah, but there are some who say there have been moving images for thousands of years in development. We're talking about surface and penetration. I mean Jung and Freud are working around the same time that cinema emerges. Jung, you could say, would say that you can tell everything from the surface and Freud will say you can tell everything from the dreams. Jung is dealing with the surface and the symbols that are expressed. Freud is penetrating deeper.

MJT: Can I bring up something you told me about when you were talking about your own films? In another interview, while discussing your diary films, you said you weren't merely recording events, but that just by virtue of your approach through the camera you were actually changing the event.

JM: There was a period when I was still following the old language of documentary film. I filmed in longer little cuts, takes of five seconds, ten seconds. At some point, it did not satisfy me. I had to break down reality. I had to introduce myself into it. When I film, *I* am looking at something. *I* have to look at that specific thing. There's a reason why I'm filming it now and the object has to reflect that reason, otherwise it will be just a thing out there. I have to introduce myself by breaking it down into single frames and by changing light varieties and speeds. That introduces the state I was in when I wanted to film it. So in other words I'm filming the tree but still I'm putting myself, merging myself with it so that you see the state I was in when I perceived it.

MJT: So why is it important to do that?

JM: For years I filmed the snow, snowing and snow, and I was always unhappy. I kept something going, the same subject until I thought, "Ahh, I've got it, this is what I feel, this is what I feel when I see snow." So, it's not just straight filming. It's filming in a certain way, merging myself with the subject and the instrument that I'm using. Of course, what I'm filming is my memories. There's some reason, and I don't know that reason, but it comes from the past. I will give you one anecdote: I used to visit Richard Foreman some summers. We would drive and look for the places where we could stop. We would drive around for sometimes half an hour, and nothing would appeal to us. I realized that we were looking for places that seemed familiar, but that meant that we were not discovering anything new. We were only stopping because it was familiar to our memories or dreams. So, we decided that we would use our watches and decide to randomly stop at fixed times no matter what. We eliminated memory and familiarity and had a great time. You stop and discover something new and different. Very often we just keep relying on memory.

MJT: So why is that important?

JM: I just have no choice. It's like an obsession. That's how I am, I just have to. I admire poets like Jackson Mac Low, that period where he was very mathematical. He had a system. His feelings, memories, emotions are bracketed. I don't know if you are familiar with what he did in the sixties, seventies in his poetry. He applied mathematical systems to his poetry. It's totally mechanical but it's great. I don't do that. I guess my past has something to do with it. I was so rooted in my village, so much in my community when I grew up. I was so deep in it that, when I was uprooted by the War, I was pulled away from it so abruptly. To tell the truth, only now am I beginning to come to a point where I'm a little bit more free.

MJT: This interests me because of what you were saying before about filming, about yourself, about the way you see it changing the object. This reminds me of Wordsworth with the poem "Tintern Abbey" when he talks about how my vision actually changes the object and the result is the poem.
JM: Those who do experiment change the context.

MJT: So is your conception then more romantic, the idea that the human being, the emotions take precedent over any kind of abstraction?
JM: Yes, I think I am walking a very, very delicate, very dangerous balancing line like a tightrope walker. When I was watching my most recent film, *As I Was Moving Ahead Occasionally I Saw Brief Glimpses of Beauty*, I became very conscious of that because when you work with material that is so close to you, in this case my family, then it is very easy to fall off into being too romantic, too sentimental, too emotional. But I think I have managed to leap across that stretch without falling down, but it was an effort. I cut out for instance a lot of material consciously that would have dragged. It's very, very close to falling down. That is what one has to be conscious of. That is a problem with this kind of diary film.

MJT: You have spoken often of your films as "efforts to preserve bits of paradise."
JM: Again, I think it comes to my childhood. I think I had a very happy childhood. I enjoyed the nature and the work. Now, when I go through my life with my camera, be it film or video, there are certain moods, there are certain situations, that awaken those feelings. Some memory of something familiar is awoken. So it is still connected with my childhood. But then it gets more complicated because then you see what I came to believe in, what humanity is all about, what my function here is, that belief doesn't have to be so pronounced, it's maybe in the background somewhere. Often examples come from eating and drinking. It could also come from poetry.

I feel one of my duties is to try to preserve what has been achieved already by those who lived before me. I have to do everything to help it remain here and preserve for those who will come after me. I consider it a duty almost. I'm more and more aware now of those who lived in other centuries. I would be betraying them, the best minds of humanity. I have to help continue their works.

MJT: Especially during this ebb.
JM: Yes, yes. I just finished this project called Utopia Station. A dozen artists from

all over the world were invited to present reports on the subject that could be exhibited. In segment number four, I pledged to all those who lived before me not to betray their work but continue their work. Those are the fragments of paradise.

Short Films from a Long Life

Wired / 2006

From *Wired*, December 19, 2006. © Condé Nast. Reprinted by permission.

Wired News: Where did the idea of making 365 films in 365 days come from?
Jonas Mekas: I have so much footage. I've been videotaping my life, my friends' lives, wherever I go since 1987. That's twenty years' worth of video, thousands and thousands of hours. I never knew what to do with it. I made one compilation. But otherwise there it sits.

Most of my videos consist of fragments, one or two minutes long. They are haikus or sketches. I have thousands. So now, beginning January 1, I'll finish one film a day. Maybe one-third will use old material, and two-thirds will use new.

WN: Are you plotting it out?
JM: No, no, no. I'll go through some of the old material and choose some things to use. But with the new material, I prefer not to know. It'll be a totally unpredictable project. That's what excites me about it.

WN: You used 16mm for thirty years until switching to video. Can you describe what's different about shooting on digital and on film?
JM: A few years ago, I taught a class at Cooper Union called "The Absolute and Beautiful Interrelationship between Technology, Content and Form of Cinema." Once you change the technology—from a film camera to a video camera, or from an 8mm camera to 16mm—you change completely the content.

With 8mm, a leaf on a tree will be made up of maybe four grains. So it's very impressionistic, almost like Seurat. If you switch to 16mm, the technology gives you hundreds of grains on that leaf. It's more deeply detailed, more naturalistic.

Some cameras are heavier and need to be on tripods. Others are small enough to hide in your pocket. There are places where you don't want to feel like you are disturbing anything, so I may use a camera like that.

WN: Back in the 1950s, Stan Brakhage dreamed of a 16mm projector in every living room, of families shutting off their TVs and watching independent films.

JM: That was also the dream of the mid-1960s, when Super 8mm came. All the filmmakers thought, "Now we can make our films and put them out into the world." It just did not happen. It still was too complicated.

In 1967, in the United States, there were nine million Super 8 cameras. People were filming weddings and their travels. Most of the time, they were used one time, maybe on a honeymoon, and then into the closet.

WN: Do you think digital video and the internet can fulfill that promise from the 1960s? Can innovative films lure audiences from Hollywood to independent cinema?

JM: Yes, they are already doing that. Not necessarily on their iPods yet, but on DVDs. The edition of Brakhage films that was brought out by Criterion sells very well, thousands of copies. It's maybe not the way he wanted to have them seen, but the quality is good.

Before, through the Film-Makers' Co-op, you might show something in the three places where they show independent film in New York and reach fifty people or three hundred people. That's it. Now you can make an exchange with everyone.

WN: But most filmmakers want their films to be shown in communal situations.

JM: Less and less. Movies can be private and personal. Books are written for everyone and published, millions of copies for some. Everyone has their own. They are accessible to all. That hasn't diminished the value and importance of literature. It's the same with films.

WN: So you don't worry that watching films on iPods and computers will wreck the cinematic experience, the experience of sitting in a theater with a group of people?

JM: That can exist also. Listen, to really see the great paintings of, say, the Renaissance period, you have to go somewhere, to Florence. How many people can do that? I haven't seen many of them. I've seen only reproductions. But you can still get something from the reproductions.

I myself saw the great works of Western civilization for the first time in my high school in Lithuania in bad black-and-white reproductions on miserable paper. That was, for many years, what art was for me. But from those miserable black-and-white reproductions, I got something, something unmistakable.

When I went and finally saw the originals, it didn't give me that much more. I had got their essence already. Same with video. You've got the film on the big screen, with three hundred people; that's one thing. But it can also work on a small screen.

George Maciunas had a six-inch Sony television. The screen was tiny, almost like an iPod. He'd watch westerns and action films, everything. I said, "George, get something bigger." He said, "It works."

So I sat there and watched. At some point I forgot the dimensions. The movie pulled me in completely. This could have been Radio City Music Hall. You forget the size. It's like looking through a microscope—everything in you can be seen in a little bit of DNA.

WN: Do you watch films online?

JM: No, I have no time to watch anything. I am a maker. I'm so involved with what I'm doing. I try to keep in touch but I have little time.

WN: Do you get a sense what the scene is like for young experimental filmmakers?

JM: It's exciting for them because they can immediately throw their work into the world and get responses back. That simply did not exist for us in the fifties, sixties, seventies, eighties.

WN: There's so much garbage out there, though. Who has the patience to sift through it all?

JM: Some of the more intense pieces, films you want to see again and again, will survive. It's natural selection of cinema. Only the best will remain. Do you really think what you see on YouTube today will still exist in five years?

Nam June Paik used to laugh at filmmakers: "Your films will crumble in a few years." Then we discovered that video lasts seven or eight years. The same with DVDs—they have a limited life. Technologies will disappear. Only things that people really like will be transferred. And that's a very good thing.

WN: You talked about the nine million Super 8 cameras in the 1960s. Today, even more people than that are using digital video. Do you think all these filmmakers will change cinema?

JM: I mentioned that number, the nine million, when talking to (director Pier Paolo) Pasolini in Paris in 1968, during the student revolution. "Maybe something interesting will happen with their cameras," I said. "These cameras can change the nature of communications." And he said, "There are more typewriters than cameras. Did that change the world? Did that make this revolution?"

WN: But the digital cameras must be having an influence.

JM: Yes, yes definitely. New technologies make more money than old ones.

WN: Do the digital cameras and editing help push the form, too?
JM: The content changes with the technology.

WN: How has that happened already?
JM: Kenneth Anger—he has more time to read than I do—he sent me several clippings having to do with the explosion of short films. An article from the front page of the Sunday edition of the *LA Times*. So maybe there will be more short films. People go where you can make more money. If short films work, they'll go there. It's something interesting to watch.

WN: So can the internet and digital video help make experimental cinema more viable?
JM: Yes, yes. That time isn't exactly here yet. Brakhage is dead, and now the films are finally being distributed and being seen. But all of the money that now comes from his films didn't come in time for him. It didn't come for most filmmakers. It's too late for them.

As for myself, I'm not waiting for the money. And the dream in the sixties really wasn't about money. The filmmakers wanted to reach more people.

WN: Maybe you'll do that with your 365 series.
JM: My dream doesn't even have to do with reaching more people. This 365 project is more about the unpredictability. I'm curious to see what will happen with this adventure. All I know is that at the end I'll have 365 films.

Keep Dancing, Keep Singing

Benn Northover / 2012

Jonas and I met in 1998 in New York, while I was an intern at Anthology Film Archives. Over the years we have become close friends and allies, working together
on numerous film and gallery projects. This conversation took place one hot June
day in Brooklyn. Jonas had just returned home from a week of "rumination" at the
Brooklyn hospital. Being of strong Lithuanian farming stock and with, as Jonas
put it, help from his angels, he was home and well.

To many, such an experience would be a hindrance, but for Jonas this event
marked a new period of change to be embraced with a characteristic sense of
adventure. With an exhibition at London's Serpentine Gallery this winter, the
publication of his second volume of written diaries, *I Seem to Live: 1953–1964*, the
DVD release of his key film works and two retrospectives at the BFI, London and
Centre Pompidou in Paris, it's looking to be another busy year for Mr. Mekas.

Jonas Mekas: Since this conversation is taking place towards the end of the ninth
decade of my life, I do not envy you, the problem you are facing, because you will
have to decide which of my many lives you want to cover, or how to jump from one
to another. My Lithuanian life, my life as a filmmaker, my life as the minister of
defense for independent cinema, or as a writer in the *Village Voice*, editor of *Film
Culture* magazine . . . So where shall we begin?

Benn Northover: Well, in another of our recorded conversations you once said
that you wear many hats and ride many horses. Your life has been a series of different chapters.

JM: Yes. I have lived many lives. Until I left Lithuania it was all literature. During
the German period, between '45 and end of '49, until my arrival in New York, I was
freely grabbing everything from every possible source and direction and culture
and civilization. Then I landed up here in New York, and cinema immediately comes

in. At the end of 1954, with my brother Adolfas, we brought out the first issue of *Film Culture* magazine. In '58 I jump into the *Village Voice*, with my Movie Journal column. Then I go into the creation of all of those organizations: Film-Makers' Cinematheque, Film-Makers' Cooperative, Anthology Film Archives.

BN: Much of your activity in cinema seems to come from a sense of necessity.
JM: Yes, there was no coherent focused film magazine in America. We had to do it. There was no film venue open to the independents as a permanent situation. So I had to create the Film-Makers' Cinematheque. There was no real film preservation work being done for avant-garde film. Yes, I did whatever I did from necessity.

BN: You started keeping a kind diary very early on.
JM: I went to primary school very late because I was needed at home on the farm. I only learned to read and write when I was nine. But I kept a picture diary from age six. The written diaries were very factual, like "Today father went to the mill," or "Today we sowed the barley."

BN: Similar to your films . . .
JM: Yes, very down to earth, exactly.

BN: How did you get involved with the anti-Nazi underground movements?
JM: We were against the occupation by the Russians at first, and then against the Nazis. We were powerless. They were big. All we could do was try to appeal to the United States, to other free countries, to come to our aid. We did that via underground publications. And since I was literate enough, I was pulled in to help edit the texts. I had a special typewriter which I used only for this underground newspaper. But the German Secret Police, of course, were following all those newspapers, trying to locate who was publishing them. The only way of tracing it was by the typewriter face—if they found a typewriter in your house that matched the publication that was it: you were done. The typewriter I used was, one night, stolen. I was hiding it in a huge pile of firewood, but somebody who came maybe to steal wood, was lucky to find a typewriter. So now, of course, he would sell it. And there was a chance that it would come to the attention of the German Secret Police, the Gestapo. So I had a meeting with my underground friends, and they insisted I disappear—they were endangered too. Chances could not be taken. The underground helped to make the papers for me and Adolfas to leave for Austria, to enlist in the University of Vienna. Adolfas just thought we were going to study. He did not know about my involvement in the underground at all. It was very secret because the lives of many people depended on it. And that's why he could take his diaries—they were innocent farmer boy's diaries. But I could not take mine

because politically we were young and naïve, and I was writing down details about our meetings. So I buried my picture and written diaries when I left Lithuania so that they would not fall into German hands.

BN: When did you become interested in cinema?

JM: The very first movie I saw was a Walt Disney cartoon. The teacher took our graduating class. Even before the Soviets came, I saw some movies shown by traveling movie entrepreneurs, with electrical power generators running the projectors. They were very noisy! Mostly we saw early comedies. Some Chaplin, and a lot of Pat and Patachon—comedians that were popular in the Netherlands area. And then the Soviets came with their propaganda movies, and the Nazis came with their propaganda movies. They put tents in the city markets to show them. But I began going to movies with Adolfas more regularly after the war, in the displaced person camps, because there was nothing else to do. There were screenings arranged by the American army, cheap, cheap movies. The first one that impressed us was John Huston's *The Treasure of the Sierra Madre*. We were not impressed by the dramatic situations but by the visuals, the desert footage. And then postwar German cinema came in, which used actual locations, because they had no money to build sets. Visually it was very strong. But our real life in cinema began in New York.

BN: You immediately got very involved in the growing cinema scene when you arrived.

JM: Immediately. The next evening, we went to the New York Film Society, run by Rudolf Arnheim, and we saw *The Cabinet of Dr. Caligari*, and *The Fall of the House of Usher* by Epstein. We arrived in New York starved for culture. It was in New York that I saw an avant-garde film for the first time. Everything was there: the theater, the music!—It was so incredible after five years of displaced person camps. I had no time to think about the past anymore, it was all here, now, new, fresh! I was twenty-seven, and I decided to remain twenty-seven. Because I had lost those ten formative years; they were taken away from me. I was like an empty sponge craving to be filled, and I absorbed everything.

BN: People have often called you the "godfather of underground cinema." You've never liked that term.

JM: I hate that term, because the pioneers of the avant-garde were in the twenties—French, German, and Italian filmmakers. In the United States, before 1950, before I even put my foot in America, there was Maya Deren and a whole gang of filmmakers emerging in San Francisco. Markopoulos and Kenneth Anger . . . I came to New York at the right moment. The excitement was already brewing, coming from all the dark corners of America. The golden period of the American avant-garde began with Kenneth Anger's *Fireworks*. It ends, practically, with Michael Snow's *Wavelength* in 1967. The whole body of American avant-garde film was created with nobody's help, no foundations, no arts councils. Just from necessity. And cinema was changed forever.

BN: People still wrestle with the definitions of terms like "avant-garde" or "experimental cinema" . . .

JM: When I arrived in the United States and began going to the Museum of Modern Art and screenings at Cinema 16 and other film societies, the term was always experimental. But people like Brakhage and others were not "experimenting." That was simply how they, themselves made films. The word "independent" began coming in around '57 or '58. And then around '58, '59—the word "underground" began appearing.

BN: Wasn't that Duchamp?

JM: The promoter of the term "underground," the one who really planted it in New York was Stan Vanderbeek. But yes, he picked it up from Duchamp. To me personally, I am against all such terms. To me cinema is cinema. Cinema is one big tree with many branches. The same as literature. In literature, you don't just say, "Oh, I bought some literature." No, you say, "I bought a novel" by so-and-so , or a book of essays by so-and-so. In the narrative cinema a certain terminology has already been established: "film noir," "Western," even "Spaghetti Western." When we say "film noir" we know what we are talking about. But in the nonnarrative cinema, we are still a little bit lost. So sometimes, the only way to make us understand what we are talking about is to use the term avant-garde. The term avant-garde is lately returning back to cover all that other areas. The other important term that is around is "independent," referring to the filmmakers who are not working within the established industry; that means, working with lower budgets. They are sort of independents. Cinema is still a little bit too young; we do not yet have developed terms for all the different, small branches of the cinema tree.

BN: How did you move into the diary film form?

JM: A month after we landed in New York, we thought, we have to get a camera. We befriended Klybas, the mayor of Papilys, near where I grew up in Lithuania. He had already come to New York with his family. He guaranteed to the Peerless photo store, that we could take the camera on time payment. So it's thanks to him that we got our first Bolex and began shooting around Williamsburg. And that developed into what became my film diaries. A year later, Adolfas was called into the army, so for the next couple of years I was on my own. I filmed the Lithuanian immigrant community settled in the Brooklyn, Williamsburg area, material that ended up in *Lost Lost Lost*. That was still a period when we were only talking about Lithuania: "Will we be able to return someday, or is that it?" But soon I gravitated towards the American arts community. I found out where all the poetry readings and film screenings were. In the spring of 1953, I escaped from Brooklyn into Lower Manhattan, to 95 Orchard Street. That was the beginning of my new life. I began filming my new friends.

BN: And in 1960, you made your first feature-length film, *Guns of the Trees*.
JM: During the making of *Guns of the Trees*, I realized it was the first, and probably last of my attempts into novelistic cinema. Alberto Moravia, the Italian novelist, wrote after seeing it: it follows the post-Eliot and Ezra Pound poetry structures, which I thought was the right observation. It sort of has no logic, no continuity. It grows piece after piece, to achieve a certain effect. The best footage was not acted but free improvisation footage—fooling around by the East River in the rain, around the train tracks. I made one more attempt at narrative by filming *The Brig*. It was a critique of cinéma vérité. I filmed it with the Auricon camera that recorded sound directly on film. The next day I projected it. Andy [Warhol] happened to be at that screening. He said, "Really? This can be done?" I am guilty of ending Andy's silent cinema. When he saw you could shoot film with sound and project it the next day, he got very excited!

BN: You've often described yourself as a "filmer" as opposed to a "filmmaker."
JM: A filmmaker is thinking about scripts, a producer, actors. I do not do that! I walk through life with my camera. The result, eventually, is a finished film, shorter or longer. But the film is determined by the material. I'm not collecting material to illustrate a certain idea. The scenes in *Scenes from the Life of Andy Warhol* were made up of visiting Warhol, summers in Montauk. *As I Was Moving Ahead* or *Sleepless Night Stories*, they are all scenes from my "real life" with real friends, real people. I'm a filmmaker, but my working process differs.

BN: How did your move to video affect your approach to filming?
JM: It took me ten years to master my Bolex, and about the same to master the video camera, to make it an extension of myself. A good musician never thinks about his instrument, he just plays. With the Bolex, the fingers control the speed, lighting, shutter. It was more like playing a musical instrument. Video is something else. Much of my later videotaping is like anthropological vignettes. Like in *Letter from Greenpoint*, there's you (Benn) and I wrapping a present for Louise Bourgeois. It happens millions of times, across the world, when somebody is preparing a gift for somebody one loves. But it's something unique. There is an intensity, a concentration in that moment; it's not theater, it's not artificial, it's real. That's

where my Bolex and my video cinema differ. I seek those moments; sometimes I get them, sometimes I totally fail.

BN: In 2003 you moved back to Brooklyn and this seemed to mark a new chapter in your life.
JM: Yes. I devoted thirty years of my life to Anthology Film Archives, but around 2000, it was running by itself, and I could focus on my own work. What I'm concentrating on now is very personal. My aim is still how to really record life around me—catch the essence of the moment without interfering or destroying it. The same as for a haiku writer. It has to be short, to the point, you have to catch the right moment. Some people just identify me with my sixties work. But I am completely somewhere else, content and technology-wise.

BN: You said before we sat down today that you felt you were entering a very new period in your life, yet another chapter.
JM: This interview is taking place, one day after the summer solstice, the end of my ninth decade. Recently I spent one week in hospital. To sum it up: it was very useful and timely. I would even suspect it was specially arranged by angels. I had time to think, look back, I had nothing else to do. And I also went through the most up to date, technological inspection of my body machine. Of course, they discovered the machine was there, but it was quite used up, so that one has to be more subtle when one handles it. For nine decades I ran a hundred miles per hour. When you go that speed, it's only a blur. So I decided, "Okay, the machine needs small adjustments, we'll switch to another gear, let's say, speed 65." At a slower speed, unpredictable new things will be happening. They are already happening. Like, I began taking T'ai chi. And I feel I will be moving more out of Western civilization, and more towards Basho and Issa and the Orient. I'm entering a new, unpredictable period. With adventures and expectations that are totally unknown and mysterious and exciting.

Remains of the Day

Gilda Williams / 2013

From *Art Monthly* 363 (February 2013): 1–4. Reprinted by permission.

Gilda Williams: The title of the central film of your recent Serpentine Gallery exhibition is *Out-takes from the Life of a Happy Man*, 2012. This year you celebrated your ninetieth birthday. Is this exhibition a satisfied reflection on your long life, one spent immersed in art and film?

Jonas Mekas: *Out-takes from the Life of a Happy Man* really is made up from out-takes, the footage I did not use, that did not fit into any of my completed films—ends and bits. I discovered I had a lot of it; time was passing, and the films were slowly fading. It will all be gone soon, and I was worried about it. I thought on this occasion, on the occasion of the Serpentine Gallery show, I will do something with all these remains.

GW: When you returned to these out-takes and were re-editing your footage after perhaps thirty or forty years, could you remember most of it?

JM: I know exactly where I shot every bit, every little piece. I remember where I filmed it and every different circumstance. Yes, I remember every moment of it.

GW: Is your filmmaking a kind of prosthetic memory for you; is it part of your memory?

JM: Not the usual memory that people talk about, or what we usually mean by "memory." I do not work with "memory." I work with actual material, physical material, film—that's very real. I don't think of myself as working with memory but with real recordings of moments in the past, with whatever we have left. I work with concrete pieces of film that happen to contain moments from a certain place and a certain time, a certain situation. It is very real. And I don't think they are just personal. I think they are universal.

GW: In contrast to the art gallery, in a cinema your sense of the actual space you are in disappears.

JM: Yes, of course. To be cinema, it has to be that way—just you and the screen.

GW: How do you choose when or what to film? Do you always carry a camera with you?

JM: Oh yes, always. I have my camera with me right now, in my bag. But I don't make rational decisions about what to film; I don't plan. Whatever I film is a moment when something happens that triggers something—suddenly I have to take out my camera and film it. There is no explanation, no planning. The reasons I choose to film are invisible; they are never rational.

GW: Obviously, sound is added afterwards. How do you decide how to join sound and image?

JM: In this case the sounds are from my sound library. Just as I have collected images, I have collected sounds—thousands and thousands of cassettes. The music in this film is actually my wedding music. My wedding took place in Kremsmünster Abbey in Austria, a very old abbey, like twelve hundred years old. You can hear the monks singing, the nuns singing—these are from my recordings. The piano is played by a Lithuanian musician and painter, Auguste Varkalis, a very good painter and a very good friend. Everything in this work is part of my life.

GW: You write in one of the wall texts how your life has witnessed so many tremendous twentieth-century events—the rise of Soviet power and the invasion of the Nazis in your homeland of Lithuania, your subsequent imprisonment in a forced labor camp near Hamburg during the Second World War, then your time in displaced persons camps across Germany after the war.

JM: Unfortunately—or fortunately, perhaps—I was born shortly after the Communist revolution and shortly before the arrival of Hitler. I went through all the horrors of the twentieth century. Yes, that was my fate, what can I say?

GW: Yet you always seem able to focus on the redemptive moments of your life, the happy episodes of your everyday life

JM: Yes. I don't remember the unhappy parts—I don't try to remember. That's my nature. I don't remember for very long the horrors that were close to me. I could, I suppose, spend my time brooding on or remembering the horrors of the twentieth century, but I'm not interested in that; that's not my nature. I concentrate in my work and in my life only on the celebration of life. That's what I am all about. I am celebrating life and having a joyful relationship to life. I am a propagandist for happiness and beauty. This show, this exhibition, is my manifesto: a manifesto for the celebration of life and happiness and beauty.

I think that too much in contemporary art—too much time, too many exhibitions, too much space—is dedicated to horrors, to the darkness of our civilization. If you surround yourself with darkness, it begins to affect you; those images start to affect you. When you go into a cemetery, you think about death; it has an effect on you. When you visit the Museum of the Inquisition . . . you are affected by those horrible things. You leave depressed, you need a drink. But if you are in a field of flowers, you are affected by the flowers—you smile.

GW: You were relocated by the UN Refugee Organization with your brother Adolfas to New York in 1949, and by the early 1960s found yourself at the center of the avant-garde, working with filmmakers like Jack Smith, Maya Deren, and Kenneth Anger, with poets Allen Ginsberg, William Burroughs, and John Giorno, and with artists including Andy Warhol, George Maciunas, and so on.
JM: You didn't mention music, which was also at the center—John Cage, La Monte Young, and others. All the arts were being reinvigorated at the time, so much began in those years, or was brought up to date. But maybe we have been stuck too long on the 1960s. For decade after decade the interest was always on the 1960s, but now I think attention has moved forward—people are discovering the 1970s. Maybe that is good.

GW: You have always worked independently, securing your own funding and working outside established institutions—in fact often inventing your own institutional models. I am interested in the strategies you invented to finance and organize your many ventures—*Film Culture* magazine, from 1955, or the Film-Makers' Cooperative, which you founded in 1962 and which was funded by the artists themselves.
JM: Luckily, for my own personal work, I did not need money. My kind of films do not require money. But my struggle and all the fundraising—oh all the fundraising!—was always directed towards other projects. *Film Culture* magazine, the Film-Makers' Cinematheque (now Anthology Film Archives)—that is where all my work and effort in fundraising was needed. Film preservation, for example, takes quite a bit of money. I have spent much more time, many times more time, on fundraising than on making my own work. Fundraising is not easy for us independents—it never was and still isn't. We have always had very little support from the city or any official bodies. I'm still fundraising.

GW: Did you fund your projects through cooperatives or through individual donors?
JM: Mostly individuals. I have spent a lot of my life writing letters, making calls, trying to persuade rich people to support us. It is hard work. Fundraising is hard work; it's no joke. Some artists supported us too, by donating their art, which we sell. I bought the Anthology Film Archives building from the city for $50,000 in an auction in 1968 or so with an outright donation. But to fix the building cost me $1.8 million. To transform this former courthouse and prison into a film

museum . . . you can imagine what it cost! I spent ten years of my life raising that $1.8 million, but I needed to create the Anthology. It was a nightmare. I still have bad dreams about it.

GW: Were you surprised when film and video moved massively into gallery and museum spaces from the 1970s into the 1990s?

JM: No, I wasn't surprised. I thought it was natural. It was hard work to convince some galleries and museums to embrace film, but not all of them. For example the Museum of Modern Art included film right from the start, since the 1920s. The Pompidou also included cinema from its very beginnings in the 1970s, thanks to Pontus Hulten, who was a visionary. But in the private galleries, it was really the introduction of video art that marked the change, mostly for practical reasons. It was much easier to present a video on a monitor than to project a film, which requires a projector and someone who knows how to operate it. Film projection is a much more complicated business than a video show. For the galleries it became very simple to show moving-image art because of the videocassette. The simplicity of the technology opened the door first to video and then to film.

GW: In your films, you are not interested in staging events but in recording the everyday events going on around you

JM: That is my challenge. The everyday, the invisible, life around us, the daily life which we don't even notice—especially the art world, which seems to be totally uninterested in reality. They aren't even interested in color. The art world seems to like things that are so boringly black and grey. But I crave color. When I walk into the art opening, I search for color, and most of the time I don't find it. So I'll go back to my movies. My challenge is how to see and record moments of daily life that pass as if invisibly. That is my challenge.

   So much of the contemporary art making I see around me—it's all an artificial, invented reality, with artists trying to be "creative." I'm very old-fashioned in that sense. I am interested in living things, like an anthropologist who is going with a tape recorder and recording old songs that humans, somewhere, are still singing or dancing to. I'm interested in catching these moments of contemporary humanity, recording it. I don't need to create it.

GW: Today everybody carries around with them in their phone a fairly sophisticated digital camera, recording daily minutiae, and we can instantly distribute this imagery over the internet. Would this have been the ideal means for your "everyday" films? You have a very comprehensive website, jonasmekasfilms.com, and in 2007 you created there the internet project *365 Day Project* in which you presented a new short film every day, like a visual diary.

JM: The internet, to me, is just an extension of the telephone. It continues the history of correspondence, of having conversations by other means than face-to-face talk. This history is as old as the world itself, and the internet is just an extension of that history. It is a very vague thing for me to try to define what my art is, or what film art is. In fact it is hard to define what any art is, or how best to distribute it. I'll give you an example: a friend of mine from Naples, Giuseppe Zevola, worked in the Banco di Napoli, which is about four hundred years old. He showed me stacks and stacks of ancient records in the bank—you know, checks cashed, that sort of thing. And the bank employees from long ago, obviously very bored with their work, doodled in these books. These bank registers are full of doodles, hundreds and hundreds of these improvised little drawings, which Giuseppe collected. They look like the work of many contemporary artists that I see everywhere today—in fact they are often more interesting than a lot of what I see in the galleries.

So how can you say what "art" is and what it isn't, or where best to show it or to find it? Where would you place these doodles? What's being exchanged today on YouTube or other websites is part of the everyday exchanges and conversations that have been documented in the past in other ways—why do we need to call things "art"?

GW: Do you call your films "art"?

JM: No! I am not an artist! I refuse to call myself that. I am not an artist. I am a maker, a filmmaker. I make films. I film with a camera, or I videotape. To decide what is "art" and what is "not art" makes no sense. We must always remember that what we have left of art, what we call "art history," is just what managed to survive. It is not the whole story. We know only about what religious fanatics and political fanatics did not manage to destroy, to say nothing of the earthquakes, fires, and wars that destroyed plenty more. We call it "art history" as if this history is complete, but in fact very little is left. I was just told that Botticelli destroyed almost all his late work, something like twenty years' worth of works, hundreds of paintings, only because the religious fanatics around him told him it was sinful to paint the works he did. Botticelli was said to have been pressured into destroying much of his work. What is left of Botticelli, like all art, is just a fragment. What we see in the museums or what is written about in books, what we study in schools as "art history," in truth is only the miserable leftovers that happened to survive the horrors of the past.

The same is true now. We have this visual flood of images, produced by all the tools at our disposal for recording and disseminating moving images. What will remain of it all will be only random pieces, fragments. Consider how quickly technology is changing. Already it is difficult for me to see material I recorded just five years ago. Recording formats become obsolete, the machinery dies out, and vast quantities of recorded material turn invisible. They are only as permanent as the technologies that support them.

You have to remember that decisions about formats are made solely by businesses, making business decisions not artistic ones. Motion-picture film is disappearing purely for profit-driven reasons. Business people realized they could make more money with video than film, so everything moved to video. The production of celluloid has been discontinued and you can no longer find film labs, which are all closed. Business determines formats: it is certainly not the artists who are making decisions about dominant formats. Every two years or so, formats have to change for business reasons only—for money, for profit. We all have to buy and change everything. We are spending a lot of money now at Anthology Film Archives to transfer video art from the 1970s and '80s to new formats. We have to do all this work because we can no longer watch these works on the original machinery, which has disappeared. And of course this is bound to repeat itself as even newer formats will replace the current formats.

GW: And there is always a loss in quality in any transfer of this kind.

JM: Of course, there is always a loss. If a painting is made in oil, the content could only have been captured using oil paint. There are different contents that can only be caught in watercolor or inks. The exact same thing is true with moving image—what you can do with 35mm you can't do with 16mm, and what you can do with 16mm you cannot do with 35mm—much less with video or digital recording. The tool you use to make the image and the result are inseparably connected, you cannot transfer film to video and think it is the same thing. You are no longer seeing the film, you are seeing something else. The texture is different, everything is different—it is a completely different thing. All that is left is "the story."

GW: Were you appalled when the Museum of Modern Art showed Warhol's films on video, as they did in 2010?

JM: Yes, I called it a crime. It is a crime! For the Museum of Modern Art—and other major museums—to show films like Andy Warhol's *Screen Tests* on video when it is still possible to show them as films—to project them—was criminal. In ten years' time it really will be very difficult to project them, but in 2010 it was still possible to screen them properly. To present Warhol's films as videos really was a crime.

GW: I would credit you with being among the first to take Warhol's art seriously—not just in the light-hearted context of Pop. Already in the early 1960s you understood him as a radical artist and filmmaker.

JM: Of course we should take Warhol very, very seriously. The *Screen Tests* are incredible: hundreds of portraits, unique in the history of portraiture. Warhol's early silent-film period, I think, is especially important. But even the sound period—I mean, *Chelsea Girls* is a monumental work; its complexity and richness still hasn't been understood. We still haven't understood enough how important that film really is.

GW: Do you remember the circumstances behind the making of Warhol's *Empire*, 1964?

JM: I was walking with my friend John Palmer, carrying *Film Culture* magazines to be mailed. The post office happened to be in the Empire State Building. We stopped and we looked at it from a distance, and Palmer said, "Ah, this is a perfect subject for Andy Warhol!" because Andy was interested in iconic images. "Why don't we tell Andy?" I said, so we did. John Palmer's name appears in the *Premiere* announcement of the film.

GW: That is very rare in Warhol's lifetime—he didn't like to openly share artistic credit, especially in writing. Despite all his assistants and collaborators, the art was always signed "by Andy Warhol" alone.

JM: Andy actually thanked John later for giving him the idea. Marie Menken, a filmmaker and Warhol friend, worked at *Time Magazine* in Rockefeller Center, on the fortieth floor or so. She let us in at night—without permission, of course. We went there with some sandwiches. I did most of the work. I set up the camera and loaded the film. We waited until each reel ended, then I changed immediately to another reel of film. It was quite boring, we just sat there nibbling at our sandwiches. But the film—it's a great movie. That kind of idea—duration art—was in the air already. La Monte Young had already made music by extending one single note into four or five hours, for example, and, of course, Andy had already made *Sleep* the year before *Empire*.

GW: You have always been a writer alongside your image-making work—you wrote anti-Soviet and anti-Nazi propaganda, then you were a journalist and a poet, and text is often interspersed in your films. Are they parallel activities for you, writing and filmmaking?

JM: Yes, but I wear many different hats, not just those of writer and filmmaker. They are all me.

GW: A word that comes up often in your writing is "paradise." You use that term to describe your early childhood in a farming village in Lithuania, for what you found in New York when you arrived in 1949 and, later, in the 1960s.

JM: Paradise means "innocence"—where there are still patches of innocence, of nature, an innocence that has not been destroyed by any of the poisons produced by our civilization. In every area you pick—what you drink, or what you eat, what you dream—you can find little that hasn't yet been poisoned. Whenever you find something that is still pure, where you know that what you are getting is not contaminated, by chemicals or whatever, that is innocence, that is paradise. There are still some fragments of paradise. And some of us are still trying to protect them, to see that they remain. That is what I am trying to do. Preserving films—it is like keeping seeds for the future, when maybe they can grow. There are still some fragments of paradise around us, but they are being eaten away, attacked, all the time. Like the corals in the ocean, eaten away by the pollutants. I think we are doomed, actually. I think our civilization is doomed.

GW: You have said that in Lithuania you are mostly a poet, in Europe a filmmaker, in the US a kind of maverick promoter, supporter, enabler, and friend to avant-garde film.

JM: That is still so. In Lithuania I am a national poet. When I work on my films they think I'm just wasting time. In the US some institutions have started recognizing me as a filmmaker, but mostly they think of me as an organizer, a writer for the *Village Voice*, founder of *Film Culture* magazine. They admit and recognize now my contribution to the development and changes in cinema. In Europe, I would say they recognize all those aspects, in Paris especially. But now other countries in Europe are beginning to see my work too and accept me as a filmmaker, like here in the UK.

GW: Do you have a favorite way that you like to be described?

JM: One description of me that I liked was coined by Vincent Canby in the *New York Times* who said, "Jonas Mekas does everything with the shrewdness of a farmer." It's true, I grew up in a farming village, and I am still a farmer. I plant many things. I water them, I see that they grow. I defend them—I see a lot of what I do as defending. I function as minister of defense, minister of finance, minister of propaganda. I do all those things, out of necessity. No one else was doing any of this, showing our films, preserving them, protecting. It had to be done—and it still does. I have done all those things without stopping since the 1960s. I did it all for the glory of cinema.

I Am Still a Farmer: A Discussion with Jonas Mekas

Hans-Ulrich Obrist / 2015

From *Document*, Issue 6 (Spring/Summer 2015). Reprinted by permission.

Rightly known as the godfather of American avant-garde cinema, Jonas Mekas has inspired the careers of artists and directors from Andy Warhol to Martin Scorsese. A pioneer of the video diary and the founder of the Anthology Film Archives, Mekas, now ninety-two, has set to work building a largest cinema library in the US. Mekas catches up with Hans-Ulrich Obrist from his loft in Brooklyn to discuss being from a pre-radio generation and witnessing the internet generation, why he's not an archivist, and his pantheistic roots.

Hans-Ulrich Obrist: Hello, Jonas!
Jonas Mekas: Yes, I can hear you, but I don't see you. Can you see me?

HUO: I see you. Do you see me?
JM: No, I do not see you. I can see you in my mind. [*laughs*]

HUO: That's strange.
JM: Oh, now I see you!

HUO: You see me?
JM: And I hear you!

HUO: We are almost ready, Jonas! How are you?
JM: So far so good. We have a comparatively nice early January day in Brooklyn. That's where I am—in Brooklyn.

HUO: You are in Brooklyn, I am in London, so this is a London/Brooklyn interview. Can you tell me what you have been working on today? What are you working on right now?

JM: I am slowly every day putting some time into organizing all my materials around me. It's a huge job because I have so much stuff. That's why some people call me an archivist. But I am not an archivist, as I do not collect stuff: I only do not throw out anything that comes into the house. That's why I have so much stuff. But the reason why I do not throw out anything is that everything that comes into my loft immediately becomes part of my working materials, even if I do not know what and when I will need it. So that's what I was doing night now, organizing, But mostly this year I'll be working on building a library for Anthology Film Archives, a paper materials library. I am going to build it on top of the present building. This will be probably the largest such library—a library devoted to cinema—in the States. But it's a $6 million project, so it may take me some time to do it. Is there anyone who wants to build it? We'll put your name on it! And next to Anthology I am go-ing to build a café, Heaven and Earth Café, named so in honor of Harry Smith. It will serve our patrons and the neighborhood. It will provide additional income to Anthology Film Archives which is operating at a deficit. So my work this year will be mostly fund raising. But while do that, I'll be also finishing final touches on a huge twelve-hundred-page volume of five decades of my written diaries.

HUO: Can you tell me about the most recent entries to your video diary?

JM: Every week I put on my website one or two new diaristic pieces about what's happening around my life. Yes, I continue doing that.

HUO: So it's like an ongoing video diary?

JM: Yes. Sketches, notes. Some new, some old. I have so much old video material that is unique as history.

HUO: Can you tell me about the most recent entries? Of January? It's nice to mark that moment, the beginning of a new year.

JM: What I am going to put on my website today—I hope I'll have time to finish it today—but it may not appear on my website until tomorrow—is my visit to St. Petersburg. Actually, it took place in September 2013. But I am putting it on the website today because I was just reminded, reading this Sunday's *London FT*, that it's the one-hundredth anniversary of Malevich's *Black Square*. So I remembered my St. Petersburg footage.

The occasion was the opening of George Maciunas's exhibition, *Russian Atlases*, and my *365 Day Project* exhibition at the State Hermitage Museum's newly built contemporary art wing. After the opening, Mikhail Piotrovsky, the director of

Hermitage, wanted to show me something. He took me took me to an adjacent gallery room, and there, right in front of my eyes, on the wall, there it was: Malevich's *Black Square*! Right there. Someone had just donated it to Hermitage. And there it was, in its full humble, fragile black glory. I must tell you one anecdote related to this exhibition. You see, all the stuff from my personal Fluxus collection a few years ago ended up in Vilnius, Lithuania. The Hermitage Fluxus show was a selection from that collection. And one of the pieces that Piotrovsky decided to include in the exhibition was a huge die (dice), you know, one that you throw, roll in some games. George had made it from wood for one of his Fluxus games. After George died, it ended up in my loft. It sat there for years collecting dust, the children and the cats used to hide in it, before I sent it to Vilnius. So now it was at the Hermitage and there was Piotrovsky, and there was me, and there was this huge wooden dice, now clean and in a museum situation. So I said, "Yes, but you can also open the top and get into it, if you want." And I began opening it, and Piotrovsky said, "No, don't touch it, don't touch it!" [*laughs*] Because now it was upgraded to the status of art, and it was clean, you weren't supposed to touch it. ... That's what happens with the pieces that are in your private home, and then at some point they end up in a museum and they become something else. I thought it was a really funny situation.

HUO: Obviously you anticipated a lot of what's happening now with digital technology: the blogs, the video blogs, through your diaries. Do you remember how you invented this idea of doing video diary? How did it come to you?

JM: The initial idea was just to put on the website a few pieces and try to sell them via website. But it didn't work, the process was too complicated. But it made me interested in the possibilities of a short form. Next I made forty short pieces using mostly old footage, as an exercise in short film form. That was in December of 2006. January was coming so as a joke, I said, "Okay, beginning January 1 I should make one short film every day and see if can do it." As said, so done. And that's how it began. Once I began, I could not stop. And I didn't miss a single day the entire year 2007. I am still continuing, but not with same crazy intensity. Now I put only one or two pieces weekly on my website.

HUO: And early on, you already did something which now in our digital age is extremely widespread and actually rejects this idea of time being linear in a way. I am sort of wondering what prompted that, I mean Manuel De Landa talks about a thousand years of nonlinearity. What prompted you in nonlinearity?

JM: Theoretical thinking is not my stuff. I am still a farmer. I refer to myself as a farmer boy. I am down to earth, practical, dealing only with what's in front of me. I never think about time, linearity, practically or theoretically. Time does not exist to me, and memory does not exist to me either, because all the materials that are in my house, all the books, what's written in them, all the documentation, all the junk that I have, and all the video cassettes and film reels, they are all materials, they are not memories to me, they are working materials, and I work with them. Like when I go and film in the street, there is a reality there and there is me filming, taping it. It's all real. The same when I begin to work with what is on the shelf: I pick up a roll of film or a video cassette, and I am working with it, here and now. Or I open a book: what's in it is all real. And now.

HUO: When we met for the first time in Paris—thanks to agnès b. twenty years ago—you said that you never film the past, that you cannot film the past, that you don't want to film the past, that you are always in the present. Then obviously you have a huge archive now of many decades of past footage, but in this footage . . .

JM: You know, I believe that even what we call "memory" and "thoughts" they are also real, "physically" real; they are also my working material. Memory is as much a matter as any piece around me. [*knocks on the table*] No thing is "nothing."

HUO: That is such a beautiful sentence!

JM: By the way, since we are talking, I want to ask you about talking: What do you think about what Matisse once said that one who wants to be an artist, the first thing he has to do is to cut out his tongue? You are interviewing, you are talking to so many artists. But don't you think that all this talking is really . . . just talking? Because I know that I am not answering the same questions the same way as I was answering them ten years ago.

I am answering them completely differently, sometimes in total opposite. So it's just talking. . . .

HUO: For me it started when I read the interview with Francis Bacon and David Sylvester, and it was such an amazing document which somehow got me into art.

JM: But it's always a reflection of the period when that talking is taking place, and with what the artist is doing at that time, so of course, it has validity . . .

HUO: Of course Matisse, you know there is a big book of Matisse interviews which now came out. It was a Swiss critic who went to interview him, but at the end Matisse decided that he didn't like to be pinned down, so the book never came out. It only came out now because the copyright had ceded over many decades, so they could publish it. But Matisse objected to the publication; he didn't want that interview book to be published.

JM: So that goes with what you said.

HUO: Now also I wanted to ask because we started with January 2015. I was in Paris last week when there was the terrorist attack. I just wanted to see in a way because I remember we discussed terrorism when you were in London a couple of years ago. I wanted to see your reaction to what happened.

JM: I may disagree here with some of my friends on this subject. I don't think this was an attack on free speech: this was response to an insult. I think that one has to respect, one has to pay consideration to other people's feelings, be they your neighbors, your compatriots, or people of other countries—especially other countries which have very different social, religious, etc., makeup. Not to pay attention to it is both impolite and foolish. Or, if calculated, then close to a provocation, and then you have to take what comes. To say that "we are not afraid to laugh at you" is the same as saying "we are not afraid to insult your feelings, to hurt you." I do not think much about people who can say that kind of thing. So you see, I have some essential questions re: this subject. I am against unnecessary, insensitive provocations; we have too many of them already.

HUO: Now we have also of course an incredible moment in technology once more in 2015. 3D printing takes over and becomes very present. And at the same time we have also the internet of things, objects becoming . . .

JM: I saw the other day on TV, a car, printed out . . . and it runs!

HUO: So I was wondering, you were always ahead of the game, doing things before. How do you feel about these latest developments of technology and if it's something you use or if you're interested in it?

JM: I am not part of the consumer society, so most of it will be useless to me. But technology cannot be stopped. It's out of out of control. It's running on its own, with the encouragement of the corporate elite. Have we reached the limits of it? I do not think so; I believe that after we complete harnessing for our daily use the atom, all that quantum engineering can give us, we'll go beyond the atom, beginning with the "emptiness" in which all those atom particles exist, and beyond. In a way, the computers work already in the area, the suburbs of the "spirit": we don't see it, we only know it's there because it works. . . . The spirit works!

HUO: Now another thing which is interesting in this generation. Simon Castets and I are doing a mapping of all these artists of the '89-plus generation who grew up with digital technology. Tim Berners-Lee invented the internet in 1989 which is also the year the Berlin Wall fell. It's Tiananmen Square. It's the year the first GPS satellite was launched. So we started to do this project where I am making a cartography, a mapping of generation of artists who are born with the internet—the first digitally native generation. We have mapped so far more than five thousand artists of this generation in their early or mid-twenties, and one of the patterns we have observed—which are very fascinating—is that there is a big return to poetry. A lot of artists are writing poetry. There are new forms of poetry appearing on the internet, and you've always had a very big link to poetry. Czesław Miłosz whom I was friends with gave me text he wrote on you and told me a lot about your poems, amazing poetry. So I was wondering if you could talk about this aspect of your work, because in terms of alternate reality your work as a filmmaker is much more well known.

JM: That sounds very illuminating, your digitally native generation project. Yes, poetry is here to stay! The poetic feeling—read Paul Valéry, Edgar Allan Poe—can exist, can make manifest itself in any art, any medium, or life itself. So I am not surprised at all about its emergence on the internet, the net poetry. I am all for it. But personally, I have to say, you know that I am not even from the TV generation: I am from the early, primitive radio generation, even before radio. And I grew up with no radio, no TV, no telephone, no electricity . . . was like a *tabula rasa*, technologically, when I was dropped in New York in 1949. Now this, curiously, instead of creating a need for me to attach myself to any one old technology, made me very open to all new technologies. It may have come also from my background, my years of displacement, exile—I am not a settler, I am a vagabond, always moving. . . . But, to cut it short: I see it all happening, but it's not always easy for me, me being from before the radio times, to jump into new technologies. So my knowledge of what's happening in net poetry is very limited. But I think it's a very open, rich field of activity there, and the net poetry will develop its own, new, forms specific to the medium.

HUO: There is an amazing new generation of poets: Andrew Durbin, Luna Miguel, and Bonnie Rogers. There is an amazing generation of new poets emerging on the internet, but you have been writing poetry for a long time, and your films are much more known than your work as a poet; however, Czesław Miłosz told me, "Mekas is a great poet." You once said that a haiku is what comes closest to reality.

JM: Yes, the condensation of reality—place, time of the day, the weather, and your thoughts, feelings at that moment. When Issa or Basho sits there on that mountain or by the brook somewhere, it's the same as when now a filmmaker tries to reach a similar state of intensity in some situation. It's the utmost concentration, the utmost condensation of what one sees, how one feels that moment. That's a haiku. That's what my ideal in cinema is.

HUO: Exactly, and a haiku comes close to reality. You said it's about a struggle also with reality and both haiku and the cinema is about this struggle with reality. Can you tell me about this?

JM: The struggle is inside, between the content that wants to be "expressed" and search for the form in which it can be "expressed" best. It's about how to put in words, or on canvas, or on film the essence of that moment, the divinity of that moment. It can drive you to insanity, trying to keep yourself in the most open, highest state of readiness, ready any moment. It's a dangerous way of life. To really be an artist, a poet, is dangerous.

HUO: Another thing which is related to this reality when you talked about reality before and that is also something we wanted to come back to: how things arrive in the world because we still said art happens, and you said reality actually very often jumps at you; it suddenly pops up. It's unexpected, it's surprising.

JM: Yes. It's like what one calls empty conversation or small talk. Let's just talk. As you talk, and it's about nothing, it's like you clean yourself out, there's like a certain emptiness—and then suddenly something jumps into that emptiness, totally unexpected. Very often when I sit down by my typewriter—I still use my Olympia for most of my writing—I know only very vaguely what I have to write, something presses to be written. I know it approximately; I can feel it, but I do not see it clearly yet. So the only thing I can do is just start typing, almost blindly. So you just write, and the typewriter begins to pull you in. And suddenly it all jumps out, and you can barely follow your fingers. It's the same in filmmaking, painting, and music, I think it's the same in sciences too, and I'd say in human relationships.

HUO: So can you tell me a little about your work with poems? Because there is a book of your poems, and Czesław Miłosz wrote the preface.

JM: Yes, I wrote that cycle of poems when I was twenty-two or twenty-three in Germany, in Wiesbaden and Kassel Displaced Persons camp. It's in Lithuanian. It's available in German [Matto-Verlag], English [Black Thistle Press and Hallelujah Editions], Japanese, Polish, etc. But that's one part of my work that I usually do not talk about because who speaks Lithuanian here? But very possibly it's the best thing I ever did. That's why I care so little about what I did after. It's a cycle of twenty-six poems about life in a small farming village of Semeniskiai where I grew up, describing the work the farmers do during the four seasons. "In free-verse 'idylls' that recall Virgil's *Georgics*, Hölderlin, Stifter, Clare, Leopardi, Rilke, Pasternak, and William Carlos Williams, and are as direct as cinematography," quoting John Ashbery. It's a very factual series of poems, I used to describe them as "documentary poetry," very much of what I am doing now in cinema: trying not to be "poetic," same way as now I am trying not to be "cinematic." Trying to record, almost like any anthropologist, moments where seemingly nothing much happens. The sacredness of the moment . . .

HUO: What do you think is the role of mistakes in all of that? Because Cedric Price, the architect, always said that it's very difficult now in society to make mistakes, but mistakes are very useful.

JM: Yes. Mistakes are very similar or exchangeable with chances. Some of the most beautifully surprising moments in my own filming has happened when, stuck on some one spot, in order to move forward I consciously permitted chances or mistakes to happen. Sometimes I used two cameras: I film, and then I put the camera on the shelf until I forget what I filmed with it. Then I pick it up again and film. So the two images connect totally unpredictably. But in architecture, of course, today, with all the money involved, you cannot afford mistakes or take chances. Everything is written down and calculated to the penny. And the possibilities and chances that the computer designing permits are not the same as taking chances, or permitting and using mistakes. That's why Raimund Abraham, the visionary Austrian architect, left Cooper Union when hand drawing was replaced by computer designing. That signified, according to Raimund, abandoning of poetry and personal in architecture.

HUO: One thing that is also striking in the new generation of emerging artists of the '89-plus generation, I observe that artists are even writers or also poets or architects. So this idea of being in these alternate realities, and you obviously have been doing this a long, long time. You know you have been a poet, a filmmaker, a curator, many, many different roles. Can you talk a little bit about these alternate realities, and how it comes together, how you fluctuate? It's almost like in quantum physics; there are parallel realities.

JM: And the amazing thing is that, in my case, it didn't happen "horizontally," in time,but mostly simultaneously, all at the same time. Like living in a big mansion and just stepping into different rooms. There was a time—in the sixties and seventies—and it continued when I was a curator, running Film-Makers' Cinematheque; often was also the projectionist. I was also writing the weekly Movie Journal column in the *Village Voice*, and publishing *Film Culture* magazine, and running the Film-Makers' Cooperative, and acting as the minister of propaganda and minister of finances. And at the same time, of course, I was writing my poetry and making my films. . . . On any given day, I had to change hats many, many times. How did I manage to do it? I don't know. I simply didn't think about it. I just did it. With no thinking, no planning. And of course, it was easier to do it all then than now, things were smaller. . . .

HUO: Peter Fischli said that with his students and the younger generation of artists, we can observe a return to an almost Fluxus type of spirit, because Fluxus made art out of nothing. Maybe that leads to the question of Fluxus and Pop. I think it is just so interesting. It is interesting also as the only question the editors of the magazine asked me to ask you is about Fluxus and Pop. Obviously we are doing this interview very much about the present because it's much more interesting than to talk about the past.

But it's the only question about the past because it's interesting. At the moment there are big shows everywhere about Fluxus, and at the same time Jessica Morgan is preparing a big exhibition on global Pop on all continents. A lot of revising of Pop and Fluxus is very much not only part of this but also inspiring. You've inspired Fluxus and you've inspired Pop, you've inspired Warhol and you've inspired the Fluxus people. Yoko Ono told me you've inspired her generation, but you inspired also Andy Warhol. So for this reason, I wanted to ask you and I promise it's the only question from the past: Could talk a little about Pop and Fluxus and how you define Pop and Fluxus now?

JM: Strange as it may sound to some, I think that there are many similarities between George Maciunas and Andy Warhol. Beginning with their productivity and ending with politics. It's not very productive to talk about the political art of Lichtenstein or Oldenburg or any other Pop artist, but there is the *Electric Chair* and the *13 Most Wanted Men* of Warhol, and *American Flag* and the *12! Big Names!* of Maciunas. Maciunas was creating his own Fluxus reality, he didn't care about what was around him, everything that he did was invented, made up, including SoHo. He wanted to change the architecture of New York, to introduce the Japanese architecture, in order "to change the Americans, to make them lighter, to civilize them." And Andy's permissiveness, his proverbial YES YES, never NO, came from the same not caring, not giving a damn to what was going around, doing his own thing. Andy had a great respect for George, he told me that; and George, although more critical of Andy's work, respected him enough to invite him to his famous dumpling suppers.

HUO: So there is actually an encounter somehow?

JM: Yes, I think so. And not only in their attitudes: also, as I said, in their productivity and multifacetedness. Just think how many BIG shows have already been of Warhol! And each one revealing always a new face, different aspect of his work, of his oeuvre. And we still haven't seen the end. We still haven't really seen his private videos, and heard his thousands of hours of audio tapes, and we have seen only a fragment of *Screen Tests*, etc., etc. Same with Maciunas and Fluxus. Shows are beginning to pop up in various museums, including Hermitage, with always a different focus, and it's only beginning. And as you and Fischli have noticed, there are neo-Fluxus attitudes popping up on all continents. About how many other artists of the last fifty years can you say that? It's only Andy and Pop, and George and Fluxus.

HUO: I have one or two last questions I was going to ask about religion. Religion is a very big topic now.

JM: I have read all the key religious texts, from all the way back: Asian, African, American Indian. Name any, I have them right on my shelf. And all of them, essentially, tell, yes, to worship God is good and to belong to a church, but when it really comes down to it, you are alone—God and you, alone to talk between yourselves. God and yourself. So I never cared about organized religions. Actually, I believe that their contribution to humanity is negative, and these days, maybe even very negative, because—to standards—they have all become sort of pagan.

Myself, you see, I come from pantheistic roots. Lithuania even after it was Christianized in the fifteenth century and until today remains very much pantheistic; that is in union with Gaia, Earth—its various manifestations, celestial bodies, nature. Of course, even pantheists had certain ceremonies, festivities, but not to the degree that the organized religions have. But I know very little, I have little interest in the rules, ceremonies of organized religions. . . . I would like to tell you one anecdote from my life in Brooklyn, in connection with this subject: I was taking a taxi the other day, and the driver happened to be from Bangladesh. So I asked him if he was Muslim. So he said yes, he was a Muslim. So I said, "How does one become a Muslim? Is it difficult? Do you have to go through some complicated ceremonies?" "No," he said, "it's actually very simple: there is a mantra, you recite it, or someone recites it to you, if you don't know—and you are a Muslim." So I said, "I am curious what the mantra says. Can you recite it for me?" So he recited it to me, and I said, "It sounds very beautiful." "Yes?" he said. "So now you are a Muslim," said the taxi driver. [*laughs*] That how I became a Muslim. A week later I took another taxi. It was another Asian driver. "Are you a Muslim?" I asked. "No," he said, I am a Sikh." So I said, "I don't know much about the Sikh religion." "Oh, it's a very simple religion. Anyone can be a Sikh." So I said, "What do you have to do to become a Sikh?" "Nothing much," said the good Sikh, "You maybe just go to the gatherings sometime. But you don't have to go, I don't go," he said. "I just believe I am a Sikh." So now I am a pantheist, a Muslim, and a Sikh too. [*laughs*]

HUO: Sounds like a great conclusion. I have one last question: A long time ago I asked you about your unrealized projects, and I wanted to ask you again, now in 2015.

JM: One of those unrealized projects I was telling you some about ten years ago is about to be realized. It's a twelve-hundred-page volume of my written diaries covering the years from 1950 till 2000. It's done. Only the photographs are missing. The other one was completion of Anthology Film Archives. The original plans of Raimund Abraham included a paper materials library and a café. I managed to find money only to complete the theater spaces, but now I feel the time has come to complete what I call the "Cathedral of Cinema." I am going to build two additional library floors on top of the existing structure and a Heaven and Earth Café, dedicated to Harry Smith, on the side of it. It's a $6 million project, so it won't be easy, but it must be done. This is what will be my work for this and probably next year. Is there anyone who wants to have his or her name on the library? What other unrealized projects do I have? When I am one hundred, I want to go to the Himalayas, to travel to Tibet. We'll talk about it in 2023, when I come back.

HUO: My last question is about the archives. We spoke earlier about the archives, and you once told me that we have a good reason to be paranoid about digital technology because everything might actually disappear. What is your advice for the duration? Because we live in a crazy moment with every year or every couple of years, the formats change. We can't play old formats anymore, and we're not sure how long hard drives will last.

JM: That is one of the frustrating aspects of the present digital technologies based on corporate profits. We go through great pains at Anthology Film Archives to retransfer, to protect early video artworks. Equipment and formats change, and the materials themselves are fragile. Proper storage, control of humidity and temperature helps, but there are limits. It's the same with books: A few years ago, in Lisbon, I bought a volume of Petrarca. It is 250 years old, but the paper is perfect. It's like it was made yesterday. But much of my library from thirty years ago—the new books—their pages are crumbling already.

HUO: What's your advice, Jonas?

JM: My advice is to do nothing. Nobody can stop the movement of time and changes of technology. But it's like with food lately: there are some young people who are beginning to care about what they eat, how the food is produced, etc. The same will happen, and I think already is happening, with the young printers of books. And I wouldn't worry too much that so much video stuff disappears because of changing technologies. I see it almost as a positive thing. It's a part of Darwinian law. It will come down to love. What will be retransferred, as technology changes, what will be preserved and exchanged with friends, will be works, videos pieces that we love and want to resee and exchange. Yes, it will come down to what we love, to love itself.

HUO: You also have your beautiful printed still work. Can you talk a little about the role of these stills? We have never really talked about them.

JM: Some of my colleagues, filmmakers, they complete a film, and they show it—and that's it. They see it as almost sacrilegious to do something else with it. But while I leave my films as they are, once I complete them, I continue working with the individual frames of my films. While in a Hollywood movie in the span of twenty-four frames, there is practically no big change, in my case, within even three frames there are drastic changes because I do a lot of single frame filming. So there are dynamics between two different frames. That's what I am interested in. I am interested in exploring that aspect. I have pulled out thousands of three or four frame units and printed them on photographic paper. Especially I find interesting what's happening when you just snap a face of someone with a still camera, and when you do it with a movie camera, in action. A completely different content is recorded, the result is very, very different. So I do a lot of that.

HUO: Now my last question is . . . Rainer Maria Rilke wrote a little book to young poets. What would be your advice to young artists?
JM: Just the other day when I was looking through my bookshelves filled with my poetry books, I noticed this great book. I don't know how and when I got this book, *Angel Without a Permit*. It is translated from Spanish by Allen Ginsberg. Here it is. [*holds the book up to the webcam on Skype*] My advice is all young poets should read this book.

HUO: Who wrote it?
JM: It's by Carlos Edmundo de Ory.

HUO: Why is it so important?
JM: It's amazing and is great poetry for anyone to read.

HUO: So the advice is to read this book by Carlos Edmundo de Ory.
JM: Yes. De Ory. It says Vanguard Edition, Gas Station, New York, 1988. It's not a new book, but it's amazing. You see what one can find by chance. It's really amazing.

HUO: Now I have one very last thing. As I continue my project against the disappearance of handwriting on the internet, and you've participated before, you wrote: Don't forget 3:30. That was a mysterious appointment, I don't know what it was. And you put down a good idea where you actually drew a flower. So I was wondering if you'd talk a little bit about this previous post, and maybe do a new one for me now.
JM: What was the last sentence?

HUO: What about 3:30? Why shouldn't we forget 3:30?
JM: Oh, it's very important, 3:30. It could be important!

Jonas Mekas

Peter Bogdanovich / 2015

From *Interview* magazine, October 26, 2015. Reprinted by permission.

Jonas Mekas: Hello, hello! Where are you?

Peter Bogdanovich: I'm in Beverly Hills, staying at a friend's house. And I'm waiting for my new film to come out in August.
JM: Ah, good. It's about time that we see a new film by Peter Bogdanovich.

PB: Well, thank you. It's called *She's Funny That Way*. It's a kind of screwball comedy about the theater.
JM: Well, we met, actually, in the theater. That's what brought us together. I went upstate to see your production of . . . was it the Tennessee Williams?

PB: Yes, you're right. You have a good memory. It was *Camino Real*, a wonderful play of Tennessee's. I'd forgotten that that's where we met.
JM: The New Yorker Theater times, where we spent a lot of time when you did the programming there. We had so many nights upstairs with Emile de Antonio and Dan Talbot, in the early sixties. And then, of course, we got more involved because of *Film Culture*, which I was editing and wanted you to write for. You did a lot of good writing. Are you still writing? Your writing somehow always went together with your filmmaking and your television work—all the biographies of filmmakers.

PB: I have a new book that I may publish. I'm not sure about it because a lot of people are still alive.
JM: Oh?

PB: Well, it's a diary book. I kept a diary from the middle of '65 to the middle of '71. And that was a very big period for me because I went to California and I got into pictures. And it's a good book, but I'm worried about some of the people being insulted by it, you know?

JM: [*laughs*] That is always a challenge, yes. I am publishing almost fifty years of my diaries.

PB: Wow.

JM: They begin in the fifties and end in the year 2000. When I had my video camera in the nineties, I somehow phased out the written diaries. The video replaced my written diaries. You appear in my video diaries. And, of course, you appear in my written diaries, too. [*laughs*]

PB: You have a fascinating life. Where were you when the Soviets invaded Lithuania?

JM: When we noticed the tanks and truckloads of soldiers on our dusty small village road, I grabbed my camera and ran—I was a farmer boy—my older brothers had just given me my first still camera, so I thought, "Oh, this is fantastic. Some of my first images will be of those trucks full of soldiers on a dusty village road entering Lithuania." I ran to the road and snapped the first picture in my life. And one of the Russian soldiers comes running to me, grabs the camera out of my hands, rips out the film, throws it into the dust of the road, rubs it in with his boot, points a finger to the house and shouts, "Run, you stupid boy! Run home before anything else happens to you."

PB: How old were you?

JM: Fourteen, fifteen. Something like that.

PB: It didn't discourage you, though, obviously.

JM: You see, on a farm, there is no money, no income. We couldn't afford to take snaps, like, wildly. You'd wait for special occasions to take a picture. When I graduated the fourth grade, our teacher took all of us to the city to see a movie. The city was about fifteen miles from the village, but I had never seen a movie before. It was some kind of American melodrama, and a Mickey Mouse cartoon. I don't remember the melodrama. I still remember the Mickey Mouse cartoon. [*both laugh*]

PB: And you joined the resistance in 1941, is that correct?

JM: Yes. When the Germans came in, I joined other young people in the resistance. My function was to do the typing for the underground newspaper. It was against the Germans and the Soviets.

PB: You and Adolfas?

JM: I was more than two years older and already in high school. I was in the city, and he was still in the village on the farm. Actually, I don't think he knew about my involvement at the time. I could not tell him. I could not tell anybody. It had to be very, very secret. But my work with the underground was the reason why I ended up in the West. My typewriter was stolen and I could not take chances that it would be discovered by the German police because they were searching for typeface that would match that. I was advised to disappear, the further the better. So I persuaded my brother Adolfas to join me. We were very close, so he felt that he had to go with me. And we boarded a train for Vienna to go to the University of Vienna, but on our way there, the German military police got us and sent us to a forced labor camp near Hamburg. And that's where we spent the last year of war.

PB: I heard you escaped.
JM: We managed to escape, and we thought that if we could get to Denmark and from Denmark maybe to Sweden. . . . But it was all a pipe dream. We ended up on a German farm together with some German refugees, and that's where the end of war found us. What followed was five years of displaced person camps. Like the refugees that you have now in Lebanon and all those other places—all those millions of refugees, homeless. Our situation was very similar to that. And, then, on October 29, 1949, the United Nations International Refugee Organization brought us to New York. I was twenty-seven. And that's when I decided to remain twenty-seven.

PB: [*laughs*] Were your parents still alive?
JM: They were. We did not know, though, at that time. We connected, like, ten years later. It was not possible to write. They didn't know what happened to us, and we did not know what the situation was there. Those were very hard days.

PB: Were you always interested in art?
JM: I did a lot of reading, and I began keeping a diary when I was about six years old. Not a written diary; I learned to write comparatively late, but I made a diary of drawings. But those drawings are all gone. When I had to leave Lithuania, I buried everything in the ground, and it's all rotten now, of course. I began writing poetry when I was about ten. Bad poetry, but you start with bad poetry. [*laughs*]

PB: How did the hardships of the war affect you?
JM: One result is that I missed my teenage years. I was never a teenager. There is a big hole there, and then it's in New York where my life begins. But forced uprootedness is not the same as when you leave home on your own, seeking luck or adventure abroad. An adventurer can always return home; an exile cannot. So I decided that my home would be culture. But the deeper I went into culture, the

more confused I got. So I needed something more real. I said, "Okay, from now on, my country will be cinema." But an exile is still never at home. I will always be split. I'm not schizophrenic. I am not two parts; I'm split into, like, seven parts. There was a time, maybe, I was in, like, one hundred parts. I managed somehow to put them together—thanks to New York and to my new friends, including you. But I will never be able to put myself back together completely. I am still Lithuanian. My early life is poetry, Lithuanian poetry. It never really disappears. And now I am here in New York, and I go to Paris, and I feel like, "Oh, maybe I should live in Paris." When I lived in Manhattan, I looked west, to New Jersey, across the Hudson River, toward California. Where I am now in Brooklyn, I seem to look east. I'm very happy in Brooklyn; it is much more alive than Manhattan. But at the same time, Brooklyn is not exactly America. [*laughs*] When I first came to New York, I came to Williamsburg, which was very poor and miserable in those days. Like all immigrants, I stayed around there for a couple of years, earning my bread by taking any job I found, but then I had to run. I had to run to Manhattan. I ended up on Orchard Street, and that's where my real New York life began. At some point I ended up in a place called Graphic studios, doing photographic work, working with huge cameras. Actually, we did work for the international edition of *Life* magazine. As soon as I moved to Orchard Street, I met Jackson Mac Low, LeRoi Jones, and Allen Ginsberg. It was very simple, you went to poetry readings, to film screenings, to theater, and you met people—especially when you're ready for anything, any excitement. I was starved for culture. Adolfas and I would go to theater or movies every evening. We didn't miss any new opening, be it ballet or theater or movie or poetry readings at the 92nd Street Y. It was amazing. Or you could go to the White Horse Tavern, where Robert Flaherty and Dylan Thomas were holding court. Yoko Ono, I met through George Maciunas, the father of the Fluxus movement, whom I met when he was seventeen. I met Yoko in '61 or '62, I think. She was already holding her own court in her loft on Chambers Street. I helped her during her first show at AG Gallery on Madison by the old Whitney Museum. And we became friends. I gave her her first job in America, at *Film Culture*, so she could stay in the States. We're still friends. I also met Maya Deren very early on. That was in the spring of '53. I visited her because I could not find her little book, *An Anagram of Ideas on Art, Form and Film*. I'd heard a lot about her essay, but I could not find it anywhere, so I called her, and she said, "Come, I will give you one." That's how I met Maya Deren. And we became good friends.

PB: And when did you meet Dalí?

JM: [*laughs*] That was in '63. I was already on 414 Park Avenue South. That was my apartment and the headquarters of the Film-Makers' Cooperative, which became a very busy place, a meeting place for filmmakers, poets. You'd see Robert Frank and

Ginsberg and Barbara Rubin, Kenneth Anger, Harry Smith, Larry Rivers, painters. . . . And one evening, there was Salvador Dalí. He was a very curious person and was interested in what was happening in this so-called underground at that time. And that's when he met some of the people that he used later in some of his own "happenings." Of course, Andy Warhol also came and met all the filmmakers and some of his future superstars. He wasn't so well known yet. That's where he met Jack Smith and Mario Montez and Taylor Mead, etc., etc. And then he decided to make a movie himself.

PB: You became friends with Jackie Kennedy around that time, didn't you?

JM: What we are doing here is dropping names. [*laughs*] All those names. By chance, the fates led me to many of those people—people who are very big or famous. It's just how it happened, I don't know. But as far as Jackie, she needed somebody to tutor her children in cinema and photography. Peter Beard was tutoring them in art history, and when Jackie asked who could help to introduce them to cinema and photography, he said, "Oh, I know the person—Jonas!" So we spent a lot of time, in New York and Montauk. They spent their summers at Andy Warhol's estate in Montauk—well, an old house and some shacks around the house—the children used to spend a lot of time during the summer there. So we both, with Peter, kept them company and, unofficially, performed the duties of bodyguards.

PB: And then you started *Film Culture*, in '54?

JM: The first issue came out in December '54.

PB: That magazine was quite revolutionary, wasn't it?

JM: There really was nothing else at that time. In Paris there was *Cahiers du Cinéma*; in England there was *Sight & Sound*. There was nothing in the United States. So *Film Culture* was the only serious publication dedicated to cinema. We managed to get some very exciting young writers with new and exciting points of view and ideas about cinema, about the history of cinema and where cinema was at that time. Andrew Sarris brought his friend Eugene Archer who later went to the *New York Times*. And Arlene Croce, before she joined the *New Yorker*. And, of course, Andrew went to the *Village Voice*. I began my *Voice* column, "Movie Journal," in '58. But around 1960 or '61, New York was so busy already—I couldn't cover everything that was happening. So I brought in Andrew Sarris to cover the more public cinema, or what they call commercial cinema, and I restricted myself to the independent productions.

PB: So that's how you met [John] Cassavetes?

JM: Yes, I met him during the shooting of *Shadows*. Actually, I met him during the screening of *Shadows*, but later we became friends during the reshooting of *Shadows*. It's a long story, but there are two versions of *Shadows* [1957 and 1959].

PB: Yes, the first version, which you liked, and the second version you didn't like as much.
JM: The first version was more open, more like a jazz piece, and the second one was more carefully structured, and closer to what he was doing later. I would have liked him to continue in that more open kind of style. But *Shadows* was, for him, like school, like an exercise for what he did later.

PB: Did you like his films later?
JM: I like his work very much. Unique. You cannot compare him with any other filmmaker.

PB: Was *Film Culture* successful?
JM: I think it created enough discussion and enough interest, and it produced an entire generation of writers. It did what we wanted it to do, I guess. It was hard work. I had to work at Graphic studios because I needed money to pay the printer. Everything I earned went into the magazine.

PB: And then you opened the Film-Makers' Cinematheque, which eventually became the Anthology Film Archives.
JM: That was in '64. In the spring of '64, I ran into problems with the police because there was a law requiring that every film presented publicly should be licensed, and I was against it. I felt films shouldn't need to be licensed, shouldn't go through the committees that can decide what should be cut, what can be left in. And that happened to too many, many films. So I refused to do it, and that's where I clashed with the police—for screening *Flaming Creatures* [1963], a Jack Smith film, and Jean Genet's *Un chant d'amour* [1950]. I screened them without licensing, so I was arrested. I got six months of suspended sentence. But it provoked discussion that sped the abandoning of licensing. The censorship affected other areas, like performances. Lenny Bruce had problems around the same time. It took a few more years, but by the time I opened Anthology Film Archives, in December 1970, in Joe Papp's building, 425 Lafayette, the licensing of films was gone.

PB: I didn't know anything about all this, about your adventures, like you shooting Andy Warhol's film *Empire* [1964].
JM: I think that was in '64 maybe? Yes, I was the cameraman on that one. It was shot just facing straight at the Empire State Building, through the window from the forty-first floor of the Time-Life Building. So I set up the camera, I framed it,

and it took all night, but we did it. But during this whole time, when I was editing *Film Culture* and running Film-Makers' Cinematheque and starting Anthology, I was also making my films. And, of course, I was writing, which is continuing. But as of fifteen years ago, with me focusing on video and embracing the digital, I am completely somewhere else: installation art, multiple projections and monitors, etcetera. But that's why—that past that we were just talking about, it's history— but to me it's boring. It's enough. It has been written about enough!

PB: I understand. Let's talk about where you are now.

JM: Right now, I just came back from Venice, where I have exhibitions in two different places. One of them, "The Internet Saga," is at the only Burger King in Venice. It's a Burger King, but it's a palace. [*both laugh*] Somebody referred to it as a cathedral, because I put frames from my films, colored frames in transparencies. I covered all the windows, and inside I have screens, several different screens running constantly with different images that are from different video cycles. It's a busy place. At the same time, there are some people eating hamburgers. It's a simple people's place. And a few streets further, there's the official Venice art Biennale sponsored by ministries of culture and very expensive, million-dollar boring installations—whereas mine cost only a few thousand. And just before that, I had a show in Karlsruhe, in Germany, with fifty-two monitors running my 365-day project where, in 2007, I made a film every day and put it on my website. On fifty-two monitors, running simultaneously, it was like a symphony of images. So that's what I'm doing, and that's what makes me excited.

PB: Do you think that the relative inexpensiveness of digital equipment to make a movie is helpful?

JM: Yes. Even for the very commercially minded films telling some very complicated, big, monumental story, they do it digitally now. But also you can use less-complicated digital technology, just little cameras that you can carry in your pocket, to find more personal subjects and personal approaches. Just as in writing, there are novelistic and sort of pedestrian ways of telling a story, to write a postcard with your little pocket camera and put it on websites. I think that's where the most exciting kind of imagery and content is being recorded and exchanged today.

PB: Since you have worked in a variety of mediums, is there some way that you can define what your artistic practice is? What continues to interest you in terms of subject matter?

JM: I never did anything because I was "interested" in it, but from a certain kind of compulsion. Obsession. Passion for something that pulls me into it. So I am pulled into different media. I cannot resist. Maybe it is a sickness. I have to do it and exchange that with friends. [laughs] And what we want to record today, it can only be recorded with the newest, most up-to-date technology; it cannot be recorded any more with the old technologies. So I use what's available, the technology that helps me to do what I want to do. I think if I would ask you why you do what you do, Peter, you would have the same difficulty—you just have to do it. Otherwise you would have a nervous breakdown. [laughs]

PB: Exactly. That's true.

JM: On the other hand, I don't trust people, artists, who never have a nervous breakdown. [Bogdanovich laughs] Because a certain kind of sensitivity is needed for an artist—be it a musician, a dancer, a filmmaker, or the poet. We don't lead normal lives. We don't think normally. We don't feel normally. We are not normal in that sense.

PB: I've always thought of you as a revolutionary, Jonas.

JM: [laughs] They called my Venice show a manifesto. Like a protest, in a way.

PB: Definitely.

JM: But that was done as a normal thing, without thinking. It's just following what one's feeling. That's how it has to be done.

PB: I look at the titles of your films, like *Reminiscences of a Journey to Lithuania* [1972] or *Lost Lost Lost* [1976] or *As I Was Moving Ahead Occasionally I Saw Brief Glimpses of Beauty* [2000]. They all have a kind of sadness to them.

JM: I'm not so sure there is much sadness there, but sadness is a very essential, necessary feeling—state of human experience. Sadness means . . . I don't know, I've never thought how to really describe what is sadness. Not so easy to describe.

PB: Well, a lot of your films are dealing with memories, no?

JM: I'm not so sure my work is about memories. My films are the celebration of reality, of life, of my friends, of actual daily life that passes and is gone tomorrow. We don't pay attention to it when it happens. Later, of course, we look back, we remember. But, for me, to catch, to celebrate the reality and life and friends and everything around me the very moment it happens—that's what is, that's what I'm possessed by.

PB: I remember Adolfas wrote a script called *Hallelujah the Hills* back in the late fifties, early sixties, and he wanted me to be in it, and I rejected it because I didn't want to be running around without clothes on. [laughs]

JM: And in the snow . . . Peter Beard ultimately did it. You know, a couple of weeks ago, I was looking through some of my old film material that I still have on the shelf, and there it was: Peter, the first screen test! I have the footage; it's right there.

PB: My God. [*Mekas laughs*] What did I do?
JM: You were just sitting there, and you and a young woman are having a little conversation. I think I shot only twenty-eight seconds. [*laughs*] I have twenty-eight seconds of footage of you, because Adolfas wanted to know how you look on film. How you move.

PB: What's next, Jonas?
JM: There is a big celebration of the Velvet Underground in Paris next March. A lot of my time will be spent on that. You can imagine—a volume of two thousand pages or so of text, and there are about five hundred illustrations and documents, each of which needs captions and credits, and each detail requires research. But while I do that, my main work this next year will be building an extra floor on top of Anthology Film Archives, for its library. It will be the largest library in the world dedicated exclusively to books and periodicals on cinema. I will need all the help I can get. I mean it will cost me $6 million . . .

PB: Wonderful! We need such a library. I hope you get support from some film industry people.
JM: I hope so. One thing I know: there will be one shelf dedicated to your books. And, next to it, a surprise: Orson Welles's shooting script of *Citizen Kane*, with his personal notes, which we have.

PB: Wow! And here is my last question: What do you think of movies as they are now?
JM: It's easy to laugh at and put down what's being done today, but I cannot. To begin with, I see very little today, I am too busy working on my own stuff. But we thought that there was nothing of interest being done in the fifties or sixties in Hollywood, and now when we look back, we see that we were wrong. There was a lot of good work done. One needs perspective.

A Conversation between Film Legend Jonas Mekas and Director Jim Jarmusch

Benn Northover / 2017

From *AnOther* magazine, Spring/Summer 2017. Reprinted by permission.

In the ever-changing cultural landscape of New York City, Anthology Film Archives has stood strong as the bastion of independent cinema for the past forty-seven years. It is one of the world's largest and most important repositories of independent and avant-garde film and a New York cultural landmark.

Anthology is about to embark upon an important new expansion project led by its founding father, the filmmaker Jonas Mekas. Like so much of what Anthology has achieved over the years, it will be a team effort. The international artistic community has come out in force to support the project. Artists such as Chuck Close, Ai Weiwei, Julian Schnabel, Matthew Barney, Michael Stipe, Jim Jarmusch, and Patti Smith have all pledged their support for the planned fundraising events. They need to raise $7 million to secure the future of Anthology along with the films they preserve for generations to come.

Mekas and Jim Jarmusch first met in the late seventies, both part of an energized downtown film scene still infused by the cultural revolution that swept through New York over a decade before. It was a decade when a fierce independent voice had put cinema in the hands of its makers, changing it forever.

The following conversation took place one rainy day in December. I met Jonas and Jim in the lobby of Anthology Film Archives, and we decided to head over to a small bar across the street, on the corner of Second Avenue. The two began to talk as we walked through the rain . . .

Jonas Mekas: Where is poetry in your life?

Jim Jarmusch: It's important to me. I read a lot of poetry. I studied with Kenneth Koch and David Shapiro at the New York School, and I've been guided by poets all my life. When I was a teenager in Akron, I first discovered the nineteenth-century French poets in translation—Baudelaire, Rimbaud, and Verlaine. Parts of my life William Blake has been my guide. I wish someday when I'm gone, someone will consider me a descendant of the New York School of poets, they've been my guides because of the sense of humor, the kind of exuberance, you know, of Frank O'Hara—

JM: Yes, Frank O'Hara and Kenneth Koch. They have a humor, but there's also something very real and down to earth. Koch still has to be recognized properly.

JJ: Joe Brainard I love also very much, and Ron Padgett. Ron Padgett wrote the poems for our new film. The character is a poet.

Benn Northover: The character's named Paterson, right?

JJ: I called the character Paterson, in the film, because of the poem "Paterson" by William Carlos Williams. He makes a metaphor in the poem of a landscape above the waterfalls there as being like a man. And then I just kept this metaphor; "I'll make a film about a man named 'Paterson' who lives in Paterson, who writes poetry," you know.

JM: When I first read *Paterson* I thought that I should meet William Carlos Williams and maybe make a film based on his poems. I knew LeRoi Jones, Amiri Baraka—so we went and visited Carlos Williams. We discussed the project; he had no patients that day. We agreed I would make some notes, and then he would make some notes, and then we would meet again. But I do not remember what happened next. Those were the first years of *Film Culture* magazine, and I became very busy, and I never pursued the project. But I'm curious if some of the Carlos Williams notes would be in his archives. To me he was very important.

JJ: I heard a funny story that Allen Ginsberg, when very young, because he lived in Paterson, gave some of his poems to William Carlos Williams. William Carlos Williams responded but said: "These poems are terrible. You must find your own voice. These poems are rhymed; they're just not good. But if you desire to be a poet you must continue to work at it. Find your voice."

BN: Thank God he kept writing. I've always loved Emily Dickinson.

JM: I don't know if you saw, a new book just came out. They've published a selection of her envelopes and tiny pieces of paper, where she scribbled little poems or thoughts. It was in today's *New Yorker*. She's my favorite English-speaking poet.

JJ: Ah, one of my favorites, certainly, American poets.

JM: Amazing, what she did with the language.

JJ: So modern and beautiful, amazing. And you read in German and French and English and Lithuanian, of course.

JM: And I can get to Italian and, with a dictionary, Spanish and Russian.

JJ: Kenneth Koch once gave me a poem of Rilke's, in German, and said, "Jim, come back in two days and translate this poem." And I said, "But, Kenneth, I don't read any German at all." And he said, "Precisely." He wanted me to take anything I wanted. The number of lines, anything, and make a new poem.

JM: What Zukofsky did from the Latin poets—he translated by sound. And of course Robert Kelly did that together with Schuldt. They took Hölderlin's poem and by sound translated into English, then read the English and by sound from the English—which was already second water from Hölderlin—retranslated it into German.

JJ: Oh wow. Fantastic.

JM: They published the project.

JJ: That's fantastic. It's so playful.

JM: We all have those memories: when you don't know the language, and you listen, and you seem to understand, but you get completely something else. Yet the amazing thing is, like with Zukofsky's translations and the same with what Robert Kelly and Schuldt did with Hölderlin—you get some of the same spirit, there is something that remains.

JJ: I think it was e. e. cummings who said, "You can understand a poem without knowing what it means."

JM: The same with music and films in a language you don't understand. Somehow you know what the characters are feeling and saying.

JJ: When I went to Japan in the eighties I was obsessed with Ozu and Naruse and Mizoguchi. I couldn't get their films here, so I bought so many on VHS, but they were, of course, not translated. I would watch them endlessly without any knowledge really of the dialogue at all, but I still would understand so many beautiful things, and I learned a lot about acting and people's eyes and camera positions, and just the tiny ways you make a film.

JM: People say you should not watch video copies of the films. But sometimes that is the only way for somebody in a remote part of the world to see those films. It's the same in art. When I went to primary school in a remote village in Lithuania, there was a shelf full of books, and there was one book on Renaissance art. It was on black-and-white, miserable paper and already old. I was so impressed with those miserable black-and-white reproductions; I always wanted to see the originals. Somehow in those miserable reproductions, the essential came through. So I'm not against films made available for information and on digital materials, as long as there are places like Anthology Film Archives where they can still be seen and projected film as film, or video as video.

JJ: I was just looking through a small amount of different artists—film artists—that you have preserved or celebrated. This is only a small amount of people that have really moved me: Peter Hutton, Hollis Frampton, Nam June Paik, Bruce Conner, Hans Richter, Taylor Mead, Danny Lyon, Rudy Burckhardt, Shirley Clarke . . .

JM: And we have not only their finished films, but unfinished materials. Outtakes of Hans Richter, Maya Deren, Hollis Frampton, and even Tarkovsky.

JJ: . . . Man Ray, Joseph Cornell, Robert Frank, Harry Smith, Jack Smith, George and Mike Kuchar, Kenneth Anger, Lizzie Borden, Stan Brakhage, Bruce Baillie, Ron Rice, Michael Snow, Andy Warhol, Ken Jacobs, Maya Deren . . . on and on.

JM: Anthology is the bastion of poetry and cinema, and we are here to stay. This is the building where the poets of cinema live. It is a metaphor, this building.

JJ: I love that. It's a very strong metaphor: we're not going away, you know, we are here. I always thought, visually that it is a badass piece of architecture. I wanted to ask you about the name, because I've always loved Anthology Film Archives, because Anthology is sort of anti-hierarchical in a way.

JM: Myself, Stan Brakhage, and P. Adams Sitney, we all came from a background of poetry. The first idea was to establish an essential list of films that have contributed something to what is known as the "art of cinema," to establish an anthology of the films we love and are willing to defend with our bodies and our minds and all our passions. Researchers often come from Europe because they cannot find the materials we have anywhere else. Not only the film materials but also the extensive paper material collections in our library. This includes publications, periodicals, scripts, correspondences, filmmakers' working materials. We have for instance, the original shooting script of *Citizen Kane*, with Orson Welles's notes, cross-outs. Things like that. We have Joseph Cornell's working materials: magazines, books from which he cut out angels and stuff that he used in his collage work. But we also have hundreds of boxes of materials that are not available to researchers, as we simply do not have the space. This is why right now we're trying to raise money to expand the Anthology building. We have all these materials, and nobody can see them; it's very important we build our library.

JJ: And the library will be on top?

JM: Yes, one new floor on top of the current building.

JJ: Fantastic.

JM: We will also improve film and video archival facilities and will have a gallery space, so we can protect, preserve, and display all these incredible materials properly. As well as improving the two film theaters we have now.

JJ: It's incredible.

BN: It seriously is. It has to happen.

JJ: It has to happen.

JM: All of this is now a $7 million project. That's why right now I am in the process of organizing an art auction, trying to raise those seven million . . . I really hope that between the auction and donations we can raise the budget needed to complete the project. So for the past months, it's been my main job to get artists and collectors involved. I'm working hard, and I'm sometimes not sleeping nights.

JJ: Well it's got to happen. I remember when you were struggling years ago, when you were just starting to renovate—we shot the first *Coffee and Cigarettes* there. I didn't realize until I was just reading up more about Anthology Film Archives, this gangland murder that took place in 1923, right outside the front doors of what is the Anthology building. Where a guy, a young gangster named Kid Dropper was assassinated by Louis Cohen—a notorious gang member—and he killed him right outside of the doors there.

BN: Of course, it was a courthouse.

JM: The building was built in 1914, and the original plans were for a twelve-story building. But the war started, so the building remained on two and a half floors. The structure as it stands now is very strong and could carry another ten floors.

JJ: Wow, fantastic.

JM: So next to the library, we are going to build a café, which my dream is, should become like a tribute to Café Voltaire and Café de Flore.

JJ: Oh man.

JM: We want to make it very, very special.

JJ: I want a new hang out, and I need a new hang out.

JM: Yes. Yes. There is no place right now in New York where, you know, poets, filmmakers can go—like in the sixties there were several. Now there's no place. Can you name one?

BN: No.

JJ: In Williamsburg?

JM: But we need one in Manhattan. We need one in downtown Manhattan. It will be just wine, good simple food—not a restaurant. It will be a café like some French bistros.

BN: And with good coffee!

JJ: Well that would be fantastic.

JM: The "cathedral of cinema" will be completed. The cinema is like a big tree with many different branches, and although Anthology's mission is to serve primarily the independents and the avant-garde, the cinema of poetry—we are equally devoted to all of the branches of the tree called cinema. Of all styles, forms, periods, genres, countries.

JJ: We mentioned the people whose work has been preserved, but we also have to mention how incredible a living place it is, with an incredible catalogue of programming and amazing people coming through and speaking, appearing, presenting. So there's this preservation that's so important for these kinds of films, but there is also the living thing—that's why I love the café idea. There's value to all of these things. It's like molecules of so many things there. And history too. Can I ask you, how do you feel about the present? When you think about all these people that you've known and worked with, do you still feel optimistic about the present and artists?

JM: I'm always optimistic because the future is always full of possibilities. It can go bad, or it can go well. But then you see I was very involved during the past sixty years, very involved in whatever was happening. I'm less involved now in what's going on. But I must say that I don't feel that much passion and craziness in the contemporary art-making generation of today. You see, my feeling is that we are still in a period, which I describe from Joseph Conrad, as after "the shadow line." Before the shadow line you don't care what you do, you just do it. No matter who says what, you just do it. "Fuck you, I'm doing what I do." But after the shadow line it becomes reverberation; it's like so much is being done after the black square and after abstract expressionism and after Warhol, that is just reverberations. I feel we are still in this transitional period when we have so much respect for all that, that we are rehashing the same. There is no new explosion. We need like a new booster. But I think that the computer—there is something to that, there in this computer generation, I think there is something new beginning that is there.

JJ: We're waiting for the explosion.

JM: Yeah, I think we are before the explosion.

JJ: And are you worried, as cycles of history, are you worried about repression of speech and ideas?

JM: I don't think it will happen. I think that people will protest. I don't think Trump can do what he wants to do; I don't think he'll be able to. We have to see what he does, and that's when the people will revolt. If he does something against immigrants or women—they will really fight him. When people rise up with passion, anything is possible.

BN: Very true.

JM: I will show you what I'm reading now. I don't know if you know Paul Celan's poetry; he is one of the great German language poets. I found one of the best recent descriptions of what poetry is in this book. You can read the whole passage silently for yourself. But he ends with this: "The search for ground lights is not enough. There is the axis to be followed and"—dot dot dot—"forgotten. You must above all find lightness, buoyancy, the permanent defiance of gravity."

JJ: That's fantastic. The permanent defiance of gravity.

Index

About the Editor

Gregory R. Smulewicz-Zucker is managing editor of *Logos: A Journal of Modern Society and Culture*. He has edited several books, including the second edition of Jonas Mekas's *Movie Journal: The Rise of the New American Cinema, 1959–1971*. He worked closely with Mekas for twenty years.

Printed in the United States
By Bookmasters